The Power "To Coin" Money:

The Exercise of Monetary Powers by the Congress

The Power "To Coin" Money:

The Exercise of Monetary Powers by the Congress

Thomas Wilson

M. E. Sharpe, Inc.
Armonk, New York
London, England

Library of Congress Cataloging-in-Publication Data

Wilson, Thomas Frederick.
The power "to coin" money : the exercise of monetary powers by the
Congress / by Thomas Wilson
          p.   cm.
ISBN 0-87332-794-2–ISBN 0-87332-795-0 (pbk.)
1. Monetary policy—United States—History. 2. Money—United States—History.
3. Money—Law and legislation—United States—History. 4. Implied powers
(Constitutional law)—United States—History. 5 I. Title.
HG501.W684   1991
332.4′973—dc20   91–340
                                                             CIP

Printed in the United States of America
The paper used in this publication meets the minimum
requirements of American National Standard for
Information Sciences–Permanence of Paper for Printed
Library Materials, ANSIZ39.48-1984.

∞

MV   10 9 8 7 6 5 4 3 2

To Darren,
Charlotte,
and Tim

CONTENTS

PREFACE

> *... authorizing Congress at all to emit an unfunded paper as a sign of value, a resource which, though useful in the infancy of this country, and indispensable in the commencement of the revolution, ought not to continue a formal part of the Constitution, nor ever, hereafter, to be employed, being, in its nature, pregnant with abuses, and liable to be made the engine of imposition and fraud, holding out temptations equally pernicious to the integrity of government and to the morals of the people.*
>
> *—Alexander Hamilton*

Alexander Hamilton in 1783, although supportive of an "infant country case" for fiat currency, expressed the consensus underlying the framing of the United States Constitution. Yet few today seem to understand the transition in constitutional interpretation that gives legitimacy to the emission of an unfunded paper and the significance of that transition in the construction of the U.S. monetary system.

This book traces the history of the monetary powers exercised by the Congress under the Constitution. Interpretations of the Constitution's monetary provisions underlie the evolving construction of the U.S. financial system. The monetary powers, on the one hand, have been instrumental in forging the institutional arrangements for the conduct of the nation's financial affairs, but on the other hand, the Constitution has been interpreted by the courts in a manner to accommodate bold assertions of power by the Congress. The Congress is now limited legally in monetary matters only by self-restraint. Yet, the institutional setting reflects the history of constitutional interpretation and the restraint of the Congress in exercising those powers. This history, then, provides a meaningful orientation to the contemporary debate on money, banking, and monetary policy.

A perusal of the literature has left me with a profound sense of dissatisfaction with the casual references to the constitutional underpinnings of our financial system. Careful reading of the Constitution and its historical interpretation would scarcely lead one to suppose that the Federal Reserve System, for example, is legally grounded on the power of the Congress "to coin money." The Federal Reserve does not issue coins, nor does it "regulate the value thereof, and of foreign coin," as set forth in the narrowly defined monetary provisions of the Constitution. The Federal Reserve System, however, may be a "necessary and proper" means for the execution of an aggregate of powers expressly granted to the government, while issuing a paper currency as a requisite of banking in a historical sense.

It is my impression that mainstream writers feel compelled to establish, as apologists, the legitimacy of the current exercise of monetary powers by the Congress, seemingly justifying the present institutional arrangement as some form of stationary state. Other, perhaps less respected writers are found at the other extreme, declaring the illegitimacy of paper money, fractional reserve banking, or even the Federal Reserve System. While I do not piously claim complete neutrality in historical interpretation, this book seeks to provide a more balanced treatment of the subject.

Court decisions sanctioning assertions of congressional authority are typically viewed as "correct" interpretations of the Constitution. While I am not suggesting that all interpretive modes are equal, and recognize considerable latitude in reasonable construction of the document, I am not prepared to dismiss as "incorrect" the opinions (one formal) of two successive chief justices of the Supreme Court that the "greenbacks" were unconstitutional, even though the ruling was subsequently reversed. The Constitution can obviously accommodate very different legal opinions.

Constitutional interpretation is manifest historically in the institutional structure of the financial system. Close fidelity to the express language of that document appears in the nation's early history under the Constitution in its money, banking, and monetary policy. Implied powers were soon enlisted, however, in the accommodation by the courts of bold actions taken by the Congress. Even so, institutional arrangements were long influenced by the distrust of lodging the monetary powers directly in the federal government. This distrust reflected the fears of the founding fathers that governments tend to substitute paper money for taxes and arbitrarily redistribute income in favor of special interests. Under our fiduciary currency standard today, this distrust seems only weakly expressed in the "independence" of the Federal Reserve System and in the maintenance of competitive markets for banking services, limited, of course, by regulation-induced redistributions of income and wealth to preferred constituencies.

In short, the Constitution, in its original meaning, was not supportive of the issuance of an "unfunded" paper money by the Congress, but we have experienced, nonetheless, a transition in constitutional interpretation, lifting the exercise of the monetary powers by the Congress to a plenary status. The historical transition in constitutional interpretation can be traced to the expansive exercise of powers by the Congress and their accommodation by the courts. The evolution of institutional arrangements reflects this history. The institutional setting today, while respecting constitutional underpinnings to some extent, as expressed in an "independent" monetary authority and the allocative function of competitive markets, remains logically grounded as well on the constitutionally ordained structure of government and the division of delegated powers.

The power "to coin" money, as contained in this book's title, refers to the specific monetary provision in the Constitution. Yet it also captures, it would seem, the sense that a more expansive construct might be applied. In the author's estimation, the words "to coin" do not translate so facilely into the words "to issue," for example; other provisions of the Constitution must be examined before concluding that the Congress possesses plenary powers in monetary affairs.

Proposals for restructuring the financial services industry, it is contended, should recognize the history of constitutional interpretation. I suggest that there is some value in (1) insulating the central bank from close political scrutiny in policy formulation and implementation, (2) relying on the budgetary process instead of central bank regulations as conduits for income redistribution, and (3) allowing the private sector to employ protective devices against inflation, e.g., gold coins, gold clauses in contracts, price indexation of contracts (including bonds), floating-rate debt instruments, foreign currencies, and private money substitutes.

The theme running through the chapters of this book accentuates the distrust of the assumption by the Congress of those supposed claims of sovereignty in manipulating the money supply and credit flows. As a matter of self-restraint, the Congress may be better served to mollify "the anguish of central banking," as former Federal Reserve Board chairman Arthur Burns described it, by stepping back from the policy process and simply setting the broad guidelines and objectives for the management of the money supply. Otherwise, setting a policy course that is sensitive to transitory developments blurs the limited long-run vision that may be critical as the nation risks an inflationary solution to today's debt overhang. The Federal Reserve, in one sense, manages a bond portfolio. As an analogy, I—on a vastly diminished scale, of course—have managed some bond portfolios, and have not been surprised to find that close surveillance by fund sponsors tends to shorten the horizon for measuring investment returns, to cause frequent changes in the performance standards, and to increase portfolio turnover. The longer-run investment return suffers in the process.

The reader may not be convinced that policy inferences in this book are at all appropriate. Nonetheless, I trust that the reader will find the rich history of constitutional interpretation of value in understanding U.S. monetary history and in the contemplation or critique of proposals for reforming the financial system. The

U.S. central banking tradition, moreover, may serve as a useful reference in the search for a model by those countries undergoing economic transformations and the countries of Western Europe as they develop integrative structures.

Special appreciation is expressed for the research assistance of Brent Taylor, an attorney with Baker and Daniels, the encouragement of Kenneth Boulding, Janos Horvath, and George Geib, and the close editorial advice and supervision of the editor at M. E. Sharpe, Richard Bartel.

The Power "To Coin" Money:

The Exercise of Monetary Powers by the Congress

CHAPTER 1

Introduction

*The Congress shall have power . . . To coin money, regulate
the value thereof, and of foreign coin.*

—Article I, Section 8

The power to coin money is found [...] powers expressly delegated to the [...] reference to money in the Constit[...] powers, for example, "to borrow m[...] States" and "to provide for the p[...] of counterfeiting the securities and current coin of the United States." Specifically absent from the document, however, are powers granted to the Congress for the emission of paper money, i.e., "bills of credit," and for the incorporation of a bank. Indeed, those powers were rejected at the Constitutional Convention. The courts, of course, have sanctioned the expansion of the power exercised by the Congress over money, lifting it to a plenary status, as the nation's fortunes are now attached to the management of bills of credit by a central bank, the Federal Reserve System, under its authority.

The transition in constitutional interpretation obviously broke down the constraints imposed on the Congress by that social contract's express language, but this history is not regrettable, as we might suppose that only the powers expressly delegated to the Congress 200 years ago would not be entirely appropriate today. Yet, we might suspect that certain aspects of our founding fathers' vision in writing the Constitution remain relevant, so that the Congress may be well advised to exercise some self-restraint in the management of the nation's monetary system.

The history of money and banking under the Constitution weaves a pattern of institutional structure and practices respectful of a distrust in lodging the power to exercise discretionary management of the money supply directly under the authority of the federal government. Now, however, the absence of legal checks accompanied by frail market checks pose a real danger that the Congress is becoming less and less distrustful of itself in exercising the monetary powers in the face of mounting debt and financial market instability.

Monetary Powers in the Constitution

The Constitution, we might say, incorporates a matrix of powers divided among the federal government, the states, and the people. There are powers expressly prohibited, as well as powers expressly delegated. Within the confines of the Constitution's express provisions, one can derive a reasonably clear understanding of the "original intent" of the framers in their formulation of the monetary powers. Beyond those provisions, other interpretive modes may leave much to implication. What monetary powers may be implied ordinarily involves a marshaling of an aggregate of express provisions, coupled with reference to the broad, enabling clauses, e.g., "to make all laws which shall be necessary and proper for carrying into execution the foregoing powers." As we shall see, the monetary powers so conceived may be drawn from numerous provisions of the Constitution, which constitutes the construction underlying the legitimacy of the Federal Reserve System.

The express language of the Constitution provided for a monetary standard based on gold and silver coins in conformity with international practice. Congress, of course, was given the authority to coin money, meaning precisely that: Congress was granted the power to regulate the quality of the circulating media, i.e., to define the metallic content of U.S. coins and to assign legal tender status to those coins and comparable foreign coins. This does not mean that the regulation of coinage related to the quantity of money as such. The money supply was left to market determination. Provisions for the Congress to emit bills of credit and to grant charters of incorporation were rejected at the convention, as noted.

The states were expressly prohibited to "coin money; emit bills of credit; make anything but gold and silver coin a tender in payment of debts; pass any bill of attainder, *ex post facto* law, or law impairing the obligation of contracts." The states, therefore, were stripped of all monetary functions, except the power to charter (and regulate) banks. Note-issuing banks existed in 1787, and their notes, devoid of legal tender standing, were presumably compatible with the Constitution—banking was viewed as a right of individuals or corporations to form business enterprises under the common law tradition.

Interpretation of the Constitution's monetary provisions, of course, has evolved a considerable distance from their original understanding. Three major steps account for much of the distancing of interpretation from the express language of the document.

• Alexander Hamilton summoned the implied powers to convince the Congress and President George Washington to grant a charter of incorporation for the establishment in 1791 of the Bank of the United States. Chief Justice John Marshall in 1819 adopted Hamilton's reasoning in upholding the constitutionality of the bank in *McCulloch* v. *Maryland*.

• In financing the Civil War, Congress authorized the issuance of greenbacks, the first legal tender paper money emitted under the Constitution. The Supreme Court initially ruled that the greenbacks were unconstitutional, but, after changes in the Court's membership, the decision was reversed, and greenbacks were declared to be a proper expression of sovereignty.

• The Great Depression prompted emergency measures, including steps to relegate gold to a commodity status, as the governing role of gold was replaced by the management of a fiduciary currency. In upholding these steps, the Supreme Court recognized the full power of the Congress to preside over the monetary system.

The Congress has allowed some "independence" in the central bank's conduct of monetary policy and the operations of competitive markets in the allocation of credit, diverted to some extent, of course, by regulations and at times strict controls. The financial system retains these features associated with its constitutional origins. Yet the powers exercised by the Congress in certain respects resemble the practices of the states proscribed by the Constitution: the issuance of legal tender paper money, the printing of money in place of taxes, and the use of monetary policy as an instrument for redistributing income to special interests. Just as the unwinding of the market constraints imposed by the New Deal legislation amplified the urgency of the Congress to draft new guidelines for its regulation of the financial system, the exercise of its monetary authority should be reconsidered in view of those developments and deficiencies in the framework for the conduct of a stabilizing monetary policy.

Capsule Comments on the Contents of This Book

The broader issues examined in chapter 2 encompass a society's choice of the monetary standard, the structure of the financial system, and the associated implications for economic stability, inflation/deflation, and the distribution of income. Monetary policy within this context is constitutional in nature, and the founding fathers recognized the importance of these fundamental policy choices in drafting the Constitution. Monetary policy in a narrow, conventional sense refers, for example, to the policy of the central bank, presuming an institutional setting formed on constitutional principles. Within the broader context, the chapter treats rules versus discretion in contrasting the "society" theory of money and the "state" theory of money, control of money as a requisite of sovereignty, the profit from the issuance of money, and income stabilization and redistribution. While addressing recurring issues in U.S. monetary history, the chapter clearly contrasts monetarist and Keynesian attitudes toward money and monetary policy.

Besides these broader issues, orientation to the historical theme is provided by chapter 3; it reviews the interpretive modes of the Supreme Court, a critical element in understanding the application of constitutional principles in monetary decisions. The express language of the document, perhaps aided by inferences about the intent of the framers, as noted above, contrasts in constitutional interpretation with a marshaling of implied powers, perhaps supported by inferences about the general tenor of the instrument. "Clause-bound" approaches, for example, differ sharply from "value-laden" opinions that rest on some perceived, overriding social objective. The purpose of this survey is not primarily to critique the reasoning of the courts, but rather to understand the bases of the courts' decisions. Within this context, it is also important to recognize the structure of the government and the associated matrix of powers delegated under the Constitution.

Chapter 4 explores the roots of the Constitution's monetary provisions in the experiences and observations of the founding fathers. The roots extend back to the colonial period, when the colonies issued bills of credit and regulated coins. The dramatic depreciation of the "continentals" in financing the Revolutionary War lingered in the minds of the framers, but more distressing were the unstable financial conditions under the Articles of Confederation, when the states issued fresh batches of legal tender paper money, undermining private contracts, and Shays's Rebellion, which raised their fears of a "leveling" radicalism to an alarming pitch. The ferment leading to the drafting of the Constitution reflected a broadly based hostility toward the government's issuance of paper money.

The framing of the Constitution's monetary provisions is examined in chapter 5. Given the historical backdrop of chapter 4, the language and intent of the framers are understood more clearly in devising the monetary provisions establishing a specie standard, along with the implications of adhering to that standard. Special attention is attached to the bases for striking from a draft of the document the power of Congress to emit bills of credit and for denying Congress the power to grant charters of incorporation, as described above. Emphasis is given as well to the exclusion of the word "expressly" from both the "necessary and proper" clause and the Tenth Amendment. The absence of outright prohibitions and the limiting word "expressly" allowed room for more expansive interpretations of the monetary provisions.

The next six chapters, while not strictly in chronological order, give attention to the maintenance of a narrowly prescribed constitutional standard but amplify the issues surrounding the departures from the express language of the Constitution cited above: the granting of a charter for establishing the Bank of the United States; the formation of a bimetallic standard; the issuance of legal tender paper money to finance the Civil War; the reestablishment of the gold standard under a national currency; the creation of the Federal Reserve System; and the abandonment of the gold standard during the Great Depression. Attention is given to the exercise of monetary powers by the Congress and to the performance of the economy and the financial system, focusing on certain persons who influenced the course of events.

Chapter 6 reviews the constitutional debate surrounding the chartering of the Bank of the United States. James Madison, the "Father of the Constitution," opposed the granting of a charter to establish the bank, and one of his collaborators in writing *The Federalist*, Alexander Hamilton, was, of course, the bank's intellectual architect. A quarter of a century later, Madison, as President, signed the bill incorporating the second Bank of the United States. Chief Justice John Marshall, as noted, relied on Hamilton's constitutional arguments in upholding the bank in *McCulloch* v. *Maryland*. Hamilton's bank was essentially a private organization with minority government ownership; the second bank had minority government representation on the board along with minority government ownership. President Andrew Jackson's veto of the bill to recharter the Bank of the United States and the subsequent withdrawal of the government's deposits, under the direction of Treasury Secretary Roger Taney, ultimately led to the demise of that institution.

Chapter 7 sweeps across the period from the ratification of the Constitution to the Civil War. This was the era of state bank notes, and important to this time was the fidelity to the constitutional precepts underlying a specie standard. The Congress was very active in the exercise of its power to regulate the nation's coinage. The free banking era that followed the Bank of the United States fomented another constitutional issue: that was, whether the notes of state-chartered institutions were indeed the proscribed bills of credit. The Court ruled that they were not. In the state banking era, the money supply was grounded on specie and the banks operated under a competitive market regime. In the absence of the Bank of the United States, the Treasury did furnish notes to shore up the banking system during financial crises, when private nonbank organizations issued both tokens and scrip more abundantly. Long-run price stability was administered by the underlying dependence on specie, but money, prices, and economic activity were highly unstable in the short run.

The Civil War brought a major transformation in the nation's money and banking, marking sharp departures from strict constitutional moorings and enhancing the monetary powers of the Congress. The advent of the greenbacks and the creation of the national banking system highlight these changes, sparking controversy and framing the institutional structure for the remaining decades of the century, as set forth in chapters 8 and 9. Chapter 8 examines the legal tender cases, while chapter 9 reviews policies and performance under the national banking system. Under the latter system, the evidence suggests, the behavior of money, prices, and economic activity compares closely with that behavior in the state bank note, "free banking" era, and private money issues again accompanied financial panics. Treasury Secretary Salmon Chase was a strong advocate of a national currency under the auspices of nationally chartered institutions, on which he stamped legal approval as the chief justice. Ironically, his portrait appeared on the greenbacks, but it was he who ruled them to be unconstitutional, an opinion with which his predecessor, Chief Justice Roger Taney, might very well have concurred.

Changes in membership of the Supreme Court, however, brought a reversal of the ruling, again with a single vote margin. In the aftermath of the Civil War, the Supreme Court recognized, as a matter of the national government's sovereignty, that the Congress held the power to preside over a national currency and that the matter was not appropriately left to judicial scrutiny afterwards.

Greenbacks and free silver occupied the center stage in opposition to the gold standard, and the Congress was very active in the exercise of the newly granted power to issue paper money. The regulation of coinage assumed a secondary, but not inconsequential role.

William Jennings Bryan, the exemplar of populism, denounced the gold standard as crucifying mankind on a cross of gold. It was Bryan, as Woodrow Wilson's secretary of state, who was nonetheless influential in securing passage of the Federal Reserve Act, as described in chapter 10. The original plan for a central bank was associated with Republican Senator Nelson Aldrich, who envisioned a banker-dominated board with minority government representation. The political tides shifted, however, as the leadership role devolved to Democratic Representative Carter Glass, who favored some banker representation on a government-dominated board. Given respect for the Jacksonian tradition, the Owen-Glass Bill created a decentralized central bank, though largely fashioned after the Aldrich Plan; but Wilson sided with Bryan, insisting on having a fully government-appointed, though independent, Federal Reserve Board and a government-backed currency. The nature and extent of central bank "independence" have been the subject of debate since the inception of the Federal Reserve System.

Chapter 11 recites the story of the Federal Reserve's failure in its mission to prevent a financial crisis, as the banking system collapsed in the early 1930s, accompanied by a deep contraction in business activity. Private money issues emerged once again, though largely as a sign of this debility. The Great Depression was shortly to bring to a close the governing role of gold in the monetary system. Devaluation of the dollar was accompanied by nationalization of private gold holdings and the nullification of gold clauses in contracts; these steps were narrowly upheld by the Supreme Court as constitutional measures of the Congress in presiding over the nation's currency. The Federal Reserve, then, after the Accord of 1951, possessed monetary powers well beyond those contemplated in 1913, when the gold standard was still intact.

Chapter 11 also draws contrasting portraits of the economy and financial market behavior under the two regimes: the gold standard and the fiduciary currency standard governed by the Federal Reserve. The market-oriented gold standard maintained long-run stability in the price level but allowed considerable short-run economic instability. Moderation in the cyclical amplitude of business activity in recent decades under the Federal Reserve, of course, has been accompanied by chronic inflation. While validating the founding fathers' observations on the government's management of a fiat currency, the political consensus today apparently approves the trade-off of long-run price stability for less short-run economic instability, so long as inflation is reasonably well contained. The Congress, while obviously cognizant of these developments, now often seems preoccupied by redistributive issues, as seen in credit allocation and interest rate regulations, in contrast to the earlier devotion of energies to the regulation of coins and paper money in order to maintain a viable currency system. The revolutionaries, of course, had formulated the monetary provisions of the Constitution in order to foreclose the use of the monetary powers as a political instrument.

The concluding remarks made in chapter 12 present the case for a "Supreme Court of Finance," an obvious allusion to "independence" in setting the course of monetary policy by the central bank. While the Congress should establish the guidelines and objectives for the management of the money supply, a set of rigid "rules" seems inappropriate, as too confining. At the other extreme, it has been asserted that an independent monetary authority is tantamount to having an independent Pentagon. Subordination of the central bank to the executive branch clearly runs against the constitutionally prescribed structure of the government as well as against the historical current. This chapter also represents a convergence of themes, as central banking and the management of a fiduciary currency came together under the Federal Reserve. The transition in constitutional interpretation that lends legitimacy to this arrangement is summarized as well.

Summary

The theme running through the chapters of this book emphasizes the relationship between constitutional restraints and the exercise of monetary powers by the Congress. The breakdown of constitutional restraints, understood in the express language of the document and manifest in the establishment of a bimetallic standard, was dramatized by the chartering of the Bank of the United States, the issuance of legal tender paper money, and the removal of gold as an impediment to expansive policies. The absence of legal constraints on the Congress in the exercise of monetary policies has, nonetheless, been accompanied by some respect for an "independent" monetary authority and for competitive markets, while leaving in the wake of constitutional interpretation in U.S. monetary history a financial structure very different from that which might otherwise have developed.

The underlying logic for implanting constitutional restraints supposed that monetary policies otherwise would be inflationary, subject to arbitrary redistributive practices, and would serve as a source of revenue in lieu of taxes. The outcome has fulfilled expectations. The expressed powers have not restrained the Congress from exercising those powers expansively over the broad sweep of history, and self-restraint exercised by the Congress has proven to be insufficient. The Congress would be well advised to exercise greater self-restraint in the employment of monetary policy devices to meet its competing set of objectives, one of which is, of course, an "independent" central bank.

CHAPTER 2

The Scope of Monetary Policy

A nation's monetary policy in a broad sense encompasses the choices of that society in determining the monetary standard, the division of monetary powers, and the structure of the financial system. Constitutional principles should play a meaningful role in the delegation of powers, as they carry serious implications for the stability of the economy and the distribution of income. The exercise of monetary powers by the government may be limited and thereby leave a large role for market forces by simply establishing the rules, or these powers may be less constrained in the discretionary conduct of policy.

The monetary powers are clearly articulated in the Constitution, in language that appears to express the intent of the framers. The monetary provisions, moreover, conform to the general tenor of that document. The founding fathers envisioned a form of government that, on the one hand, should be sufficiently responsive to the people to avoid the causes for rebellion set forth in the Declaration of Independence, while on the other hand, it should be sufficiently orderly to avoid the confused state of affairs that prevailed under the Articles of Confederation. That form of government is characterized by a network of checks and balances in the federal government and by a sharing of powers among the central government, the states, and the people. The Constitution also prescribes the structure and operating processes of a representative democracy in which citizens and minority groups are protected from the oppressive exercise of power by the majority, a protection strengthened, of course, by subsequent amendments. While we should not reasonably suppose that monetary policy today can conform precisely to the thinking of those who framed the Constitution two centuries ago, we should expect policy to fit into the conceptual framework of the Constitution around which the government is structured and through which its powers are given legitimacy.

The express language of the Constitution projects a division of monetary powers designed to prevent the federal government from using inflation as a policy instrument. The specie standard allowed considerable market determination of income distribution and the price level. Instead of resorting to the printing press, the government's fiscal affairs were supposed to be conducted through borrowing, taxes, and the appropriation of funds. Inflationary policies were viewed as a deceptive practice outside the constitutionally prescribed policy channels, practices that could shift the cost of government and lead toward controls of wages, prices, and interest rates that further adversely redistribute income.

The Supreme Court has accommodated the transition to a tightly governed fiat currency standard by effectively delegating, based on implied powers as a requisite of sovereignty, an unconstrained authority over money, thus expanding the role of the government in the determination of income and the level of prices.[1] The distribution of income generated by adherence to the original monetary policy prescription favored the wealthy, as the framers recognized, and the monetary regime often proved to be unstable and highly deflationary. Preference might have been for constitutional amendment rather than expansive interpretation, but the authority assumed by the Congress nonetheless received substantial political support, effectively ratifying the broader exercise of monetary powers by the government. The ascendancy of discretion over rules and market determination of outcomes, of course, has left a legacy of chronic inflation and inefficiency in the use of redistributive devices in meeting the nation's economic objectives. Indeed, these deficiencies in the conduct of our financial affairs correspond closely with those that the founding fathers sought to foreclose in the conduct of monetary policy.

The "Society" Theory of Money

Monetary powers in the United States derive their legitimacy from the Constitution, a social contract that specifies the checks and balances in the distribution of powers among the national government, the states, and the people.[2] Convention, market dynamics, and the institutional structure affect the expression of those powers. Within this setting, monetary powers are shared powers, and they are limited, despite many expansive interpretations of the Constitution.

A nation's money supply is governed by market forces and/or by the government. At one extreme, the supply of money and the level of prices are determined through an equilibrating process by competitive markets, with money providing an integrative function yielding social gains over barter. The exchange economy thus wields the organizing mechanism, and monetary powers are private. At the other extreme, governments employ monetary powers to gain revenue, to foster social and economic stability, and to redistribute income. While money may be used in a quasi-legitimate fashion to confiscate property, the value of money ultimately rests on confidence in its value and restraint in its issuance. A government's powers are limited by the ballot box, passive resistance, and revolution, but in the monetary area, they are also limited by a reversion to barter and competing monies, whether of domestic or international origin, or the use of protective devices, e.g., indexation. Monetary powers in this sense imply a sharing of those powers.

This perception of monetary powers is consistent with the "society" theory of money. The "society" theory holds that money is simply something that serves as a generally accepted medium for transactions. This view can be found in Montesquieu's *The Spirit of the Laws,*[3] and possibly traced to Aristotle's writings.[4] The "society" theory for many decades essentially formed the basis for U.S. law. In *Thorington* v. *Smith* (1869), for example, the Supreme Court upheld contracts stipulating payment in Confederate currency.

The "state," or nominalist, theory of money, in contrast to the "society" theory, maintains that money is what the state proclaims as money.[5] The "state" theory of money seemingly underlies legal thinking in the United States at least since the 1930s, such that legal scholar Gerald Dunne could conclude:

> The government and only the government can declare what shall be money, emit it, enforce it, and protect it. In short, power is power.[6]

This position may accurately reflect the opinion of the Supreme Court and other legal scholars, as well as of the typical pedestrian. At best, it is a tautological statement: money is what the government proclaims to be money, and nothing else is money. Beyond that, legal definitions of money may not correspond closely to what serves as money, and the government may not be sure exactly what is money. Interpretations of the Constitution, of course, have evolved some distance away from the "society" theory that is implicit in the express language of the document, toward compatibility with the "state" theory, but legal rulings tend to lag behind the evolution of money within practical market operations. Nonetheless, these fundamentally different views of money appear intermittently throughout U.S. monetary history, and they still prevail today when, for example, the "independence" of the Federal Reserve is debated.

The "society" theory, in my estimation, more accurately reflects the legal framework and the practical employment of monetary powers. Governments establish threat systems and engender integrative relationships in their conduct of monetary policy, but they must respect the limits of power, especially when money transcends the boundaries of the state. Laws against competing monies may be enacted, but simple counterfeiting of the official issues could be a serious problem. "To counterfeit is death" was often printed on early American paper money, but to little avail, since the issuers of lawful money were incapable of carrying out the threat.[7] "Legal tender" may mean no more than that the money is worth less than the note proclaims, and may scarcely retard depreciation. Laws may define money and "compel" circulation, but the marketplace will determine its acceptance and may inspire entrepreneurial creations of what will actually serve as money.

Some economists, perhaps of a Keynesian persuasion, favor the use of money as a policy instrument, consistent with the "state" theory of money. Others, perhaps monetarists, seek to establish a set of rules to impede discretionary authority. In contrast to the Keynesian view of money, Oxford professor S. Herbert Frankel offers the earlier notion of a free monetary order, which "postulates the existence of principles, enforced by custom, convention and law, which ensure that its operation will not be arbitrarily, capriciously, or lightly altered in favor of particular groups, individuals, or interests."[8] And Frankel adds:

> The basic difference between the two philosophies of money which I have been considering is that the one endeavors to incorporate the view that the monetary system should be regarded as a means for the achievement of specific and immediate goals of public policy, while the other regards this view as incompatible with a monetary order: the pursuit of changing goals of action will make it capricious and uncertain and prey to conflicting and varying political objectives.[9]

Money as a tool of government policy subverts the role of money as a standard for the conduct of "free economic and social relations."[10] When used as a policy tool, money no longer serves primarily as a reliable vehicle for operating the exchange economy, according to Frankel's view, and the inevitable erosion of trust in the value of money spawns a variety of defensive, speculative activities in the private sector. At the same time, however, the rules set to obviate discretionary management of the money supply may prove to be too rigid in an institutional framework characterized by unpredictable evolution, and the market-generated outcomes may be unacceptable.

Sovereignty

"State" theory adherents often allude to the claims of sovereignty. The issuance of money was of private origin, however.

The earliest coins of Lydia were issued by those who performed banking functions, or by merchants.[11] The earliest stamped ingots, which were similar to Chinese chop marks of more recent vintage,[12] bear the impressions of private issuers as well. Later, punch marks were made by bankers, merchants, mine operators, and state and church officials, all of whom had no superior authority. While in China a system of parallel public and private issues prevailed for many years, the power to issue money in other areas generally was seized by the state.[13] In Lydia, for example, economic historian A. R. Burns observed, "When coining was established as a state monopoly the exercise of that function became an attribute of sovereignty."[14] It should not be supposed, however, that this early assumption of the coinage power was final, or that it was a natural (divine or economic) right of the government. The circulating media have historically fluctuated in composition, often being essentially of an international character or dominated by competing issues of petty princes, while private money has been primarily, though not exclusively, associated with banking.[15]

Coinage has been used to expand the market for precious metals and to facilitate commerce and public administration. Governments have also used their monetary powers to promote unity, to relieve debts, and to gain profits. Devaluation—that is, raising the exchange value of coins—has served as a device to reduce the burdens of debts, including those of the sovereign. Debasement—that is, decreasing the intrinsic value of coins by reducing their weight or fineness—has enabled the state to increase the money supply (and concomitantly its expenditures, including the repayment of debts) with a given stock of precious metals. This practice was noted as a sign of decadence in ancient Israel,[16] but the Romans were particularly adept at exploiting coinage. During the Middle Ages, the right of coinage degenerated into an explicit source of profit to the sovereign, who levied a charge ("seigniorage") in excess of costs ("brassage").[17]

National currencies are a symbol of unity, which further contributes to the integrative function of money. The first coin issued under the authority of the United States exhibited a thirteen-link chain arranged in a circle, although the legends "Mind Your Business" and "Fugio" (because time flies) had a less certain integrative function. A portrait of the sovereign is depicted on the currency of a number of countries.[18] The United States, with only a few exceptions, one of whom was Senator Carter Glass,[19] eschews the portrayal of living persons on its coins. "Miss Liberty" or historical figures (from George Washington to P. T. Barnum)[20] are generally depicted, along with the legends "E Pluribus Unum" and "In God We Trust." Also, symbolic of soundness in the nation's currency, the government has tended to portray on its fiat notes the likeness of the country's staunch "hard money" advocates, e.g., Andrew Jackson's portrait on the current $20 Federal Reserve note.[21] A rationale for certain legislation on money has been to provide uniformity of the nation's money—an integrative function—and the case for federal authority in money matters has been built in part on the presumed claims that such authority is an attribute of sovereignty.

Competitive markets historically have been viewed as alternatives to the government's application of the law, as evident in the gold standard, free banking, and the structure of financial markets. Privately issued bank notes and deposits have been recognized as regular components of the money supply. In several chapters of this book, private nonbank money is also reviewed as an element of competition with the government's money. Such private money has ordinarily served a useful role in arresting the degeneration of the economy into barter during depressions, and has the potential to serve as a constraint on the government's exercise of monetary powers. Indeed, a fully competitive private money has been contemplated by some monetary economists, but the prospect still remains remote. The historical record nonetheless suggests that the public would seem to be receptive to such ventures under times of financial distress, even though the government would obviously frown on private entrepreneurs intruding on its sovereign claims to issue and preside over the nation's money supply. Inflations, however, foster protective devices beyond the traditional reliance on gold and foreign currencies, e.g., the indexation of contracts, thus limiting the government's sovereign claims. The Constitution is silent on private money, bank and nonbank, but under the law that domain has fallen to state and federal authority. United States monetary history often records a tolerance of money issuance outside the law, suggesting that what is legally money and what actually serves as money may not be exactly the same thing.

Seigniorage

Hamilton and others warned that when governments were granted the authority to issue paper money, they would tend to substitute paper money for taxes, thus reaping seigniorage gains. The profits accruing to the federal government today from the issuance of currency and the creation of reserve deposits vastly exceed the profits of the private financial sector. While some students dismiss this matter as simply a manifestation of sovereignty, the distribution of this "tax" does carry efficiency and equity implications for the conduct of monetary policy. The issue relates chiefly to the payment of interest on deposits, both demand deposits and bank reserves.

The concept of seigniorage aids in understanding the transition of government money powers from elementary regulation to manipulation of money for gain, whether specifically for the government itself or supposedly for the general welfare. Seigniorage is defined here as the difference between the full resource costs of producing (or issuing) money and its value on the market. A competitive equilibrium in the supply of commodity money (e.g., gold) implies no seigniorage. Paper money, deposit money, and commodity money when overvalued through monopolistic control imply the extraction of profit. Governments have often seized broad monetary powers precisely for that purpose. American monetary history contains periodic debates on the cost savings of substituting paper money for specie and on the distribution of the profit from the issuance of money.

Seigniorage in a historical sense refers to the charge imposed by the agency entrusted with the power to produce coins. The term is derived from the French word "seigneurage," which means literally "the right of the lord." Congress in 1792 adopted Hamilton's coinage recommendations that the metallic value of coins be maintained at their monetary value in order to discourage counterfeiting.[22] The mint provided "free coinage" of gold and silver, except that a charge of one half of one percent was imposed for the immediate exchange of bullion for coins. Hamilton even suggested the addition of silver to the one cent piece, which did appear in the form of the silver center cent pattern.[23] Regular cents and half-cents were instead composed of copper valued below their monetary value, but without legal tender standing. The profits from coinage, which were initially very low, have expanded along with the broadening of the concepts of money and seigniorage.

Seigniorage in recent years has been accorded a broad definition, encompassing the various closely related sources of profit arising from the issuance of money. When the cost of producing a dollar falls short of a dollar's market value, there is a profit. The profit arises not only from the exchange value of coins exceeding their full production costs, as seigniorage in a strict, original sense, but from the issuance of cheap paper currency and deposits. In order to retain purchasing power, paper money supply must be restricted. Convertibility into gold could pose one such limitation, or convertibility into a national currency could also serve as a means to restrict the private component of supply, e.g., bank notes. Any private issuers must be known, of course, in order to present the possibility of convertibility, which allows monopolistic competition to prevail in contrast to pure competition. Pure competition would lead to a paper standard, eliminating seigniorage.

Money may be issued through bookkeeping entries, which is obviously a highly profitable method for producing money. Deposits in commercial banks and other institutions serve effectively as a medium for transactions as they are transferred among accounts. Under a fractional reserve system, banks may create money by writing up deposits until their reserves are fully committed to the support of those deposits. While note issues of banks stir emotional opposition, fractional reserve banking is not so often criticized as an infringement of the constitutional prerogative of the federal government to issue money.

The central bank likewise may issue money through a deposit creation process. The Federal Reserve System creates "high-powered" money by lending at the discount window or by purchasing securities. High-powered (or "base") money consists of currency plus reserve deposits owned by commercial banks and held by the Federal Reserve banks. When a Federal Reserve bank lends funds at the discount window to a bank, it credits the reserve account of that bank, thus creating high-powered money. The purchase of Treasury bills, for example, also expands high-powered money. The purchase of Treasury bills for the open-market account at the Federal Reserve Bank of New York from a nonbank securities dealer increases the dealer's account at his commercial bank and the bank's reserve account at the Federal Reserve bank. Securities may also be purchased directly from commercial banks and from the U.S. Treasury.[24] The latter transactions enable the Treasury to spend money out of its account with the Federal Reserve that is simply created with the receipt of printed bills. While the mechanics are more complicated when the Federal Reserve uses these methods, the economic implications are precisely the same as an expansion in the money supply by printing paper money. The Federal Reserve reaps a sizable profit from its earning assets, but it pays no interest on currency or on deposits held with the System—as a technical matter the System's profits transferred to the Treasury are denoted as interest on Federal Reserve notes.

The payment of interest does not eliminate seigniorage, but it transfers seigniorage to the recipient. Since the Federal Reserve does not pay interest on high-powered money, it retains that profit, transferring it to the Treasury as noted. The monetary functions of the Treasury are also profitable. The bulk of the seigniorage return of the federal government appears as profits of the Federal Reserve System. Federal Reserve payments to the Treasury in 1987 amounted to $17.7 billion—the total from 1914 to 1987 amounted to $199 billion.[25] On a national income accounting basis, the Federal Reserve System in 1987 generated $16.0 billion in profits, exceeding the $14.1 billion in earnings of the entire private financial sector.[26] Commercial banks for many years issued a large proportion of the conventional form of money on which they paid no explicit interest. This restriction has been phased out in part under the auspices of the Depository Institutions Deregulatory Committee, but a zero interest rate ceiling still applies for demand deposits. Given this restriction, competition in banking would tend to transfer the seigniorage return mainly to borrowers. Economic efficiency dictates that seigniorage be passed on to those who hold money, but regulations and the absence of interest payments to banks on reserves redistribute the profit among banking customers and to the government.[27] The government's seigniorage also operates as a tax on the "underground economy," where cash transactions prevail, and on those countries where the dollar may serve as a substitute for local currency.

The profit potential from money creation would seem to be parabolic, suggesting the existence of a profit-maximizing rate of monetary expansion for the government. A time factor would enter into the calculation, however, as rapid monetary expansion, for example, would affect the level of prices with a lag. Excessive money creation could destroy a currency and eliminate seigniorage. A contraction in the money supply could be sufficiently deflationary, reducing the demand for money and reducing seigniorage. Seigniorage gains accruing to the federal government affect monetary policy but they are clearly subordinated to stabilization and distributional objectives.[28]

Concepts of Money

Concepts of money are perhaps more amorphous than some students seem willing to accept, yet the statistical evidence linking money with economic activity appears sufficiently robust that we should not simply suppose that the conventional economic definitions of money are meaningless. Nonetheless, legal concepts of money may differ from economic concepts of money, and opinions differ on money and money substitutes. Concepts of money, of course, have changed immensely through time. Once, only gold and silver coins were recognized as money and bank notes were viewed as substitutes for money. While devoid of legal tender standing, bank notes later were generally considered to be money. A comparable transition in interpretation applies to demand deposits, as other forms of money were viewed as near-money or money substitutes, which over time have been incorporated into broader concepts of money. Definitions of money obviously must be considered within their historical context, but the appropriate concept still may not remain unambiguous.

The Federal Reserve today recognizes several concepts of money in its policy deliberations, while assigning different weights to them in setting policy. The narrow concept of the money supply, M1, consists of currency, travelers checks, demand deposits, and other checkable deposits. Beyond M1, the Federal Reserve reports weekly and sets target ranges for two additional concepts of the money supply: M2 includes M1 plus overnight repurchase agreements (RPs) and Eurodollars, most money market mutual fund (MMMF) balances, money market deposit accounts, and savings and time deposits; M3 encompasses M2 plus large-denomination time deposits, term RPs and Eurodollars, and institution-only MMMF balances. The Federal Reserve also calculates a liquid asset aggregate (M3 plus U.S. savings bonds, short-term Treasury securities, commercial paper, and bankers acceptances) and a debt aggregate (the debt of domestic nonfinancial sectors).[29]

The historical transition in concepts of the money supply clearly reflects the exercise of constitutional authority by the Congress, as expressed in laws and legal rulings pertaining to money and banking. In recent years, the concepts of money reflect as well market ingenuity, higher interest rates, and a "competition in laxity" among the various regulators to improve the market standing of institutions under their authority. These factors are intimately related to the broad-sweeping deregulatory movement and to the perceived need to rescue tottering financial organizations, which further contribute to the functional convergence of institutions, interstate banking, and the conduct of banking activities by nonbank businesses. The concepts of money are obviously subject to additional revisions.

The concept of money is closely associated with the Federal Reserve's capacity to control the money supply. The Federal Reserve for many years, for example, reduced reserve requirements, loosening the linkage between reserves and the money supply, in order to arrest membership attrition. Finally, reserve requirements were extended to nonmember institutions under the Monetary Control Act of 1980.[30] Reserve ratios are graduated, being higher for larger banks; they are uniform, as the Federal Reserve claims, only for banks of the same size. Reserve ratios also remain low, thus still sacrificing a certain degree of monetary control. The central bank possesses substantial leverage on the financial system but the fluidity of money concepts and their sensitivity to interest rates translate into less precision than would otherwise prevail in the implementation of monetary policy.

Deflationary and inflationary monetary policies historically have created private money substitutes. Deflation promotes a hoarding of currency, which then yields a positive real return to those who hold it, thus exacerbating the constriction of the money supply. When the circulating medium becomes so scarce, private monies have often filled the void to arrest the contraction in business activity. Under an inflationary regime, currency provides a negative real return. Should the primary currency be paper money, hard money is hoarded and the private sector seeks alternatives to the depreciating primary currency. That role may be served in part by private issues of money, along with indexation, foreign currencies, and other defensive measures, as witnessed in a number of foreign countries.

A serious inflation is ordinarily accompanied by an upward

adjustment of interest rates as they incorporate an inflationary premium, such that interest-bearing money and money substitutes become more attractive. Inflation and high interest rates raise the opportunity cost of holding currency and deposits subject to binding interest rate ceilings. Likewise, the opportunity cost of reserves held by the banking system increases, while the central bank captures a larger seigniorage gain and gives up part of its capacity to control the money supply. Real assets, such as gold and silver, also become more attractive hedges against inflation, along with foreign currencies, further limiting the effectiveness of monetary policy as a stabilizing tool to the extent that such assets serve as media for transactions. Interest rates on financial assets and price increases on tangible assets support their use in place of the government's money, thus retarding any drift toward barter.

The steep inflation of recent vintage in the United States inspired the use of those substitutes for the government's money, as well as speculative activities to defend asset values or to profit from inflation. At the same time, thought has been given to private money ventures as a means to compete with the government's depreciating currency. On an intellectual plain, some economists have contemplated that technological advances coupled with entrepreneurial innovations may move our society toward a system of relative price accounting where money as such is irrelevant. Indeed, the legal restrictions theory of money conceptualizes the conduct of economic transactions in abstract units independent of money as such. A system of these units might involve a set of exchange rates competing with the dollar.[31]

Economic Stabilization

The express language of the Constitution contains a set of rules for the conduct of the nation's monetary policy in a broad sense. The federal government was given the authority to regulate the value of coins in the establishment of a specie standard. These "constitutional rules" were viewed by the framers as compatible with economic stability, sharply contrasting with the instability (and inequity) of the monetary regime epitomized by state bills of credit. The rules were in compliance with accepted international practices. They provided for neither steady monetary growth nor discretionary management of the money supply. Beyond these "constitutional rules," the government was implicitly to defer to market processes for the determination of the price level as well as the tempo of business activity. The federal government on an intermittent basis certainly did promote economic development and provide for financial stability, beyond setting the rules, but laissez faire policies generally prevailed and moderate growth in the gold supply governed the level of prices in the long run, thus suggesting at least tacit acceptance of the gold standard's "rules of the game." The price level was essentially stable over extended time intervals, but in the short run the economy experienced a high amplitude in its business cycle fluctuations and instability in money and prices.

The monetarists contend that the adoption of a "monetary rule" could conceptually replicate the long-run performance of the gold standard, but in the short run, a steady noninflationary expansion of the money supply would be stabilizing as well, certainly relative to discretionary management of the money supply. Indeed, Milton Friedman has proposed the following constitutional amendment:

> Congress shall have the power to authorize non-interest-bearing obligations of the government in the form of currency or book entries, provided that the total dollar amount outstanding increases by no more than 5 percent per year and no less than 3 percent.[32]

Thus, Friedman seeks to maintain a reasonably stable, moderate growth rate in the monetary base ("high-powered" money). He suggests, in addition, a two-thirds vote of the Congress to suspend this provision on an annual basis should there be a declaration of war. A complementary restriction might also be imposed on the monetary authority to modify reserve ratios.

Friedman and Anna Schwartz have observed that the erosion

and ultimate abandonment of the gold standard under the Federal Reserve have been accompanied by greater instability in the money supply than that experienced under the monetary regime that immediately preceded it.[33] The capacity to promote economic stability through discretionary policies provides the same capacity to engineer destabilizing policies, "election cycles," or chronic inflation. Beyond that, faulty operating procedures, forecasting errors, or political influence may inadvertently generate cyclical fluctuations in business activity, and, given the lag between policy actions and economic effects, discretionary policies are very difficult to implement in a stabilizing manner.

The Federal Reserve, indeed, has underwritten chronic inflation while presiding in recent decades over the steepest peacetime inflation in U.S. history. In the process, the government has reaped substantial seigniorage gains, reduced the burden of the public debt, and benefited from automatic tax increases, even on nominal and "illusory" increases in income or wealth. Redistributive objectives, moreover, have been sought through varying interest rate ceilings, market intervention by federal credit agencies, guaranteed loans, and other regulations to divert the flow of funds, along with experiments with credit controls.

Proponents of discretionary policies fundamentally doubt the presumption that the private economy is inherently stable. Rules, then, are incompatible with economic stability. The abandonment of the gold standard stands as an emphatic rejection of market-oriented rules. Inflation, to some extent, may reflect a reasonable trade-off to avert depressions and financial panics.[34] Nonetheless, monetary policy, in the opinion of such proponents, should be supplemented by a set of policy instruments to control the private sources of instability, by directly regulating credit, for example, and intervening forcefully into the wage-price setting mechanism. Those who support discretionary policies often seem also to favor redistributive regulations of the financial sector and concomitantly a larger role of government in the management of the economy.

This is not to suggest that the advocates of rules and the advocates of discretionary policies can be so neatly segregated. The ground occupied by this writer, and by others, falls somewhere between these two positions, as we trust that a role for discretionary management of money does not necessarily encompass undue interference with the efficient operations of financial markets.

Income Redistribution

The Constitution's monetary provisions were designed specifically to prohibit the redistributive practices of the states in their issuance of legal tender paper money, and the same restriction was presumably applicable to the Congress. The interests of wealthy creditors were given protection from the abuse of monetary powers by the government—this statement is compatible with Charles Beard's thesis, but not his contention that the framers were motivated by personal gain.[35] Protection from market forces was not recognized as a responsibility of government, beyond supposing, as Hamilton did, that a solid financial footing for the nation would be advantageous for the promotion of economic development.

Another tenet in constitutional construction relates to accommodating the appeal of special interests for redistributive flows. The founding fathers were disturbed by practices impairing the obligation of contracts through the issuance of paper money, expropriating the wealth of creditors by debtors, and the general leveling undertone of dissident elements. Historically, the resolution of the monetary question favored creditors in the sense of generally providing no easy exit for debtors. One exception was the defeat of the Bank of the United States, which had administered restrictive policies. Since the Great Depression, however, redistributive devices have been increasingly employed to enhance or to maintain the redistributive gains of a wide array of debtors. These redistributive conduits have proven to be ineffective or inefficient in meeting social objectives. The constitutionally appropriate mechanism involves the explicit tax-transfer system.

The debate on the monetary standard was generally resolved

in favor of gold for nearly 150 years of the nation's history under the Constitution. The anchor, of course, was lifted periodically in times of banking crises and wars. The longer-run stability of the price level, however, was achieved with considerable short-run instability that obviously generated massive redistributions of income and wealth. The inflationary policies advocated by the Populists, under the banners of free silver and "greenbacks," were unceremoniously rejected. The political consensus was not entirely on the side of restrictive policies, however. Jackson's objective in the Bank War was ostensibly to institute a hard-money regime, but opposition to the Bank of the United States was also found among the emerging business interests whose credit demands were accommodated during the succeeding, less disciplined "free banking" era.

The distributional impact of monetary policy has been a matter of continuing public policy concern of the presiding administration since the Great Depression, and monetary policy has served as an instrument for achieving distributional objectives.[36] While limiting monetary policy as a tool for stabilization, monetary policy as a redistributive instrument suffers from what Kenneth Boulding calls "political irony," i.e., "what you do to help people hurts them, and what you do to hurt people helps them."[37]

The redistributive characteristics of monetary policy in recent decades may be viewed from several vantage points. Inflationary monetary policy constitutes a substitution for explicit taxes, as described above, redistributing income to the government, as well as arbitrarily redistributing the burden on the private sector to finance the government. The inevitable disinflation (or deflation) that follows accelerating inflation also suggests, when coupled with policy lags, a redistribution of the policy options among generations of politicians—those who must face the consequences (or opportunities) of their predecessors' policies. To the extent that this tames the business cycle, and that bailouts are potentially available, some protection is offered to the business community. The observed "competition in laxity," moreover, suggests that regulatory agencies may operate for the benefit (or are captives) of those organizations over which they exercise regulatory authority.[38] Two additional, closely related, redistributive objectives are found in the effort to shield certain sectors or groups from the restrictive policies or from an escalation of interest rates and the effort simply to aid preferred interest groups. The Federal Reserve has often been the target of charges, not without grounding, of aiding the banks, but the central bank has generally eschewed the administration of specific, selective credit controls.

The distributional impact of inflation is difficult to assess when the adjustment process is so pervasive and the longer-run effects contrast so sharply from those apparent in the short run. An unanticipated acceleration in inflation benefits debtors, while unfavorably affecting their counterparts, but an unanticipated deceleration in inflation can reverse the redistributive flows. The total returns for bond investors (creditors) may be negative under accelerating inflation, if the decline in principal value exceeds interest income, and may turn substantially positive if inflation decelerates—the real, inflation-adjusted return may experience a more exaggerated swing. The bondholders, of course, may see the debtors default on their obligations at such times. While inflation may proceed at a diminished rate, many debtors are hard-pressed if their product prices decline absolutely (i.e., a basic commodities price deflation). The rejection of the long-run Phillips curve, moreover, suggests that inflation has not been accompanied by lasting employment gains for low-income, marginal workers. The temporal symmetry in the redistributive effects of inflation/disinflation certainly would not apply to all. Persons selling their bond portfolios at the bottom of the market to invest in high-yielding money market instruments may have failed to participate in the ensuing rally, just as borrowers at high interest rates might have expected inflation to reduce their debt burden but found the debt load unbearable under disinflation. The young and the poor may escape the financial market volatility but fail to hold those real assets that may continue to rise in price even during disinflationary periods. Financial market regulations often seem to work against those persons as well, according to "Director's law," i.e., the redistribution of income and wealth from the rich and the poor to the more numerous middle class, even though they are presumably the targeted beneficiaries.

Government regulations are often designed to redistribute income, thus implicitly imposing "taxes" on one group in society in order to convey "subsidies" to other groups.[39] Deregulation recognizes the failure to achieve certain social objectives, and the reality of market forces overriding the regulations. Interest rate ceilings on savings deposits, for example, were supposed to protect home building when rates moved to higher levels. While their success is doubted, in large measure because they orchestrated a form of disintermediation, draining funds from the mortgage market, their adverse impact was clearly absorbed by small savers, who were "taxed" in an effort to "subsidize" some home buyers.[40] Usury laws have similar perverse distributional consequences.[41] Besides manipulating interest rate ceilings, the federal government in a major way continues to intervene in the markets to divert lending through legislation, e.g., the Home Mortgage Disclosure Act and the Equal Credit Opportunity Act,[42] and through the operations of federally sponsored credit agencies where the major objective has been to support residential construction.[43] The operations of these agencies and a number of agencies that provide loan guarantees encompass broad segments of the economy, often giving preferential treatment to small businessmen, farmers, students, veterans, exporters, and others besides home buyers.[44] While such groups receive implicit subsidies, others pay the implicit taxes in this pattern of "cross-subsidies." Exactly who pays is usually unclear, but no doubt in part includes less aggressive members of the same groups of persons, as well as a cross-section of individuals and businesses who pay higher prices and higher interest rates, or find credit unavailable Just as we have witnessed in several private industries, regulation-induced patterns of cross-subsidies ultimately eroded those regulations as competitors entered the market to provide goods or services at lower prices to those customers who bear the implicit taxes. This process clearly underlies the recent market response to highly inflationary policies.

The web of regulations woven by the federal government has entangled the Federal Reserve in its effort to conduct stabilization policies. The mechanical linkage between policy instruments and the money supply has become less predictable, and political pressures to subordinate monetary policy to the distributional objectives of the government have increased, threatening to eliminate the traditional insulation of monetary policy from special interests, as manifest historically in the legal ownership and structure of U.S. central banks. The rising tempo of inflation has been gradually incorporated into interest rates, eroding the balance sheets of financial institutions such that disinflation has exposed serious imbalances, threatening the financial safety net. As a result, monetary control is compromised by the weakened foundation of the financial structure, yet the amplitude of interest rate swings must be greater to produce stabilizing results, which raise political opposition to monetary restraint.

Recognition of cross-subsidies as a substitute for fiscal policy expands enormously the federal government's scale of operation, while hampering the implementation of stabilizing policies. Taxes and subsidies should be, on efficiency grounds, incorporated explicitly into the federal budget and monetary policy should therefore be conducted "independently" by a central bank free of responsibilities to meet a set of narrowly defined distributional objectives, rather than reverting to the practices of the states in their issuance of bills of credit.

Summary

The Constitution defines the relationship between the people and the government so ordained. Society ultimately chooses what serves as money, but it does so in competition, through market forces, with the state's claims of sovereignty in the determination of the monetary standard and the issuance of that money. Constitutional rules may strictly limit the exercise of the government's monetary authority, but governments may exercise discretion in conducting policies to stabilize the level of income and prices and to redistribute income to favored constituencies.

The fundamental monetary rules are expressed in the Constitution. Those rules governed the construction of financial institutions in the early decades of the nation's history. The institutions evolved, however, and the rules were altered to conform to a changing political consensus. In the absence of clearly defined rules, the government may betray that trust inherent in the Constitution, as it extracts excessive seigniorage from the issuance of money, arbitrarily redistributes income, and undermines contractual relationships by conducting inflationary policies. Society may then seek to override those abuses of the monetary powers by the government.

Notes

1. Arthur Nussbaum, *Money in the Law* (Chicago: Foundation Press, 1939), pp. 198–211; and Gerald Dunne, *Monetary Decisions of the Supreme Court* (New Brunswick, NJ: Rutgers University Press, 1960), Preface, and pp. 99–100.

2. For a broader view of the sources of legitimacy, see Kenneth E. Boulding, "The Legitimacy of Central Banks," in *Reappraisal of the Federal Reserve Discount Mechanism*, vol. 2 (Washington, DC: Board of Governors of the Federal Reserve System, 1971), pp. 1–13.

3. Montesquieu, *The Spirit of the Laws* (Cambridge, England: Cambridge University Press, 1989), pp. 398–416.

4. Aristotle, *The Nicomachean Ethics* (Cambridge, MA: Harvard University Press, 1968), pp. 283–89.

5. Nussbaum, *Money in the Law*, pp. 28–30; F. A. Mann, *The Legal Aspects of Money*, 3d ed. (Oxford: Clarendon Press, 1971), pp. 14–26; Ludwig von Mises, *The Theory of Money and Credit* (New Haven, CT: Yale University Press, 1953), pp. 461–81; and S. Herbert Frankel, *Two Philosophies of Money: The Conflict of Trust and Authority* (New York: St. Martin's Press, 1978), pp. 43–56.

6. Dunne, *Monetary Decisions*, pp. 99–100.

7. Murray Teigh Bloom, *Money of Their Own: The Great Counterfeiters* (New York: Ballantine Books, 1960). Counterfeiting was a serious matter in colonial America, as carried out by Freelove Lippencott and other practitioners of the art. (Donna O'Keefe, "Counterfeit Notes Plagued Colonists," *Coin World*, July 2, 1975, p. 72.)

8. Frankel, *Two Philosophies of Money*, p. 4.

9. Ibid., p. 89.

10. Ibid., p. 41.

11. A. R. Burns, *Money and Monetary Policy in Early Times* (New York: Knopf, 1927), pp. 76–77.

12. John M. Willem, *The United States Trade Dollar* (Racine, WI: Whitman Publishing, 1965), p. 35.

13. Burns, *Money and Monetary Policy*, pp. 75–77, 444–45.

14. Ibid., p. 83.

15. William Wiseley, *A Tool of Power: The Political Economy of Money* (New York: John Wiley, 1977), pp. 1–36.

16. Isaiah 1:22.

17. Burns, *Money and Monetary Policy,* pp. 457–64; and Nussbaum, *Money in the Law*, pp. 10–24.

18. The Bank of England from 1797 to 1804 countermarked Spanish milled dollars in order to promote their circulation, which inspired the following:

> The Bank, to make their Spanish Dollars pass,
> Stamped the head of a fool on the head of an ass.
> —Anonymous

Willem, *The United States Trade Dollar*, pp. 36–38.

The Bank of England and the Bank of Ireland issued dollars dated 1804, along with smaller-denomination tokens.

19. Senator Glass's portrait appeared on the Lynchburg, Virginia, sesquicentennial commemorative half-dollar dated 1936, honoring the senator's long career, marked by his influence on banking legislation—he also served as an ex officio member of the Federal Reserve Board. Richard S. Yeoman, *A Guide Book on United States Coins* (Racine, WI: Western Publishing, 1990), p. 219. The likeness of the governor of Alabama appeared on a 1921 commemorative half-dollar; it was the first such portrait to appear on a coin. Secretary of the Treasury Salmon Chase's portrait appeared on the early "greenbacks," and the superintendent of the national currency, Spencer Clark, had his likeness printed on fractional currency notes during the Civil War as well.

20. Yeoman, *A Guide Book of United States Coins,* p. 222.

21. This is also illustrated by Andrew Jackson's portrait on the largest denomination ($10,000) of U.S. fiat notes, series of 1878. William McKinley's likeness appears on $500 Federal Reserve notes, and the largest denomination ($10,000) is reserved for Salmon P. Chase (Coin World, *Coin World Almanac*, 5th ed. [New York: World Almanac, 1987], pp. 262–64).

22. Ibid., p. 97.

23. Yeoman, *A Guide Book of United States Coins*, pp. 10, 63.

24. Paul Meek, *Open-Market Operations* (New York: Federal Reserve Bank of New York, 1973).

25. Board of Governors of the Federal Reserve System, *Annual Report, 1987*, p. 235. The Federal Reserve's annual profits translate roughly into what

would be the government's annual cost today of maintaining the gold standard as it prevailed from 1880 to 1914.

26. U. S. Department of Commerce, *Survey of Current Business* (Washington, DC: USGPO), Table 6.18B.

27. Thomas Frederick Wilson, "Identification and Measurement of Grant Elements in Monetary Policy," in *Redistribution through the Financial System: The Grants Economics of Money and Credit*, ed. Kenneth E. Boulding and Thomas F. Wilson (New York: Praeger, 1978), pp. 38–56.

28. In the absence of constitutional monetary rules, Geoffrey Brennan and James Buchanan argue, Leviathan will tend to be guided by revenue maximization in money creation ("Revenue Implications of Money Creation under Leviathan," *American Economic Review* 71, 2 [May 1981]: 347–51).

29. Board of Governors of the Federal Reserve System, *Federal Reserve Bulletin* 71, 9 (September 1985): A3.

30. The effect conforms with expectations; that is, it lowered the earnings and stock prices of nonmember banks relative to member banks (G. J. Santoni, "The Monetary Control Act, Reserve Taxes and the Stock Prices of Commercial Banks," *Review*, Federal Reserve Bank of St. Louis, 67 [June/July 1985]: 12–20).

31. Neil Wallace, "A Legal Restrictions Theory of the Demand for 'Money' and the Role of Monetary Policy," *Quarterly Review*, Federal Reserve Bank of Minneapolis, Winter 1983, pp. 1–7. A subsequent study reviews the use of coupons as currency in Canada (Martin S. Eichenbaum and Neil Wallace, "A Shred of Evidence on Public Acceptance of Privately Issued Currency," Quarterly Review, Federal Reserve Bank of Minneapolis, Winter 1985, p. 24).

32. Milton Friedman, "The Case for Overhauling the Federal Reserve," *Challenge*, July/August 1985, p. 7.

33. Milton Friedman and Anna Jacobson Schwartz, *A Monetary History of the United States 1867–1960* (Princeton, NJ: Princeton University Press, 1963), pp 9–10.

34. Walter W. Heller, *New Dimensions of Political Economy* (Cambridge, MA: Harvard University Press, 1966); and Hyman Minsky, *Can "It" Happen Again?: Essays on Instability and Finance* (Armonk, NY: M. E. Sharpe, 1982), pp. xi–xxiv. Roy Harrod offers a conventional rationale for "incomes policy," which is tantamount to direct market intervention to alter the distribution of income in the name of price stability, while fiscal and monetary policies remain expansive (*Money* [London: Macmillan, 1969], pp. 335–38).

35. Charles A. Beard, *An Economic Interpretation of the Constitution of the United States* (New York: Free Press, 1986). Beard's classic remains the best known historical exposition of the forces motivating the framers of the Constitution. The casual reader's understanding of Beard's thesis may be very shallow, perhaps no more than supposing simply that economic considerations were dominant. Beard contends that he essentially tested two competing hypotheses:

> Did they represent distinct groups whose economic interests they understood and felt in concrete, definite form through their own personal experience with identical property rights, or were they working merely under the guidance of abstract principles of political science? (p. 73)

Beard's general thesis that economic interests were expressed in the construction of the document seems a reasonable supposition, but the framers seem to have been guided as well by certain, perhaps idealistic, political principles. The more controversial aspect of Beard's study, however, is the nature and substance of the evidence of "personal experience," e.g., ownership of public debt instruments. As such, the case appears to be built on personal gain from the adoption of the Constitution. The evidence is not very convincing. Indeed, the personal interest looms large for some of those who attended the Convention but refused to sign the document (Mason and Randolph), and Beard does not test his hypothesis in terms of the framers' participation in the rebellion or their role in the government after the adoption of the Constitution (pp. 149–51). In his introduction to the volume, Forrest McDonald reviews the evidence and subsequent research. McDonald characterizes Beard's study as "necessarily somewhat simplistic and uninformed" (p. vii). As McDonald states: "In none of the many instances in which Beard slants his data does the minor misstatement seem especially important, but the cumulative force is powerful" (p. xviii). As a result, Beard nearly doubles his list of securities holders (ibid.). Nonetheless, Beard was unaware of what "modern economic historians have discovered," . . . that the securities speculators held short positions and thus "preferred that prices remain low or even decline so that they might use cheap public securities to pay for public lands" (pp. viii–ix). Yet, "Beard's work was seminal," according to McDonald, as "it created a new and broader mode of thought than what had existed before" (ibid.). Such that in the words of Richard Hofstedter, Beard "no longer persuades, but he still sets the terms of debate" (p. xxxvi).

36. Von Mises, *The Theory of Money and Credit*, pp. 219–31, 423–52; Charlotte E. Ruebling, "Motives behind Inflationary Monetary Expansion," and Thomas Havrilesky, "The Distribution of Income and Monetary Policy," both in Boulding and Wilson, *Redistribution through the Financial System*, pp. 59–69, 70–83; and "Commentary on Monetary Economics: An Interview with Karl Brunner," *Review*, Federal Reserve Bank of St. Louis, November 1978, pp. 8–12.

37. Kenneth E. Boulding, *A Preface to Grants Economics: The Economy of Love and Fear* (New York: Praeger, 1981), p. 13.

38. George J. Stigler, "The Theory of Economic Regulation," *The Bell Journal of Economics and Management Science* 2, 1 (Spring 1971): 3–21.

39. Richard A. Posner, "Taxation by Regulation," *The Bell Journal of Economics and Management Science* 2, 1 (Spring 1971): 22–50; John Tuccillo, "Taxation by Regulation: The Case of Financial Intermediaries," *The Bell Journal of Economics* 8, 2 (Autumn 1977): 577–87.

40. David H. Pyle, "Interest Rate Ceilings and Net Worth Losses by

Savers," in Boulding and Wilson, *Redistribution through the Financial System*, pp. 87–101.

41. William C. Dunkelberg, "The Transfer Implications of Consumer Credit Regulation," in Boulding and Wilson, *Redistribution through the Financial System*, pp. 155–90.

42. Joseph Scherer, "Implicit Grants in the Financial System: The Case of the Equal Credit Opportunity Act," in Boulding and Wilson, *Redistribution through the Financial System*, pp. 149–54.

43. Patric H. Hendershott and Kevin E. Villani, "Grant Elements in the Operations of Federally Sponsored Credit Agencies in the Home Mortgage Market," in Boulding and Wilson, *Redistribution through the Financial System*, pp. 227–43.

44. Murray L. Weidenbaum, "The Use of the Government's Credit Power," in Boulding and Wilson, *Redistribution through the Financial System*, pp. 211–26.

CHAPTER 3

Interpreting the Constitution

Discussion of this topic seems appropriate in view of the transition in the interpretation of the Constitution's monetary provisions and the unfamiliarity of many readers with the interpretive modes employed by the courts. Within this context, the chapter also reviews the Constitution's characteristics, purpose, and function, along with its application and interpretation. The confusion and controversy that exist today over the appropriate manner of interpreting the Constitution, moreover, make it all the more necessary that we offer an explanation of the bases for analyzing in these chapters the judicial decisions related to the Constitution's monetary provisions.

Interpretive Rules

What is the proper set of interpretive rules has been the focus of serious disagreement among legal scholars, and particularly in the past twenty-five years, the subject of a good deal of political debate. The extent of the confusion and doctrinal and political differences is strong proof that the Constitution does not expressly or unequivocally resolve every issue that arises under it. In short, it is not a self-executing instrument. To the contrary, the application of the Constitution's provisions and principles to a particular issue typically requires interpretation.

While a full discussion of the debate over various ways of interpreting the Constitution plainly is beyond the scope of this

---

This chapter was largely written by Brent Taylor.

work, the most defensible approach to constitutional interpretation is one that emphasizes (1) the express language of the written document; (2) the plain implications of related provisions; (3) past judicial interpretations of the same provision or of related provisions; (4) the history of the drafting and adoption of the Constitution and the specific provision of the Constitution at issue; and (5) the promotion of the most fundamental political issue embodied in the Constitution—the principle that the United States is a representative democracy in which the people enjoy sovereignty and control the nature, purpose, and scope of their government through the delegation of limited powers.[1] The merit of this approach is best understood after a basic review of the Constitution's characteristics, purpose, and operation.

Characteristics of the Constitution

While it possesses the characteristics inherent in the notion of a political constitution, the Constitution of the United States is different from the constitutions of other countries in several significant ways that make constitutional interpretation necessary and important. Webster provides a succinct definition of the generic meaning of a political "constitution": "the mode in which a state or society is organized; *especially*: the manner in which sovereign power is distributed."[2] Like the constitutions of other states, the Constitution establishes the organization of the government. In its first three articles it creates and outlines the powers and operation of the three branches of the federal government: the legislative, executive, and judicial branches. Functioning as the master blueprint for our political and legal systems, the Constitution is organic, supreme law.[3] Indeed, it so provides in Article VI:

> This Constitution, and the Laws of the United States which shall be made in Pursuance thereof; and all Treaties made, or which shall be made, under the authority of the United States, shall be the supreme Law of the Land; and the judges in every State shall be bound thereby, any Thing in the Constitution or Laws of any State to the Contrary notwithstanding.

However, the Constitution is different from those of other states in that it is a single, written document, is not detailed, and is relatively "rigid."

That the Constitution is a single, written document distinguishes it from other political constitutions and fundamentally affects how it is understood and applied. Although most states now have written constitutions, the United States Constitution, as the oldest surviving written national constitution,[4] marks the beginning of the period of documentary constitutions. Even those countries frequently described as having "unwritten" constitutions have many components of their constitutions in writing. For example, Great Britain's constitution, often proffered as an example of an unwritten constitution, includes the Bill of Rights, Act of Settlement, Parliament Act of 1911, the successive Representation of the People acts, statutes dealing with the structure of the courts, various local government acts, and other statutes. Thus, the difference lies not so much in the fact that ours is a written constitution, as in that it consists of a single, formal instrument.

Compared to other constitutions, the U.S. Constitution is very short. Because the Constitution is only one document, it is less detailed than constitutions, such as that of Great Britain, that include numerous legislative acts as well as unwritten components. Even in comparison to other single-document constitutions, the United States Constitution is a lesson in brevity. The Constitution's lack of detail has allowed greater room for disagreement as to its meaning and application in particular cases, with the result that the Supreme Court has enjoyed substantial latitude in interpreting the Constitution in some cases.

The rigidity of a constitution is measured by the relative ease with which it is amended. Article V of the Constitution establishes a two-step amendment process of proposal and ratification. Amendments may be proposed either by two-thirds of both houses of the Congress, or by a constitutional convention when requested by two-thirds of the state legislatures. Ratification requires the assent of three-fourths of the states, by their legislatures or by conventions. The two-step process requiring supermajorities at each step positions the Constitution on the rigid side of the spectrum, with the constitutions requiring only an ordinary parliamentary majority falling at the other end of the spectrum. While the relative inflexibility of the Constitution is consistent with its function as a fundamental, lasting framework for our representative democracy, the rigidity, as we shall see, has placed the Supreme Court in the position of having to reconcile governmental policy arising out of economic and political exigency with the language of the Constitution, often with the result that the original intent and meaning of the Constitution were compromised in the perceived interest of responding to the exigency. In other words, in the area of monetary policy, the inflexibility of the Constitution may provide one explanation for the tendency of the Court, described below, to sanction the monetary practices of the government at the expense of the language of, and history behind, the monetary provisions of the Constitution.

Purpose of the Constitution

In describing modern constitutionalism, constitutional scholar C. F. Strong summarizes that "[t]he objects of a constitution, in short, are to limit the arbitrary action of the government, to guarantee the rights of the governed, and to define the operation of the sovereign state."[5] To understand the limits on government, the rights of the governed, and sovereign power under the Constitution, one must first locate the source of sovereign power in the constitutional scheme, a source readily apparent in the first three words of the charter: "We The People." Popular sovereignty is the basic premise in the logic explaining how the Constitution achieves the purposes common to all constitutions. It is logic that holds that the legitimacy of the state and its supreme law flows from the agreement of those governed that the state should wield only certain limited powers and that the government should be the servant of the people.

The notion of sovereignty residing in the people has its roots in the social contract theory of the state proposed by, among others, John Locke[6] and Jean-Jacques Rousseau.[7] The Lockean social compact is built on the cornerstone of man's "natural rights" and "regards government as creative of no rights, but as strictly fiduciary in character, and as designed to make more secure the more readily available rights which antedate it."[8] The familiar American constitutional values of individual rights and limited, representative government are products of the social contract described by C. F. Strong:

> By the compact men abandon certain of their natural rights, but only those necessary to the establishment of a civil condition of society. The object of political society is, therefore, to secure that the rights not so abandoned continue to be guaranteed to the citizens.[9]

Nothing provides such dramatic evidence of social contract as the purpose of our political organization—of our "constitution"—or a more eloquent statement of the principles of government by social agreement, as does the Declaration of Independence, which states:

> that all men are created equal; that they are endowed by their Creator with certain unalienable rights . . . that to secure these rights, governments are instituted among men, deriving their just powers from the consent of the governed; that, whenever any form of government becomes destructive of these ends, it is the right of the people to alter or abolish it, and to institute a new government, laying its foundations on such principles, and organising its powers in such form, as to them shall seem most likely to effect their safety and happiness.

Function of the Constitution

To realize its purpose of guaranteeing a government for the people, free of tyranny, the Constitution functions to allocate power among the people, the states, and the federal government, and within the federal government, among the three branches, so that power will be shared, not concentrated. The division of power between the states and the federal government is known as "federalism," and the allocation of powers to three independent branches of the federal government is referred to as the "separation of powers." In its most detailed provisions, the Constitution establishes and defines the three branches of the federal government and provides for a system of checks and balances wherein each of the three branches oversees and limits the exercise of power by the other branches; the framers relied closely on the work of "the celebrated" Montesquieu in devising this governmental structure.[10] The "federal" distribution of rights and powers was made explicit in the Constitution with the adoption of the Ninth and Tenth Amendments:

Amendment IX
The enumeration in the Constitution, of certain rights, shall not be construed to deny or disparage others retained by the people.

Amendment X
The powers not delegated to the United States by the Constitution, nor prohibited by it to the States, are reserved to the States respectively, or to the people.

Although the Constitution is express in its provision that it shall be the supreme law and in its allocation of governmental power and guarantee of individual substantive rights, it does not explicitly provide who shall enforce the Constitution and be the final arbiter of its meaning. In other words, the power of the Supreme Court—with which we are all familiar—to review legislation adopted by the legislative and executive branches and to declare such legislation invalid owing to its violation of the Constitution is not stated anywhere in the document. The power of "judicial review" was asserted by the Supreme Court in what undoubtedly (at least among legal scholars) was its most famous decision, *Marbury* v. *Madison* (1803).[11] Nearly two centuries after that landmark case, constitutional scholars still are trying to establish a theory that will rationalize and legitimate the power of nine unelected justices, appointed for life, to interpret the Constitution. Indeed, it is not an overstatement to say that the intertwined issues of the legitimacy of judicial review and how judicial review should be performed are the most profound and intensely debated issues among constitutional law scholars.[12] The scholarly discourse over the means and legitimacy of judicial review has been particularly vigorous in the last fifty years, following the Legal Realists' successful attack upon the proposition that the application of law generally by the judiciary is a politically neutral, scientific discovery of the single answer to a legal issue based on logic. The demise of the conception of judicial decision making as purely neutral and scientific, and the resulting crisis in American constitutional thought over the issues of judicial review make a discussion of the ground rules of constitutional interpretation important, if not essential, in any analysis of constitutional decisions.

Application and Interpretation of the Constitution

An examination of the means and issues of constitutional interpretation is best begun by contrasting "interpretation" and "application." Constitutional interpretation is a means to the goal of application. Moreover, one should appreciate that not every instance of application requires interpretation. Clearly, the application of the Constitution is a simple task when the express terms of the document address, directly and unambiguously, the question presented. Thus, for example, virtually no interpretation is required to apply the Constitution's mandate in Article II, Section 1, that the president be at least thirty-five years old and meet other specific criteria stated in the provision defining who may hold that office. However, because the Constitution is comparatively brief and is by design a statement of fundamental law and principles, it simply cannot address in express terms each of the innumerable issues that arise under it. Consequently, the application of the Constitution—particularly in the court opinions produced by constitutional litigation—generally requires that the Constitution's meaning be "interpreted."

There are many approaches to constitutional interpretation and they are not mutually exclusive. In fact, jurists and scholars almost always use some combination of interpretive modes. Often, they employ different modes in an order of preference—the "grayer" the issue, the greater the number of "levels of analysis" in the interpretation. Those cynical of the process of constitutional interpretation might argue that the various modes are chosen according to the desired result in a particular case.

There are three interpretive approaches that would be described by virtually any jurist or constitutional scholar as standard, not in the sense that any one of the approaches, or even the combination of the three, is decisive, but in the sense that these modes universally would provide a point of departure for constitutional interpretation in deciding an issue. The three standard approaches are the textual, the contextual, and the precedent approaches.

The obvious starting place for any interpretation of the Constitution is the language of the provision in question. Harvard Law School professor John Hart Ely describes the textual approach as a brand of "interpretivism" that holds "that judges deciding constitutional issues should confine themselves to enforcing norms that are stated or clearly implicit in the written Constitution."[13] Ely distinguishes "interpretivism" from a "clause-bound interpretivism," which overlooks the theme of the Constitution as a document to safeguard the functioning of a representative democracy, and the opposite category that Ely calls "noninterpretivism," a "value-laden" approach that contemplates "that courts should go beyond that set of references [stated or clearly implicit in the written Constitution] and enforce norms that cannot be discovered within the four corners of the document."[14]

To appreciate the possibilities of an approach to constitutional interpretation that is this simple and direct, one needs to study the opinions and writing of the late Justice Hugo Black, whom Ely characterizes as "the quintessential interpretivist."[15] For example, in *Griswold* v. *Connecticut* (1965),[16] the case often credited with laying the theoretical foundation for the Supreme Court's later decision establishing women's constitutional right to abortion, the Court struck down a Connecticut statute outlawing the use of contraceptives. The Court's opinion, written by the late Justice William O. Douglas, reviewed a number of the "specific guarantees in the Bill of Rights" and found that they had "penumbras" that established a constitutionally protected "zone of privacy." Vehemently disagreeing with the Court's "discovery" of the constitutional right of privacy, Justice Black offered these comments in his dissent:

> The Court talks about a constitutional "right of privacy" as though there is some constitutional provision . . . forbidding any law ever to be passed which might abridge the "privacy" of individuals. But there is not. . . . [I] get nowhere in this case by talk about a constitutional "right of privacy" as an emanation from one or more constitutional provisions. I like my privacy as well as the next one, but I am nevertheless compelled to admit that government has a right to invade it unless prohibited by some specific constitutional provision.[17]

The second standard interpretive approach is characterized as the "contextual." This mode emphasizes the importance of taking account of the established meaning of related provisions of the Constitution so that conflicting interpretations of related provisions will be avoided. The approach also is a variety of interpretivism in that the analysis still is largely textual and is "within the four corners" of the Constitution. It suggests simply that after analyzing the ordinary meaning of the language of a particular provision, one should perform a similar analysis of the language contained in the document's related provisions.

The last of the basic, noncontroversial approaches to constitutional interpretation is to look at judicial precedent. In the same way that the judicial system generally has a strong desire to be consistent in its construction of statutes and common law rules, the Supreme Court has a strong interest in being consistent in its interpretation of the Constitution. The interest in consistency is particularly strong with respect to the Court's judicial review of the acts and laws of the other branches, because the appearance of political neutrality in performing its review role explains in no small degree the success of the Supreme Court in retaining the asserted power of judicial review since *Marbury* v. *Madison*. (The Legal Realism movement, while it has caused a revolution in American legal thought, has not spread beyond the profession so as to destroy the public's traditional conception of law and judicial decision making as neutral and scientific.)

Precedent as an interpretive device plainly has its limitations and dangers, however. The chief limitation is that the Supreme Court is not infallible. Its history is punctuated with instances in which the Court "did an about-face" and overruled its prior decision. Similarly, there is the danger that a "wrongly decided" Supreme Court precedent will not be overruled, but will serve as the springboard for further deviation from the "true meaning" of the Constitution.

When the language and provisions of the Constitution and prior cases construing the provision under scrutiny do not produce a single, definitive meaning of the provision, various additional interpretive approaches frequently are used to supplement the standard initial approaches. Among these supplemental approaches, one of the most popular is the "historical," in which one attempts to determine the intent of the persons who drafted and those who then adopted the constitutional provision in question. In other words, the approach entails a search for the "intent of the framers." The search for intent as a way of ascertaining meaning is no stranger to the law. Accordingly, a court construing a private written contract will be primarily concerned with giving effect to the parties' intent under the instrument, and in construing a statute, a court will focus on the legislature's intent in enacting the law as indicated by its legislative history. The resources for an examination of the "legislative history" of the Constitution include the records of the federal convention in which the Constitution was written, approved, and offered for ratification, and of the various state ratifying conventions, along with influential commentary of the time, such as *The Federalist* (or the Federalist Papers). In addition to looking to records directly related to the political adoption of the Constitution, jurists and scholars often look to the common law and social conditions and conventions at the time of adoption to inform the meaning of the language used by the framers.

Beyond the approaches so far discussed, there are at least two categories of interpretive approach that are quite vulnerable to the criticism that they can be used selectively and with few intellectual constraints to achieve a preferred result in a given case. One category—which is not easily defined—encompasses many modes of reasoning or argument that may be used in any quest for meaning. For example, "classification" was a hallmark of nineteenth-century legal reasoning. In the context of constitutional law, it often involved the defining of "spheres of power" and then the classification of the power at issue as falling within one or the other of the spheres. The weakness of such reasoning is that the classification is made on the basis of an unconstrained characterization of the "nature" or "essence" of the power at issue. Classification clearly is not the only such mode of interpretation, as the "argument" category includes reasoning by analogy and others, e.g., the reference to practices in other countries as a warranted expression of sovereignty.

The second category of unconstrained interpretive approaches relies on a reading of the Constitution to protect and promote "fundamental values." The resort to values often occurs when the language of the Constitution is silent or vague with respect to the value. As a substitute for a documentary value, those applying the approach often rely upon some actual or perceived social consensus that the value is so important that it rises to the level of being "fundamental," and is therefore worthy of protection under the Constitution. In other cases the user of the approach is attempting to promote the "superior" value or policy.

The importation of values into the Constitution has occurred most frequently through interpretation of the due process clause of the Fourteenth Amendment, which guarantees that no person shall be deprived of "life, liberty, or property, without due process of law." In 1905, the Supreme Court awarded laissez faire economics constitutional protection in its decision in *Lochner* v. *New York*.[18] *Lochner* resulted in "frequent invalidation of various sorts of worker protection provisions during the first third of this century," but is "now universally acknowledged to have been constitutionally improper."[19] Similarly, the Supreme Court's decision in *Roe* v. *Wade* (1973)[20] held that a woman's right to privacy under the due process clause assured her the right to have an abortion during the first trimester of pregnancy without interference from the state; the decision of course invalidated the antiabortion laws in all the states. The literally violent nature of the current debate over abortion and the Court's decision in *Roe* v. *Wade* is the most vivid contemporary evidence of the weakness in resorting to values as a mode of constitutional interpretation.

The values approach has recently been defended by now retired Justice William J. Brennan, a remnant of the Warren Court. Judicial activism was the hallmark of the Warren Court, and Brennan's "noninterpretivist" approach was guided by the Constitution as a "vision of human dignity."[21] Given the understanding, in the words of Justice Joseph Story, that the federal government "is parental guardian of all our public and private rights,"[22] the judge, in Brennan's view, is assigned the responsibility to protect those enduring values in "a living Constitution," as he felt no compulsion to rely on the express language of the instrument nor to divine the "original intent" of the framers. "Original intent," in a broad sense, may indeed also be a form of "noninterpretivism," when the judges apply some supposed values of those who drafted or ratified the Constitution. The controversy excited by former Attorney General Edwin Meese, and intensified by Robert Bork's confirmation hearings, focused on "original intent" in judicial reasoning and on judicial activism versus judicial restraint. While Meese and Bork advised attention be given to the document's express language, they ultimately counseled deference to legislative majorities as a matter of judicial restraint.[23] Brennan argued that legislative majorities are suspect, and that property rights are outmoded.[24] Libertarian sentiments have coalesced around the notion of the judiciary recognizing as enthusiastically as civil rights the Constitution's protection of property or economic rights.[25] While perhaps neither majoritarian nor libertarian in persuasion, judges now seem inclined to advance more forcefully "interpretivist" modes instead of Brennan's value-laden "noninterpretivism."

Thus, the judicial elevation of certain values or policies to constitutional status can be fairly said to have created the greatest controversies in the area of constitutional law, among both the legal profession and the public. There are at least three serious problems with reliance on perceived important values or policies in the absence of express, relevant language in the Constitution: (1) the classification process deciding which values are "fundamental," and which are not, is inherently unconstrained, discretionary, and subject to result-oriented manipulation; (2) even if we assume that a list of truly fundamental values worthy of incorporation into the Constitution could be created, the analysis—free ranging, outside the language of the Constitution—has no neutral means of assessing the relative importance of competing values; and (3) the inevitability of social change makes it questionable whether any particular value will remain "fundamental" as attitudes change, public opinion shifts, and consensus deteriorates. The critics of those employing a values approach argue that the judgments about values are inherently political and therefore should be left to the people to decide through their legislatures.

There is one value, however, enshrined in the Constitution that can legitimately be used to supplement the accepted standard and historical interpretive approaches: the principle that the Constitution establishes and mandates a representative democracy. The merits of this interpretive approach have been articulated best by John Hart Ely.[26] The protection of the institutional value of representative democracy, in addition to satisfying the criteria commonly used to justify resort to other values, is uniquely appropriate because of the Constitution's provision in Article IV, Section 4: "The United States shall guarantee to every State in this Union a Republican Form of Government. . . ." Moreover, it is clear that the principle of representative democracy flows from the purpose of the Constitution as explained above, which is to preserve popular sovereignty, government to which "We The People" consent.

Conclusion

Interpretation of the Constitution's monetary provisions begins with a consideration of the text itself. The express language of the monetary provisions may be given further meaning within the context of related provisions and supplemented by studying the history of their drafting and adoption. The intent of the framers may be understood more clearly within the general theme of the document in terms of their effort to form the structure and operating processes of a representative democracy in which the people enjoy sovereignty and control the nature, purpose, and scope of their government through the delegation of limited powers. Within this setting, it seems advisable to avoid "clause-bound" interpretations that are not only unresponsive to democratic processes but also overlook the rigidity of the instrument. Yet one should also avoid, at the other extreme, those "value-laden" approaches to constitutional interpretation that rationalize contemporary policies or reshape institutions as a matter of expediency, while ignoring the principles inherent in a document that has endured for two centuries.

The monetary powers expressly delegated to the Congress are narrowly limited, as outlined in the introduction, and the provisions' textual meaning is fully consistent with their drafting and adoption, clearly reflecting the intent of the framers. Nevertheless, presented with certain exigencies, the courts have (in the manner described above) allowed a more expansive exercise of the monetary powers by the federal government, which in turn has established the precedent for further expansion of the powers beyond the confines of the language, history, and original intent of the Constitution's monetary provisions. Our task here is primarily to review this history of the exercise of monetary powers by the Congress, to describe monetary practices and institutional arrangements within the structure of government and the rubric of delegated powers, to amplify the risk of an unconstrained monetary authority, to identify the direction in which this evolutionary process is taking us, and to suggest certain steps that might be taken to alter that course in preserving certain constitutional principles.

Notes

1. The statement, "The Constitution is what the judges say it is," has been attributed to Charles Evans Hughes (Dwight D. Murphey, "Myths and American Constitutional History: The Liberal Truisms Revisited," *Intercollegiate Review* 14, 1 [Fall 1979]: 20). This often quoted opinion, of course, is incomplete. It is perhaps understood that completion of the statement would not imply, "the express language notwithstanding" (decisions ordinarily reveal some respect for the express language of the Constitution), but include, "within the context of generally accepted interpretive modes." The judges are not so unconstrained, we might suppose, that they would ignore the constitutional admonition that they "shall hold office during good behavior."

2. *Webster's New Collegiate Dictionary* (Springfield, MA: G. & C. Merriam, 1981), p. 241.

3. "Constitutional Law," *Corpus Juris Secundum* (St. Paul, MN: West Publishing, 1984), vol. 16, sec. 2, p. 22.

4. C. F. Strong, *A History of Modern Political Constitutions* (New York: G. P. Putnam's Sons, 1963), p. 342.

5. Ibid., p. 12.

6. John Locke supposed that liberty and equality were based on man's relationship with God, and that political liberties are guaranteed by a social compact:

> To avoid these Inconveniences which disorder Mens Properties in the State of Nature, Men unite into Societies, that they may have the united strength of the whole Society to secure and defend their Properties, and may have *standing Rules* to bound it, by which every one may know what is his.

To Locke, properties meant at times possessions, but alternatively it meant "lives, liberties, and estates." John Locke, *Two Treatises of Government* (Cambridge, England: Cambridge University Press, 1988, first published in 1690), p. 359. Thus Locke argued on theological and historical grounds that governments were established to preserve liberties and to protect recognized inequalities in the distribution of wealth. John Rawls, interestingly, arrives at a very different conclusion, supposing that the tabula rasa is characterized by a "veil of ignorance," under which individuals would presumably agree to equality of rights and equality in the distribution of income and wealth, providing for variation should compensating differences emerge when applying a maximin decision rule. John Rawls, *A Theory of Justice* (Cambridge, MA: Harvard University Press, 1971), pp. 14–15, 151.

7. See Jean-Jacques Rousseau, *Of the Social Contract or Principles of Political Right and Discourse on Political Economy* (New York: Harper & Row, 1984).

8. Richard Loss, ed., *Corwin on the Constitution,* Vol. 1, *The Foundations of American Constitutional and Political Thought, the Powers of Congress, and the President's Power of Removal* (Ithaca, NY: Cornell University Press, 1981), p. 124.

9. Strong, *A History of Modern Political Constitutions*, p. 12.

10. Montesquieu, *The Spirit of the Laws* (Cambridge, England: Cambridge University Press, 1989, originally published in 1748). For references to checks and balances, see especially Book 11, "On the laws that form political liberty in its relation with the constitution" (pp. 154–86).

11. 1 Cranch 137 (1803). The issue of judicial review was left unresolved at the Constitutional Convention. The concept was recognized, however: Hamilton in *The Federalist* (no. 78) stated that the courts must assume the duty "to declare all acts contrary to the manifest tenor of the constitution void" (J. R. Pole, ed., *The American Constitution: For and Against* [New York: Hill and Wang, 1987], p. 304). Marshall commented at the Virginia Convention:

> Can [the Congress] go beyond the delegated powers? If they were to make a law not warranted by any of the powers enumerated, it would be considered by the judges as an infringement of the Constitution which they are to guard. They would not consider such a law as coming under their jurisdiction. They would declare it void.
>
> To what quarter will you look for protection from an infringement on the Constitution, if you do not give the power to the judiciary? There is no other body that can afford such protection. (Jonathan Elliot, *Debates on the Adoption of the Federal Constitution*, vol. 3 [New York: Burt Franklin, 1964 reprint of 1888 edition], pp. 553–54)

In *Marbury* v. *Madison,* Marshall stated:

> It is emphatically the province and duty of the judicial department to say what the law is. Those who apply the rule to particular cases, must of necessity expand and interpret the rule. . . . Thus, the particular phraseology of the Constitution confirms and strengthens the principle, supposed to be essential to all written constitutions, that a law repugnant to the Constitution is void; and that courts, as well as other departments, are bound by that instrument. (Robert F. Cushman, *Leading Constitutional Decisions*, 14th ed. [Englewood Cliffs, NJ: Prentice-Hall, 1971], pp. 8, 11)

Jefferson, in contrast, held the view that each branch was equal in interpreting the Constitution (ibid., p. 4). Marshall's opinion may have been compatible with the consensus of his contemporaries, but in the present century, the judiciary has monopolized constitutional interpretation, and judicial review has become a policy-making instrument, thus transforming it into a matter of considerable policy debate (Alfred H. Kelly, Winfred A. Harbison, and Herman

Belz, *The American Constitution: Its Origins and Development*, 6th ed. [New York: W. W. Norton, 1983], p. 177).

12. For example, see John Hart Ely, *Democracy and Distrust: A Theory of Judicial Review* (Cambridge, MA: Harvard University Press, 1980).

13. Ibid., p. 1.

14. Ibid., pp. 1, 72–73, 87–89.

15. Ibid., p. 1.

16. 381 U.S. 479 (1965).

17. Ibid., pp. 508–10.

18. 198 U.S. 45 (1905). Lochner was convicted of violating a New York statute that restricted the work hours of bakery employees. Justice Rufus W. Peckham stated in the opinion of the Court:

> The general right to make a contract in relation to his business is part of the liberty of the individual protected by the 14th Amendment of the Constitution. . . .
>
> The question whether this act is valid as a labor law, pure and simple, may be dismissed in a few words. There is no reasonable ground for interfering with the liberty of person or the right of free contract, by determining the hours of labor, in the occupation of a baker.

Oliver Wendell Holmes stated in his dissenting opinion:

> The 14th Amendment does not enact Mr. Herbert Spencer's Social Statics. . . . [A] constitution is not intended to embody a particular economic theory, whether of paternalism and the organic relation of the citizen to the state or of laissez faire. (Cushman, *Leading Constitutional Decisions*, pp. 206, 207, 212)

19. Ely, *Democracy and Distrust*, p. 14.

20. 410 U.S. 113 (1973).

21. William J. Brennan, Jr., "The Constitution of the United States: Contemporary Ratification," in *The Constitution and the Supreme Court*, The Reference Shelf, vol. 60, no. 1, ed. Steven Anzovin and Janet Podell (New York: H. W. Wilson, 1988), pp. 166–79.

22. Henry Steele Commager, "The Constitution and Original Intent," ibid., p. 205.

23. Edwin Meese, "Interpreting the Constitution," ibid., p. 164; and Robert H. Bork, "Tradition and Morality in Constitutional Law" (Washington, DC: American Enterprise Institute for Public Policy Research, 1984).

24. Brennan's suspicion of majorities has historical roots, of course, although the minority interests so protected were to change. Madison wrote:

> It seems to be forgotten, that the abuses committed within the individual States previous to the present Constitution, by interested or misguided majorities, were among the prominent causes of its adoption, and particularly led to the provision contained in it which prohibits paper emissions and the violation of contracts, and which gives an appellate supremacy to the judicial department of the U.S. Those who favored and ratified the Constitution believed that as power was less likely to be abused by majorities in representative Governments than in democracies, where the people assembled in mass, and less likely in the larger than in smaller

communities, under a representative Government inferred also, that by dividing the powers of Government and thereby enlarging the practicable sphere of government, unjust majorities would be formed with still more difficulty, and be therefore the less to be dreaded. . . . (Max Farrand, ed., *The Records of the Federal Convention of 1787*, vol. 4 [New Haven, CT: Yale University Press, 1911], pp. 86–87)

Tocqueville also observed a judicial check on the "tyranny of the majority":

In visiting the Americans and studying their laws, we perceive that the authority they have intrusted to members of the legal profession, and the influence which these individuals exercise in government, is the most powerful existing security against the excesses of democracy. (Alexis de Tocqueville, *Democracy in America* [New York: New American Library, 1956], p. 123)

25. Stephen Macedo, *The New Right v. the Constitution* (Washington, DC: Cato Institute, 1986); and Clint Bolick, *Unfinished Business: A Civil Rights Strategy for America's Third Century* (San Francisco, CA: Pacific Research Institute for Public Policy, 1990).

26. Ely, *Democracy and Distrust*, pp. 77–104.

CHAPTER 4

Roots of the Constitution's Monetary Provisions

The monetary provisions of the Constitution are rooted in the confused state of financial affairs that existed under the Articles of Confederation, especially the disturbing inflationary and redistributive consequences of financing public expenditures by printing money. The delegates to the Constitutional Convention held strongly negative views of the states' management of their "bills of credit" (i.e., paper money), and they sensed in Shays's Rebellion an alarming drift toward more serious financial disorder. The horrendous depreciation suffered by the "continentals" during the Revolutionary War was also fresh in their minds. A precedent had been firmly established, however, as the issuance of paper money had been a major source of revenue for the colonial governments, who also had coins struck under their authority and "regulated" the value of foreign and domestic coins, as well as of other circulating media.

Components of the Money Supply in Colonial America

By the time of the revolution, over half the colonial money supply consisted of paper currencies that had been issued by all the colonial governments. During the colonial period, the money supply was composed in varying proportions of a curious mixture of exotic commodities, coins and tokens issued under governmental authority and as private business ventures, private bank notes, and foreign and British coins, as well as the bills of credit.

After the revolution, notes issued by commercial banks were added to this mixture.

The legal authority to issue coins was granted expressly under its charter only to Virginia, but other colonies assumed this power (possibly by inference from general provisions of their charters). The colonies and the states under the Articles of Confederation recognized reality in their monetary policies by accepting the array of circulating media. While the governments attempted to regulate coins by specifying their value in exchange and by setting coinage standards, they did not pretend to be able to secure a monopoly over the issuance of money. The "monetary base," so to speak, was specie, which had an international footing. Governments did effectively maintain monopolistic control over the issuance of paper money during the colonial period, although there was competition among the governments, and they entered into contracts for the issuance of coins; private coinage, however, was permitted.

The Constitution revoked the monetary power of the states (as discussed in the following chapter), and conferred on the federal government certain powers previously exercised by the colonial and state governments to issue coins and to regulate the value of foreign and domestic coins. The Constitution did not prescribe a federal monopoly over the issuance of coins and no powers were delegated for the issuance of paper money or for the incorporation of a bank.

Money in Colonial America

Several commodities served as media of exchange in colonial America. Wampum, beaver skins, tobacco, and other items circulated as money. The General Court of Massachusetts in 1637 conferred legal tender status on wampum for sums of less than twelve pence. Although the legal tender standing was rescinded in 1661, it is noteworthy that reality received such official blessing.[1]

Coins and tokens were issued under governmental authority and as private business ventures. The only specific delegation to a colonial government of the right to coin money was conveyed by the charter granted by King James to Virginia in 1606:

> [T]hey snall, or lawfully may, establish and cause to be made a coin, to pass current there between the people of these several colonies, for the more ease of traffic and bargaining between and amongst them and the natives there, of such metal, and in such manner and form, as the said several Councils there shall limit and appoint.[2]

It was not until 1773 that coins were struck for Virginia. After some delay, the Virginia coins were released for circulation in 1775. They were immediately hoarded under a monetary regime of depreciating paper money, and subsequently many coins were melted. They never circulated broadly.

Massachusetts established a mint and entered into a contract with John Hull, the mintmaster, to issue coins. Hull received fifteen pence out of every twenty shillings. The coinage (including the famous pine tree shilling) was successful and very profitable for the mintmaster.[3] The British authorities did not take actions to suppress the coinage and apparently did not view it for many years as an encroachment on their prerogatives. Most of the coins bore the date 1652, however, in order to appear as though they were struck while Oliver Cromwell was in power. The coinage was abandoned in 1682 largely on business grounds with the expiration of the coinage contract, but the legal question remained at issue.[4] Cecil Calvert, the Lord Proprietor of Maryland, had coinage struck in England in 1658 for that colony.[5]

The British government entertained several proposals for American coinage.[6] John Holt was granted a franchise in 1688 to strike tokens, the American plantations token, which was the first authorized coinage for the British colonies. They were struck in tin and valued at 1/24 part of a Spanish real. In 1722 William Wood, who owned copper mines, obtained a patent for a period of fourteen years to issue coins for the American colonies. The quantity issued was to be limited to 300 tons, and the privilege required Wood to pay £100 annual rent to the

Crown and £200 salary to the Clerk Comptroller.[7] The coins were about half the weight of corresponding British coins in an effort to secure substantial profit, but on that account they were not generally accepted by the colonists.[8]

Private coinage ventures without official sanction were also undertaken. Dr. Samuel Higley, who owned a copper mine near Granby, Connecticut, struck coins dated 1737. Higley set the value of his copper coins at three pence. Apparently their exchange value was questioned, because later issues bore the inscription, "Value me as you please," although the Roman numeral "III" remained on the coins. After his death, coins were struck in 1739. The Higley coinage business was "unquestionably profitable."[9] In 1681 Mark Newby led a group of emigrants from Ireland to New Jersey. He brought with him a large quantity of coins known as St. Patrick coinage, which were granted legal tender status up to five shillings in that colony. There were other privately struck tokens issued as speculative ventures that did not receive legal tender standing.[10] In Massachusetts, where a significant volume must have been in circulation, such pieces were prohibited by law.[11]

The regulation of the value of foreign coins was a significant aspect of colonial monetary policy. British coins and many different foreign coins circulated. The Spanish dollar, an international currency, was a prominent component of the money supply in the colonies. In order to maintain circulation of specie, the colonial governments raised the exchange value of the Spanish dollar and certain other coins. While recognizing the inflated price level of the colonies, the Crown sought to encourage the flow of specie to England. The Queen Anne proclamation of 1704 cited eleven types of foreign crown-sized silver coins, and the Act of Parliament of 1707 set a six shilling maximum to the legal value of the Spanish dollar and proportionate ceilings on the values of other silver coins.[12] Beyond the important point that the colonial governments sought to regulate the value of foreign coins, which, of course, was addressed by the authorities in London, it is obvious that a substantial proportion of the money supply consisted of coins that were not struck by these governments, despite any prerogatives of the sovereign.

Colonial Paper Money

Paper money eventually became the major component of the money supply in colonial America. At the beginning of the Revolutionary War, paper money constituted an estimated 60 percent of the currency in circulation—Pelatiah Webster estimated the money supply at $12 million, which translated into a silver value of $10 million with $4 million in coin and $6 million in paper money.[13] Massachusetts in 1690 emitted the first issue of paper money, and in 1692 its currency was declared legal tender. By 1755 all the colonies had such bills of credit in circulation.[14] Following Massachusetts, these issues were also made a legal tender.[15] While the term "bill of credit" implies a debt instrument, and the colonial governments justified their issues as a form of borrowing, there is no doubt that the bills were money.[16]

Benjamin Franklin is the best-known proponent of paper money. Although he had a proprietary interest in the printing of these bills, his arguments stand firmly on their merits. Franklin contended that paper money provided an adequate medium of exchange and augmented the supply of credit, thereby exerting an economic stimulus. Franklin set forth his case in 1729 in "A Modest Inquiry into the Nature and Necessity of a Paper Currency," where he argued:

> There is a certain proportionate Quantity of Money requisite to carry on the Trade of a Country freely and currently; More than which would be of no Advantage in Trade, and Less, if much less, exceedingly detrimental to it. . . . A plentiful Currency will occasion Interest to be low: And this will be an Inducement to many to lay out their Money in Lands, rather than to put it out to Use, by which Land will begin to rise in Value and bear a better Price: And at the same Time it will tend to enliven Trade exceedingly, because People will

find more Profit in employing their Money that way than in Usury; and many that understand Business very well, but have not a Stock sufficient of their own, will be encouraged to borrow Money; to trade with, when they have it at a moderate interest.[17]

Adam Smith in *The Wealth of Nations* offered a contrasting view. Smith argued that paper money displaced specie, such that the shortage of hard money was apparently caused by the emission of the bills of credit, and in a country where wages were higher than in England, he reasoned, it would appear to be a matter of choice, not necessity.[18] As Smith claimed: "The redundancy of paper money necessarily banishes gold and silver from the domestic transactions of the colonies."[19] Smith's position was probably valid by the 1770s, when large quantities were in circulation, but in the earlier years, especially prior to the 1740s, a shortage of specie existed, as a reflection of the exceptionally strong demand for imports. The limited supply of specie was indicated by the acceptance of commodity monies and the prevalence of barter. The value of specie in foreign trade was therefore sufficiently strong to force the domestic economy into barter before a dominant role was taken by paper money.

Adam Smith's most perceptive observation relates to the distinct economic gains resulting from the substitution of paper money for specie:

The substitution of paper in room of gold and silver money, replaces a very expensive instrument in commerce with one much less costly, and some times equally convenient.[20]

It is convenient for the Americans, who could always employ with profit in the improvement of their lands, a greater stock than they can easily get, to save as much as possible the expense of so costly an instrument of commerce as gold and silver; and rather to employ that part of their surplus produce which would be necessary for purchasing those metals, in purchasing the instruments of trade, the materials for clothing, several parts of household furniture, and the iron work necessary for building and extending their settlements and plantations; in purchasing, not dead stock, but active and productive stock.[21]

Smith, of course, was alluding to the seigniorage gains arising from the substitution of low-cost paper for precious metals in the production of money.

Seigniorage gains, when accruing to those who issue money, present an incentive for producing an excess supply of money and encourage policies designed to redistribute income and wealth between debtors and creditors and between those favored by government loans and expenditures and those who hold the depreciating currency. The bills of credit in many cases offered the prospect of borrowing without paying interest, and the money was made legal tender and backed by legal stipulations that it circulate on par with specie—despite such regulations, the bills depreciated under the weight of excessive quantities placed into circulation. While obliging certain private interests, the bills provided a source of revenue, as Smith critically observed:

> Some of the governments, that of Pennsylvania particularly, derive a revenue from lending this paper money to their subjects, at an interest of so much per cent. Others, like that of Massachusetts Bay, advance, upon extraordinary emergencies, a paper money of this kind for defraying the public expense, and afterwards, when it suits the conveniency of the colony, redeem it at the depreciated value to which it generally falls.[22]

Reliance on paper money as a source of revenue caused it to depreciate and impeded the establishment of responsible, tax-supported budgeting.

The record on the issuance of paper money on balance has been viewed favorably by recent scholars. The performance among the colonies is mixed, however, and the quantitative evidence is fragmentary. In New England, where the colonial governments competed in the issuance of bills of credit, the paper money depreciated at a brisk rate. Between 1700 and 1720, the price of silver doubled. From 1720 to 1750, the supply of bills expanded by a multiple of ten, the price of silver in Boston rose fivefold, and a comparable increase was sustained by the price of wheat in bills relative to sterling. In Rhode Island and New Hampshire the value of the Spanish milled dollar in bills more than doubled between 1751 and 1763.[23] In Massachusetts creditors inserted purchasing power maintenance provisions in contracts by stipulating payment in specie.[24] Substantial depreciation also was experienced from 1708 to 1740 in North Carolina and South Carolina, but the currencies appreciated over the following eighteen years.[25] In New York, New Jersey, Pennsylvania, Maryland, and Virginia, the rates of depreciation were moderate, and at times no measurable decline in purchasing power was evident.[26]

Private Banks and Colonial Finances

The colonial governments closely guarded their monopolistic position in the issuance of paper money.[27] No private bank cast in the mold of the Bank of England was organized until the Bank of North America was incorporated in 1781 by the Congress under the Articles of Confederation.[28] Private, note-issuing "banks" were formed in New Hampshire, Connecticut, and Massachusetts in the early eighteenth century, however. These banks were organized by merchants, one of which involved 396 participants, to provide circulating media and profits. The private "land banks" operated in much the same manner as the public loan offices of the colonial governments, which provided this banking function (i.e., monetizing mortgage debt) in addition to issuing bills of credit to finance their expenditures. These private notes specified redemption some years hence in specie, bills of credit, or goods. The promissory notes of New Hampshire paid 1 percent interest, and one Massachusetts issue was payable on demand. In 1735, Massachusetts prohibited their circulation in the colony, but the act was repealed by the Crown. Public officials did not welcome the competition or the potential threat posed by the existence of a concentration of private monied interests. With support from the colonial governments, Parliament in 1741, after a review by the Crown in 1740, extended the Bubble Act to America, thus requiring the immediate redemption of these issues.[29]

The suppression of private banks and the reliance of the colonies on paper money, instead of establishing adequate systems of taxation, might very well have hampered the development of sound financial policies and the associated dependable, noninflationary methods of financing public outlays. Although the Crown at a late date did prohibit the colonial governments from declaring their bills of credit legal tender, they were still allowed to issue public bills, in part out of respect for the common law right to borrow. Other restrictions were imposed on the issuance of paper money, however, and these restrictions themselves were cited, but with no specific reference to bills of credit, in the Declaration of Independence as an infringement on the colonies' right to determine their own domestic policies.[30]

Financing the American Revolution

Paper money served as the major source of funds for financing the Revolutionary War from 1775 to 1780, and after the currencies had sunk to a negligible value, foreign loans and requisitions on the states provided a firmer footing. Although it is difficult to reconstruct the financial situation, a comparison of expenditures and sources of funds may illustrate the role of paper money in financing the war.

Alexander Hamilton in 1790 estimated Revolutionary War expenditures at $135 million in specie, of which $92 million were actual Treasury payments.[31] Much of the latter sum was presumably covered with "continentals"; as the war dragged on, however, their purchasing power diminished. Treasury records indicate that $242 million of continentals were issued, with $168 million redeemed by the government—the total amount issued was probably substantially greater, however. The loss to the public and gain to the Treasury associated with the continental currency exceeded substantially the difference between those official figures. It has been computed at $197 million. Not only were $74 million never redeemed, but $119 million of continentals were retired in 1780 at a ratio of 40 to 1 with a special issue of state bills—these were supposedly redeemable in 1786 with a U.S. government guarantee and 5 percent interest—and the Funding Act of 1790 provided for conversion into bonds at a ratio of 100 to 1.[32] The states issued $209 million in paper money of their own. The Continental Congress borrowed some $63 million domestically, and foreign loans amounted to $7.8 million in specie. The Continental Congress did not have the power to levy taxes directly; the states did raise some revenue by taxation and the sale of confiscated Tory properties.[33]

The Continental Congress first authorized the issuance of its currency on June 22, 1775, and the first emission was approved on November 29, 1779. With the exception of fractional denominations, issued in 1776, the continental entitled the bearer to receive the face value in "Spanish milled Dollars, or the Value thereof in Gold or Silver." The continental currency initially circulated on par with specie, but commenced a steady, rapid depreciation in 1777. The convertibility provision was not honored, and vast quantities were ultimately placed (or forced) into circulation. While a total of $25 million of notes were authorized in 1775 and 1776, about $20 million more were added in 1777, and huge volumes were printed in 1778 and 1779.[34] After absorption of the early emissions, their value could not sustain the weight of additional bills and the activity of counterfeiters, despite the threat of severe punishment. Counterfeiting of the continentals reflected the efforts of the British as well as regular practitioners of the art. When New York was occupied by British forces, the Rivington *Gazette* carried the advertisement:

> Persons going into other colonies may be supplied with any number of notes for the price of paper per ream. They are so neatly and exactly executed that there is no risk in getting them off, it being almost impossible to discover that they are not genuine. This has been proven by bills to a very large amount which have already been successfully circulated. Inquire of Q.E.D. at the Coffee-house.[35]

By 1780, a continental dollar was worth about 2½ cents in specie, and they ceased to pass as currency by mid-1781, after which they traded at a fraction of a cent as an article of speculation.[36] The state issues experienced a similar fate.[37]

The sad consequences of relying on the printing press to finance the war were perceived as early as 1776. Pelatiah Webster urged the immediate adoption of a tax to prevent excessive expansion of the money supply.[38] Individual states had little incentive to fund quotas assessed by the Continental Congress, and such appeals struck an unresponsive chord when confronted with the persuasive remark:

> Do you think, gentlemen, that I will consent to load my constituents with taxes, when we can send to the printer, and get a wagon load of money, one quire of which will pay for the whole?[39]

In 1779, George Washington noted that "a wagon load of money will scarcely purchase a wagon load of provisions."[40] Webster argued that a tax would distribute the burden of the war far more equitably, and he later harshly criticized the legislation of the states compelling under severe penalty the acceptance of the continental currency as legal tender and the associated wage-price controls, with the latter ironically described as "acts to prevent monopoly and oppression."[41] Webster stated that he opposed

> limitations of prices, forcing sales of private property, tender acts, emitting deluges of paper currency, fixing the value of paper currency by law, and other absurdities which have involved America in greater calamities than the British arms.[42]

The prevailing sentiment was, nonetheless, apparently expressed in the following comments:

> There is at present no absolute necessity for high government taxes. The natural unavoidable tax of depreciation is the most certain, expeditious, and equal tax that could be devised. Every possessor of money has paid a tax in proportion to the time he held it. Like a hackney coach, it must be paid by the hour.[43]

Gouverneur Morris added:

> Depreciation is an assessor that reaches every farthing and baffles every attempt to deceive.[44]

Paper money was perhaps an unavoidable expedient. Hamilton considered it to be "indispensable," although he felt it should never be used again.[45] While not so candid, the positions espoused today are remarkably similar to those taken during the revolution.

Money under the Articles of Confederation

The Continental Congress assumed many of the powers of government, and drew up the Articles of Confederation, which were proposed by Congress on November 15, 1777, and ratified on March 1, 1781. The Articles of Confederation incorporated monetary provisions generally consistent with ongoing practice:

> The United States in Congress assembled shall also have the sole and exclusive right and power of regulating the alloy and value of coin struck under their own authority, or by that of the respective states—fixing the standard of weights and measures throughout the United States—. . .

> The United States in Congress assembled shall have the authority to borrow money, or emit bills on the credit of the United States, transmitting every half year to the respective states an account of the sum so borrowed or emitted. . . . [Article IX]

The Congress was clearly delegated the power to issue coins and bills of credit, and there was no doubt that bills of credit were money and distinct from funds borrowed. The states were not barred from emitting bills of credit, but state coinage was subject to regulation by the Congress. No reference is made to privately issued coins or paper money. The states, however, retained those powers not "expressly delegated" to the United States Congress:

> Each state retains its sovereignty, freedom, and independence, and every Power, Jurisdiction and right, which is not by this confederation expressly delegated to the United States, in Congress assembled. [Article II]

The demise of the continentals and the collapse of the state issues did not put to rest the demand for paper money. Several states issued fresh supplies in the 1780s, and, in 1786, Shays's Rebellion and the political appeal of paper-money advocates heightened fears of a turn toward radicalism. These issues also depreciated dramatically, reinforcing unpleasant memories of the continentals. By the time of the Constitutional Convention, there was a broad consensus to terminate government authority to issue bills of credit.[46] It was during this confused state of affairs that commercial banking commenced in the United States.

Several participants in the Constitutional Convention were instrumental in founding commercial banks, and private bank notes were in general circulation in the 1780s. The Bank of North America was chartered by the Congress in 1781. The plan for a bank was submitted to the Congress by Robert Morris, the Superintendent of Finance, and reflected the assistance of Gouverneur Morris and the recommendations of Alexander Hamilton, who had written a lengthy letter on the project to the Superintendent. The proposal won acceptance by the Congress, with James Madison casting one of the few negative votes. Under the supervision of Robert Morris, the Bank served as the fiscal agent of the government for several years until that function was clearly assumed by the Bank of the United States.[47] The Bank of North America was not viewed as an entirely legitimate expression of congressional authority, such that its charter

> Provided, always, That nothing herein before contained shall be construed to authorize the said corporation to exercise any powers, in any of the United States, repugnant to the laws or Constitution of such State.[48]

Charters were granted by Massachusetts, Pennsylvania (but repealed three years later, only to be reinstituted six months later, on March 17, 1787), Delaware, and New York, where the charter stated:

nothing in this act contained shall be construed to imply any right or power in the United States in congress assembled to create bodies politic, or grant letters of incorporation in any case whatsoever.[49]

After some early difficulties, the Bank's notes circulated at their specie value; small denomination notes, payable in specie, were issued in 1789 on paper supplied by Benjamin Franklin.[50]

The Bank of New York was organized in 1784, and it operated without a charter until 1791 under the common law tradition that private banking was a business. The Massachusetts Bank, the third bank, was also organized in 1784, and it was a state-chartered institution. Despite a prevailing "laissez faire" disposition, banking was soon treated as a "franchise," requiring a charter.[51] While the private banks were continually immersed in controversy, they were managed very conservatively and the bank notes were not viewed as money but as money substitutes that derived their value from convertibility into specie, a promise that was scrupulously honored—this was not true of bills of credit, which were legally money.[52] From an economic vantage point, these bank notes certainly were money.

Coinage under the Authority of Congress

The Congress under the Articles of Confederation in 1787 authorized coinage of the Fugio cent, the first coins struck under the authority of the U.S. government. The design of the Fugio cent resembles that used on the fractional denominations of the continentals in 1776 and on the continental dollar struck the same year. The design has been attributed to Franklin, who also proposed in 1779 coinage with "proverbs of Solomon, some pious moral, prudential or economic precepts."[53] The continental dollar, struck in brass, pewter, and silver, was probably a pattern, perhaps proposed as a silver dollar to replace the one-dollar continentals. Serious attention was given to coinage early in the revolution. Jefferson developed a decimal coinage system in 1776, and the Congress considered establishing a mint in 1777. Patterns for official series of coins were struck in the 1780s.[54]

Robert Morris, who was appointed Superintendent of Finance in 1781, immediately proceeded to form a national bank, but he also gave attention to a national coinage. Indeed, Hamilton, who had earlier advanced the idea of a national bank, suggested that a mint be annexed to it, and the Congress again showed interest in establishing a mint, beyond steps to ascertain the values of coins in circulation for the purpose of determining their use in receiving tax payments.

Morris proposed a silver standard, supposing that the advantage of using gold for larger transactions could be satisfied with paper money. Spanish milled dollars vastly exceeded other forms of specie in circulation by three or four to one, so that a silver coinage appeared to be practical. Morris sought to rationalize the various values in shillings assigned to the Spanish dollar by the states. He selected for this purpose the largest common divisor, which was $\frac{1}{1440}$ part of the Spanish dollar, equal to $\frac{1}{1600}$ of a British crown or $\frac{1}{4}$ grain of fine silver. Incorporating the decimal ratios proposed by his assistant, Gouverneur Morris, the coins recommended by Morris included the "mark" of 1,000 units, a "quint" of 500 units, and a 100-unit "cent" of silver—copper eight- and five-unit coins were also proposed.[55] Patterns were struck in 1783 for these Nova Constellatio silver coins, and for the five-unit copper coin.[56] As a speculative venture, Gouverneur Morris in 1785 had Nova Constellatio copper coins struck in England, but dated 1783, 1785, and 1786, with a design nearly identical to the above patterns.[57] Morris's coinage venture presumably did not conflict with the authority of Congress to issue and regulate coins under the Articles of Confederation.

Jefferson was elected to Congress in 1783 and was later to serve as chairman of the currency committee. Critical of Morris's plan, which was not well received, Jefferson viewed the coinage as cumbersome for transactions purposes, not including coins of value close to the coins in circulation, and for attempting to maintain, rather than eliminate, the valuation systems among the states. In 1784 Jefferson proposed a decimal system based on the familiar Spanish milled dollar, including a ten-dollar gold piece, and a silver dollar, half-dollar, double tenth, tenth, and twentieth, along with a copper hundredth. The values would, therefore, correspond to values in circulation of certain Portuguese and British gold coins, the piece of eight and its bits, and the English half-penny.[58]

Morris and Jefferson urged Congress to establish a mint, but a "Grand Committee" of thirteen members was formed instead in 1785. The committee reported negatively on Morris's proposal and modified Jefferson's plan, recommending a five-dollar gold piece, a quarter instead of the double tenth, and added a $\frac{1}{200}$ of a dollar. The committee recommended the dollar as the coinage unit, preferred a silver standard (silver being less readily exported than gold), and a small seigniorage gain to defray the expenses of a mint and to discourage melting of the coins. An alternative to Morris's plan was appended to the report, and a coin design was suggested—patterns were struck using this design. In response, the Congress in 1785 unanimously agreed that the unit be the dollar, the smallest coin be $\frac{1}{200}$ of a dollar, and the coins be issued in decimal ratios.[59]

The Board of Treasury in 1786 reported on the establishment of a mint and provisions for state copper coins, favoring gold and silver coins with the gold coin being the eagle. Congress, of course, did not take the appropriate steps to establish a mint. Earlier, the depreciation of the continentals foreclosed that possibility, and later the lack of funds prevented fruition of those plans. In addition, opponents to a mint felt that the nation could subsist on foreign coins and contract coinage, of which the Fugio cent was an expression of that concept by the Congress.[60]

Private and State Coinage

Massachusetts established a mint, after failing to convince the Congress to do so, and three states, Vermont, Connecticut, and New Jersey, granted the authority to private individuals to strike the coins for those states. These states issued copper coins. The state legislatures granted the power under very strict terms. Although Vermont was not admitted to the union until 1791, it apparently changed the designs on its coins to gain greater acceptance in neighboring states. New Hampshire agreed to accept any coins in the state provided that they met certain specifications.[61]

A large number of private coins and tokens were placed into circulation in the 1780s and 1790s. Sizable quantities of "Bungtown" tokens and other underweight coins were found in circulation, such that Pennsylvania, where they arrived on a regular basis in large quantities from England and contained about two-thirds of the weight of standard British half-pence, attempted to prevent their use. Also in Pennsylvania, counterfeiters of gold and silver coins were sentenced to death, and any person knowingly passing a counterfeit gold or silver coin was sentenced "to the pillory for the space of one hour, and to have both his or her ears cut off, and nailed to the pillory, and be publicly whipped, on his or her bareback, with twenty-one lashes, well laid on."[62]

There were a number of private coinage ventures in addition to that of Gouverneur Morris.[63] In Maryland John Chalmers issued his own silver coins in 1783. Even though they were underweight, Chalmers backed the redemption value, and the coins were accepted. The most prominent unauthorized coinage operation was located in New York. The petition of Thomas Machin to strike coins for New York was denied, but at Machin Mills, located at New Grange, New York, vast quantities of coins were produced in the late 1780s. Machin Mills issued Vermont, New York, George III, and Connecticut coinage.[64] A committee of the New York Assembly reported in 1787 that the copper coins in circulation passed at a value of 50–100 percent above their production costs, the difference representing the seigniorage gain to those who issued the coins. In "An Act to regulate the Circulation of copper coins," New York specified the standard and weight required for "lawful current money" of the state. All coins, including those of Machin Mills, that met these standards were lawful money, regardless of origin.[65]

Conclusion

An extraordinary range of financial practices over the decades immediately preceding the Constitutional Convention influenced the thinking of the delegates, many of whom were actively engaged in financial affairs. The colonial governments, the Congress, and the states had issued paper money, and private commercial banks were being organized. The governments issued their own coins and regulated the value of coins issued under their own authority and of foreign coins, as well as of coins struck as private business ventures.

The mismanagement of paper money under the states, Shays's Rebellion, and generally chaotic financial conditions prevailing in 1787 were such that a broad consensus favored the repudiation of government-issued paper money and the establishment of an orderly system of coinage.

Notes

1. R. S. Yeoman, *A Guide Book of United States Coins*, 38th ed. (Racine, WI: Whitman Publishing, 1984), pp. 5, 14; and Sylvester S. Crosby, *The Early Coins of America and the Laws Governing their Issue* (Boston: Sylvester S. Crosby, 1875; reprinted by the Token and Medal Society, 1965), pp. 25–28.

2. Crosby, *Early Coins of America*, p. 19; Herman E. Krooss, ed., *Documentary History of Banking and Currency in the United States*, vol. 1 (New York: Chelsea House, 1983), p. 5. Wampum was also regulated in New Netherlands. W. Keith Kavenagh, ed., *Foundations of Colonial America: A Documentary History*, vol. 2 (New York: Chelsea House, 1983), pp. 1264–65.

3. Crosby, *Early American Coins*, pp. 32–33; and Kavenagh, *Foundations of Colonial America*, vol. 3, pp. 1700–1701.

4. Crosby, *Early American Coins*, 90–115; and Kavenagh, *Foundations of Colonial America*, vol. 1, pp. 133, 145.

5. Yeoman, *United States Coins*, pp. 15–17.

6. Crosby, *Early Coins of America*, pp. 139–68.

7. Yeoman, *United States Coins*, p. 18; and Philip Nelson, "The Coinage of William Wood for the American Colonies" (reprint from the *Numismatist*, 1962).

8. Robert A. Vlack, *Early American Coins* (Johnson City, NY: Windsor Research Publications, 1976), p. 22.

9. Ibid., pp. 31–32; Crosby, *Early Coins of America*, pp. 324–27.

10. Vlack, *Early American Coins*, pp. 8, 18; Crosby, *Early Coins of America*, pp. 135–38.

11. Crosby, *Early Coins of America*, pp. 114–16, 345–47.

12. Eric P. Newman, *The Early Paper Money of America* (Racine, WI: Whitman Publishing, 1967), p. 8; Crosby, *Early Coins of America*, pp. 117–18; and Kavenagh, *Foundations of Colonial America*, vol. 1, pp. 544–45.

13. Arthur Nussbaum, *A History of the Dollar* (New York: Columbia University Press, 1957), p. 26.

14. Virginia was the last colony to issue "bills of credit," but it established in 1713 public tobacco warehouses that issued negotiable certificates based on deposits by private individuals (Newman, *Early Paper Money of America*, p. 9).

15. Nussbaum, *Money in the Law*, p. 44.

16. Newman, *Early Paper Money of America*, p. 8.

17. Benjamin Franklin, "A Modest Inquiry into the Nature and Necessity of a Paper Currency," in *Documentary History of Banking and Currency in the United States*, vol. 1, ed. Herman E. Krooss (New York: McGraw-Hill, 1969), pp. 24–25.

18. Adam Smith, *An Inquiry into the Nature and Causes of the Wealth of Nations*, ed. J. R. McCullock (Edinburgh: Adam and Charles Black, and William Tait, 1839), pp. 142, 428.

19. Ibid., p. 428.

20. Ibid., p. 126.

21. Ibid., p. 428.

22. Ibid.

23. Leslie V. Brock, *The Currency of the American Colonies, 1700–1764: A Study in Colonial Finances and Imperial Relations* (New York: Arno Press, 1975), pp. 29–30, 594–95.

24. Ibid., pp. 542–43.

25. Richard A. Lester, *Monetary Experiments: Early American and Recent Scandinavian* (Princeton, NJ: Princeton University Press, 1939), p. 24.

26. Ibid., pp. 24, 85, 114, 138; and Brock, *Currency in the American Colonies*, pp. 345–46, 386–87, 402–3, 476–77.

27. Sanford Durst asserts that these colonial bills of credit were private currencies since the charters established private corporations. In this book, they are of course treated as government issues (Sanford J. Durst, *Comprehensive Guide to American Colonial Coinage: It's* [sic] *Origins, History and Value* [New York: Sanford J. Durst, 1976], p. 3).

28. Banks issued notes in Scotland under the common law without a charter until 1844 (Nussbaum, *History of the Dollar*, p. 45).

29. Private banks were established in Connecticut (1732) and in New Hampshire (1734), and three were organized in Massachusetts (1740–41). There were also unsuccessful efforts to form private note-issuing banks (Bray Hammond, *Banks and Politics in America: From the Revolution to the Civil War* [Princeton, NJ: Princeton University Press, 1957], pp. 10–11, 24–25;

"Governor Thomas Hutchinson Comments on Massachusetts Banking and Bills of Credit, 1769," in Krooss, *Documentary History*, pp. 72–84; Newman, *The Early Paper Money of America*, pp. 9, 55, 137–38, 162; Kavenagh, *Foundations of Colonial America*, vol. 1, p. 549; and Elgin Groseclose, *Money and Man: A Survey of Monetary Experiments* [Norman, OK: University of Oklahoma Press, 1976], p. 181).

30. Hammond, *Banks and Politics in America*, pp. 24–27.

31. "Alexander Hamilton's Estimate of the Revolutionary War Expenditures, 1790," in Krooss, *Documentary History*, pp. 157–58.

32. Ibid., pp. 159–61.

33. Paul Studenski and Herman E. Krooss, *Financial History of the United States* (New York: McGraw-Hill, 1963), pp. 28–30.

34. Newman, *Early Paper Money of America*, pp. 30–42.

35. Krooss, *Documentary History*, pp. 88–89.

36. Ibid., pp. 153–54.

37. Newman, *Early Paper Money of America*, pp. 359–60.

38. Pelatiah Webster, "Essay on the Danger of Too Much Circulating Cash in a State, the Ill Consequences Thence Arising, and the Necessary Remedies," *Pennsylvania Evening Post*, in Krooss, *Documentary History*, pp. 107–12.

39. Studenski and Krooss, *Financial History*, p. 27.

40. Jonathan Grossman, "Wage and Price Controls during the American Revolution," *Monthly Labor Review* 96, 9 (September 1973): 5.

41. Ibid., p. 4.

42. Pelatiah Webster, *Political Essays on the Nature and Operation of Money, Public Finances and Other Subjects* (New York: Burt Franklin, 1969, originally published in 1791), p. 188.

43. Studenski and Krooss, *Financial History*, p. 28.

44. Krooss, *Documentary History*, p. 88.

45. Hammond, *Banks and Politics in America*, p. 29.

46. Ibid., pp. 95–103; George Bancroft, *History of the United States of America*, vol. 6 (New York: N. D. Appleton, 1890), pp. 167–76. Bancroft summarized the sad experience of paper money: the evils of legal tender paper money, property substituted for money in the payment of debt, laws for paying debt by instalments, and the "occlusion of the courts of justice." So that, "The evil was everywhere the subject of reprobation" (p. 176). Richard B. Morris, in *The Forging of the Union, 1781–1789* (New York: Harper & Row, 1987), emphasizes the role of money and credit as the underlying impetus for framing the Constitution, especially the crisis atmosphere created by Shays's Rebellion and its redistributive, leveling implications (pp. 152–58, 174, 266). Forrest McDonald, in *Novus Ordo Seclorum: The Intellectual Origins of the Constitution* (Lawrence, KS: University Press of Kansas, 1985), cited in particular Shays's Rebellion and the paper money schemes of Rhode Island in reference to the framing of the Constitution (pp. 151–77). John Marshall, in *The Life of Washington*, vol. 5 (Philadelphia: C. P. Wayne, 1807), observed that the Confederation was expiring from "mere debility," and the circulation of paper money as a means to relieve debts. Men of principle and property were

alarmed by the turn to radicalism, according to Marshall, represented by Shays's Rebellion and its "levelling principle" (ibid., pp. 112–24).

47. Hammond, *Banks and Politics in America*, pp. 48–64.

48. M. St. Clair Clarke and D. A. Hall, *Legislative and Documentary History of the Bank of the United States including the Original Bank of North America* (New York: Augustus M. Kelley, 1967, originally published in 1832), p. 13.

49. Bancroft, *History of the United States of America*, p. 29.

50. Newman, *The Early Paper Money of America*, pp. 264, 266.

51. Ibid., pp. 65–66; Nussbaum, *History of the Dollar*, pp. 44–45.

52. Hammond, *Banks and Politics in America*, p. 105.

53. Don Taxay, *The U.S. Mint and Coinage* (New York: Arco Publishing, 1966), p. 11.

54. Yeoman, *United States Coins*, pp. 30–34, 51–55; Vlack, *Early American Coins*, pp. 75–86; and Taxay, *The U.S. Mint and Coinage*, pp. 5–10.

55. Taxay, *The U.S. Mint and Coinage*, pp. 13–16.

56. Yeoman, *United States Coins*, p. 32.

57. Ibid., p. 31.

58. Taxay, *The U.S. Mint and Coinage*, pp. 20–21.

59. Ibid., pp. 22–23.

60. Ibid., pp. 24–25.

61. Vlack, *Early American Coins*, pp. 43–62, 73–74; and Crosby, *Early Coins of America*, pp. 175–224, 239–88.

62. Crosby, *Early Coins of America*, pp. 170–74.

63. Vlack, *Early American Coins*, pp. 88–105.

64. Ibid., pp. 63–65, 67–72.

65. Crosby, *Early Coins of America*, pp. 289–96.

CHAPTER 5

Drafting the Monetary Provisions of the Constitution

United States monetary history under the Constitution portrays most vividly the controversies associated with the absence of expressly delegated powers of the Congress to emit bills of credit and to grant charters of incorporation, both of which were rejected by the delegates at the Constitutional Convention. The absence of a reference to banking was also significant. The Constitution revoked the monetary powers of the states and conferred on the Congress the powers to coin money and to regulate the value of foreign and U.S. coins. The rationale for this position is critical to developing the thesis of this book; that is, the prudence of delegating limited monetary powers to the government.

Draft of a Constitution

The Draft of a Constitution, reported by the Committee of Five (or Detail) on August 6, 1787, contained the following monetary provisions:

> The legislature of the United States shall have the power . . . to coin money; to regulate the value of foreign coin; to fix the standard of weights and measures; . . . to borrow money and emit bills on the credit of the United States. . . . [Article VII, Section 1]
>
> No state shall coin money. . . . [Article XII]
>
> No state, without the consent of the legislature of the United States shall emit bills of credit, or make any thing but specie a tender in payment of debts. [Article XIII][1]

These provisions are similar to those found in the Articles of Confederation but with the important exceptions that state coinage was prohibited and the authority of the states to issue paper money or to make anything but specie a legal tender was subject to approval by the Congress.

To Emit Bills of Credit

The views expressed at the Constitutional Convention and in other forums leave little doubt that the intention was to prohibit the issuance of a legal tender paper money. Gouverneur Morris (Pennsylvania), after stating that paper money was a "ruinous expedient" that might be resorted to unless guarded against, moved on August 16 to strike the words "and emit bills," observing that if the nation had credit, the bills would be unnecessary; if not, this provision was unjust and useless. Pierce Butler (South Carolina) seconded the motion.

James Madison (Virginia) suggested that it might be sufficient simply to prohibit making them a legal tender. This would remove the temptation to emit them with unjust motives, adding that promissory notes, absent legal tender standing, might be best in some emergencies. Morris replied by indicating that striking the words would leave room for a "responsible minister" to issue such notes; however, the moneyed interests would oppose the Constitution if "paper emissions not be prohibited."

Nathaniel Gorham (Massachusetts) favored striking the words without a prohibition inserted in the document, feeling that if the words were to stand, this could lead to the issuance of paper money. George Mason (Virginia) had doubts on the subject. Congress would not have the power unless it were expressed, but, despite a "mortal hatred of paper money," Mason could not foresee all emergencies, so he was unwilling to tie the hands of the legislature, observing that the Revolutionary War could not have been conducted had such a prohibition existed. Gorham added that as far as necessary or safe, the power is involved in that of borrowing.

John Francis Mercer (Maryland), who was not present at the signing, favored paper money but would neither propose nor approve of the measure under prevailing circumstances. He felt it would stamp suspicion on the proceedings to deny that discretion, adding that it would be "impolitic" to excite the opposition of the friends of paper money when the people of property already favored the Constitution.

Oliver Ellsworth (Connecticut) thought that this was a favorable time to "shut and bar the door against paper money." The mischiefs were fresh in the public mind and excited the disgust of the respectable part of America. Withholding the power would gain more friends of influence than anything else. Paper money can in no case be necessary: give the government credit, and other resources will be forthcoming.

Edmund Randolph (Virginia) expressed his antipathy to paper money but objected to striking the words, since he could not foresee all occasions that might arise. James Wilson (Pennsylvania) contended that it would have "a most salutary influence of the credit of the United States, to remove the possibility of paper money." This expedient can never succeed while its mischiefs are remembered. So long as the government can resort to it, it will bar other resources.

Pierce Butler remarked that paper money was a legal tender in no other country in Europe, and he wanted to disarm the government of such power. Mason, still averse to tying the hands of the legislature altogether, retorted that no European government was restrained in this regard. George Read (Delaware) stated that if the words were not struck, it would be as "alarming as the mark of the beast in Revelation." John Langdon (New Hampshire) commented that he would rather reject the whole plan than retain the three words, "and emit bills."

Gouverneur Morris, who made the motion to strike the words "and emit bills," distinguished between notes of a "responsible minister," presumably notes issued by a national bank, and notes issued by the government directly, which were "prohibited" under the matter being considered. Butler, who seconded the motion, clearly understood as well that it prohibited the issuance of paper money by the federal government. It should also be noted that Mason and Randolph, who opposed the motion, clearly understood that the motion meant that the federal government would be deprived of the power to issue paper money. Gorham's view was indeed nebulous. Although he opposed paper money, he did not wish to insert an outright prohibition in the Constitution. Following Morris's comment on a "responsible minister," he may simply have preferred not to prohibit the issuance of notes under the auspices of a national bank.

Madison, whose notes constitute the best record of the proceedings, appended to his notes the comment that the affirmative vote of Virginia reflected satisfaction that striking out the words would not disable the government from issuing "public notes," as far as they could be safe and proper; and would only cut off the pretext for a paper currency, and particularly for making the bills a tender, either for public or private debt.[2]

The tenor of the debate suggests a clear consensus opposed to federal paper money, especially one with legal tender standing, although there remained an ambiguity regarding the issuance of debt instruments, as Madison indicated, that were intended for service as money.[3] The understanding was that issuance of a legal tender paper money was prohibited, made firm by rejection rather than being ignored or unforeseen by the delegates. Even in the absence of an outright prohibition, this position is buttressed by other provisions of the Constitution, which designed a government possessing limited powers, and the fact that the power to emit bills of credit, absent in the Constitution, was present in the Articles of Confederation.

Morris's motion passed 9 to 2, with nays cast by New Jersey and Maryland—New York and Rhode Island did not participate in the decision.[4]

The state conventions amplify the negative views toward paper money emissions but provide little additional information regarding the interpretation of the monetary provisions. In the Pennsylvania convention, James Wilson expressed a strongly favorable view of the restraints imposed by the Constitution on the monetary powers of the states.[5] In Virginia, several delegates offered sharp criticisms of paper money, with H. Lee of Westmoreland asking if "there can be an evil which can visit mankind so injurious and oppressive, in its consequences and operation, as a tender law?" He preferred to submit to Pandora's box than to a tender law. William Grayson added that "this engine of iniquity is universally reprobated."[6] In North Carolina, William Davie noted that a leading cause for establishing a new Constitution was "laws which basely warranted and legalized the payment of just debt by paper, which represented nothing, or property of trivial value." Discussion of paper money in North Carolina tended to focus on the treatment of the outstanding currency after ratification of the Constitution, among a wide range of issues, such as the prospect "that the pope of Rome might be elected President."[7]

The comments of two delegates to the Constitutional Convention later gave apparently conflicting impressions of the power to emit bills of credit. Charles Pinckney at the South Carolina convention seemed to hold the view that the federal government retained the power to issue paper money. After denouncing state emissions, since "it always carries the gold and silver out of the country, and impoverishes it," he added, "if paper should become necessary, the general government still possesses the power of emitting it, and Continental paper, well funded, must ever answer the purpose better than state paper." The nature of that paper money was not described, but "well funded" implies a debt instrument and Pinckney followed this comment with criticisms of paper money and the attendant legal tender laws, although presumably in reference to the states.[8]

When Luther Martin, who excused himself from the proceedings of the Constitutional Convention when he realized that the Constitution had taken shape and he opposed it, addressed the Maryland legislature, offering an opinion sharply contrasting to Pinckney's statement. Martin stated that the majority was "willing to risk any political evil rather than admit the idea of a paper emission in any possible case," suggesting that it was "a novelty unprecedented to establish a government which shall not have that authority." He added that we cannot see the future when it would be absolutely necessary, and since "the administration of the government would be principally in the hands of the wealthy, there could be little reason to fear an abuse of the power by an unnecessary or injurious exercise of it."[9]

James Madison in *The Federalist* (nos. 42 and 44) argued in favor of the federal government's powers over coinage, and in strong language on the "pestilent effects of paper money," addressed the withdrawal of the direct monetary powers of the states. Madison also reviewed the disadvantages of the states issuing and regulating coins, noting further that the "proposed uniformity in the *value* of the current coin" under the Constitution made it incumbent on the federal government to regulate foreign coins—this uniformity in a regulatory sense, of course, did not bestow monopoly powers over the issuance of coins.[10]

Alexander Hamilton was silent on monetary matters at the Convention. In 1783, however, he had recommended revisions in the Articles of Confederation, including one addressing the power of the Congress "to emit bills on the credit of the United States" (as reported in the Preface):

> . . . authorizing Congress at all to emit an unfunded paper as a sign of value, . . . ought not to continue a formal part of the Constitution, nor ever, hereafter, to be employed, being, in its nature, pregnant with abuses, and liable to be made the engine of imposition and fraud, holding out temptations equally pernicious to the integrity of government and to the morals of the people.[11]

To Appoint a Treasurer

Drafts of the Constitution until the late stages of the proceedings contained a provision for the Congress to appoint a Treasurer, e.g., "The Congress may by joint ballot appoint a treasurer."[12] The Congress, of course, had been exercising that power, but a motion to strike the provision was passed 8 to 3, thus removing it from the document.[13]

The decision to exclude this power from Congress's repertoire more clearly separates legislative and executive powers. At the same time, the monetary powers of the Congress were delimited, leaving more room for friction between the Congress and the Treasury.

To Grant Charters of Incorporation

No regulatory powers in the Constitution refer specifically to banks and bank notes. The delegates, of course, were familiar with note-issuing banks. The topic apparently was potentially too divisive to be treated effectively. Robert Morris reportedly entertained the idea of proposing to give Congress the power to establish a national bank. Gouverneur Morris opposed the idea, fearing that it would antagonize the antibank forces in Pennsylvania, and thus jeopardize acceptance of the Constitution.[14] While Robert Morris was dissuaded from formally pressing the issue, the matter was addressed earlier by the convention indirectly in the debate concerning the power of Congress to charter corporations.

The outcome of the debate on chartering corporations was similar to that involving bills of credit, as the power to charter corporations was rejected. Benjamin Franklin (Pennsylvania) moved to add after the words "post roads," a power "to provide for cutting canals where deemed necessary." Subsequently, Madison suggested an enlargement of the motion:

> to grant charters of incorporation where the interests of the United States might require, and the legislative provisions of individual states may be incompetent.[15]

Madison's proposal, which he viewed as a means to improve communications between the states, was seconded by Randolph. Rufus King (Massachusetts) thought that the power was unnecessary. James Wilson (Pennsylvania) suggested that it was necessary to prevent the states from obstructing the general welfare. King responded that the states would be prejudiced and divided into parties by it. In Philadelphia and New York, it would be considered as a reference to the establishment of a bank, which was a subject of contention. Elsewhere, it would be viewed in terms of mercantile monopolies. Wilson mentioned the importance of canals for communication with the western settlements. As to banks, he disagreed with King's fear that it would "excite the prejudices and parties apprehended." Mercantile monopolies, Wilson supposed, were included in the power to regulate trade. Mason favored limiting the motion to canals. He was afraid of monopolies, and he did not think, as Wilson did, that the power was implied by the Constitution.

The motion was modified, specifying and limited to canals, and was defeated 3 to 8. The reference to charters, then, fell as it was included in the power so rejected.[16]

Monetary Powers of the States

James Wilson moved to insert the words "nor emit bills of credit" after the word "money" in Article XII. This made the prohibition of state paper money absolute, rather than subject to approval of the legislature of the United States. This measure passed 8 to 1 with Virginia voting nay and Maryland divided. Unanimous approval was then given to add to the last amendment: "nor make any thing but gold and silver coin a tender in payment of debts."[17] This provision suggests that the states retained only a restricted power to confer legal tender standing but presumes the issuance of currency under the authority of the states.[18] The federal government would perhaps be granting legal tender status, but then only to gold and silver coins.

Some years later, Madison noted that the evil recognized at the convention was states making bills of credit a legal tender, so that notes of banks, chartered or unchartered, could not be given legal tender standing. States could charter banks, however, so long as their notes were not legal tender. The excessive note issues of banks were not foreseen, Madison added, but the banks themselves probably would not have been prohibited by the framers from issuing notes anyway.[19]

To Coin Money

The monetary powers of the Constitution now read:

> The Congress shall have power . . . To borrow money on the credit of
> the United States; . . . To coin money, regulate the value thereof, and of
> foreign coin, and fix the standard of weights and measures; . . .
> [Article I, Section 8]

> No state shall . . . coin money; emit bills of credit; make any thing
> but gold and silver coin a tender in payment of debts; pass any bill of
> attainder, *ex post facto* law, or law impairing the obligation of con-
> tracts. . . . [Article I, Section 10]

The Congress was also granted the power:

> To provide for the punishment of counterfeiting the securities and
> current coin of the United States. . . . [Article I, Section 8]

These passages clearly delegate the specific monetary authority to
the federal government and eliminate the direct monetary powers
once held by the states. The federal government could issue coins
but not paper money, and the states could do neither. The federal
government was not granted an exclusive, monopolistic power to
issue coins, but it was given the authority to regulate the value of its
coins and foreign coins, and perhaps private coins as implied by the
power to fix the standard of weights and measures. These regulatory
functions were previously carried out by the colonial and state
governments. Legal tender status, if conferred, was limited to gold
and silver coins. No regulatory powers relate to banking and bank
notes, or to the granting of charters of incorporation. The delegation
of powers, in short, reflected the framers' fears that otherwise the
federal government would adopt inflationary policies or serve vested
interests.[20]

"Expressly"

Several other excerpts from the Constitution pertain to money
and banking, insofar as they have been so applied, but the ab-

sence of the word "expressly" is the most critical in accommodating expansive interpretations of the monetary powers.

Soon after the Constitutional Convention adjourned on September 17, 1787, the "necessary and proper" clause excited considerable public debate, largely because it appeared to be less restrictive, and perhaps ambiguous, compared with the Articles of Confederation, which conferred on the Congress the enumerated "expressly delegated" powers. The controversial clause reads:

> Congress shall have power ... To make all laws which shall be necessary and proper for carrying into execution the foregoing powers, and all other powers vested by the Constitution in the government of the United States or in any department or office thereof. [Article I, Section 8]

In *The Federalist*, Madison prefaced his comments on this passage by noting that:

> Few parts of the Constitution have been assailed with more intemperance than this; yet on a fair investigation of it, no part can appear more completely invulnerable. Without the *substance* of this power, the whole Constitution would be a dead letter.

Madison reviewed alternative forms for this provision. He dismissed the wording contained in the Articles of Confederation by noting that otherwise the "new Congress would be continually exposed, as their predecessors have been, to the alternative of construing the term 'expressly' with so much vigor, as to disarm the government of all real authority whatever, or with so much latitude as to destroy altogether the force of the restriction." No important powers under the Articles of Confederation, he added, could be executed without referring to the doctrine of "construction or implication," as he preferred language allowing the Congress to exercise powers "indispensably necessary and proper, but, at the same time, not expressly granted."[21]

Alexander Hamilton marshaled a very different defense of the "necessary and proper" clause. He suggested that it stated the obvious; that it was "declaratory of a truth which would have resulted by necessary and unavoidable implication from the very act of constituting a federal government, and vesting it with certain specific powers." The clause provided the proper "means" of executing powers through the passage of necessary and proper laws, and it was "expressly to execute" the powers declared in the Constitution "that the sweeping clause, as it has been affectedly called, authorizes the national legislature to pass all necessary and proper laws." Hamilton continued:

> If there is any thing exceptionable, it must be sought for in the specific powers upon which this general declaration is predicated.

While the clause is perhaps "chargeable with tautology or redundancy," it was probably included because "the Convention probably foresaw, . . . that the danger which most threatens our political welfare is that the State governments will finally sap the foundations of the Union." Should the federal government "overpass the just bounds of its authority," then "the people, whose creature it is, must appeal to the standards they have formed, and take measure to redress the injury done to the Constitution."[22]

The new Congress first met on March 4, 1789, and George Washington's presidential inauguration was held on April 30, 1789, when the government commenced functioning with eleven states, absent North Carolina and Rhode Island. In response to requests from the states, Madison drafted twelve amendments. The last ten, of course, were ratified by the states. The Tenth Amendment, in keeping with Madison's earlier preference, excluded the word "expressly":

> The powers not delegated to the United States by the Constitution, nor prohibited by it to the states, are reserved to the states respectively, or to the people. [Amendments, Article X]

Conclusion

The founding fathers rejected provisions granting the Congress powers to emit bills of credit and to charter corporations, but also excluded from the Constitution was a limitation of the Congress to the exercise of those powers "expressly" delegated. The document also lacks reference to banks and banking, which were familiar to the framers, thus avoiding a topic that could potentially have excited controversy and jeopardized ratification of the Constitution and presumably leaving the authority to regulate banks with the states.

The monetary powers expressly granted to the federal government were consistent with the vision of a specie standard compatible with international practice, as the Congress could provide for the issuance of coins and regulate the value of those coins and foreign coins. The earlier monetary powers exercised by the states were revoked, and the states were prohibited from declaring anything but gold and silver coins a legal tender. While the quality of the underlying monetary base, specie, was regulated, the money supply was left to the determination of market forces.

Notes

1. Jonathan Elliott, *Debates on the Adoption of the Federal Constitution*, vol. 1 (New York: Burt Franklin, 1964, from the edition of 1888), pp. 226, 229.

2. Ibid., vol. 5, pp. 429, 434–35.

3. Ibid., p. 435. In summary, of the eleven members who expressed their opinion, five were adamantly opposed to paper money (Oliver Ellsworth, James Wilson, George Read, Pierce Butler, and John Langdon), three opposed paper money but understood that notes devoid of legal tender status might be issued (Gouverneur Morris, James Madison, and possibly Nathaniel Gorham), two opposed paper money but argued that future circumstances might require it (George Mason and Edmund Randolph, both of whom refused to sign the document), and one favored paper money but felt public sentiment dictated that it be prohibited (John Francis Mercer) (James Madison, *Notes of Debates in the Federal Convention of 1787* [Athens, OH: Ohio University Press, 1966], pp. 470–71; and S. P. Breckinridge, *Legal Tender: A Study in English and American Monetary History* [Chicago: University of Chicago Press, 1903], pp. 74–85).

The Madison administration did issue Treasury notes as debt instruments during the War of 1812 in denominations as small as $3, with interest calculated simply and ease of transfer. Breckinridge reported the issuance of Treasury notes with money characteristics during five periods prior to the Legal Tender Act of 1862: 1812–15, 1837–43, 1846–47, 1857, and 1861 (*Legal Tender*, pp. 101–14).

Historian Richard B. Morris observes that Madison made certain additions and alterations in the interest of accuracy, softened aspersions applied to prominent delegates, and perhaps tampered with the text to avoid embarrassment, but the notes remain "the fullest and most authoritative" source of the proceedings at the Convention. They have served as a source for scholars and jurists (Richard B. Morris, *The Forging of the Union, 1781–1789* [New York: Harper & Row, 1987], p. 272).

4. Elliott, *Debates*, vol. 1, p. 245. New York was not represented by a delegation at that time, and Rhode Island never sent a delegation to the Convention.

5. Ibid., vol. 2, p. 486.

6. Ibid., vol. 3, pp. 28, 76, 179, 290–91, 471.

7. Ibid., vol. 4, pp. 20, 173–85, 191–201.

8. Ibid., pp. 334–36.

9. Ibid., vol. 1, pp. 369–70.

10. Alexander Hamilton, John Jay, and James Madison, *The Federalist* (New York: Modern Library, 1937), pp. 275–76, 289–91.

11. Henry Cabot Lodge, ed., *The Works of Alexander Hamilton*, vol. 1 (New York: G. P. Putnam's Sons, 1885), p. 291.

12. Max Farrand, ed., *The Records of the Federal Convention of 1787*, vol. 2 (New Haven, CT: Yale University Press, 1911), pp. 594–95.

13. Ibid., p. 614.

14. Saul K. Padover, ed., *The Complete Jefferson*, "The Anas" (New York: Duell, Sloan & Pearce, 1943), pp. 1274–75.

15. Elliott, *Debates*, vol. 5, p. 543.

16. Ibid., p. 544.

17. Ibid., vol. 1, pp. 270–71; and Madison, *Notes of Debates*, pp. 541–42.

18. Arthur Nussbaum, *Money in the Law: National and International* (Brooklyn, NY: Foundation Press, 1950), p. 570.

19. Elliott, *Debates*, vol. 4, pp. 608–9.

20. James Willard Hurst, *A Legal History of Money in the United States, 1774–1970* (Lincoln, NE: University of Nebraska Press, 1973), p. 14.

21. Madison, *The Federalist* (no. 44), pp. 292–93.

22. Hamilton, *The Federalist* (no. 33), pp. 199–200.

CHAPTER 6

Establishing the Bank of the United States

Soon after the new government commenced functioning under the Constitution, the Congress established a mint, regulated the value of U.S. and foreign coins, and granted a charter to incorporate the Bank of the United States. The monetary system reflected close fidelity with the express language of the Constitution, but the establishment of a bank required constitutional reasoning grounded on the "implied powers" of the Congress. State-chartered banks were to flourish under a yet narrow conception of the federal government's monetary powers, and these institutions largely characterize the era from the adoption of the Constitution to the Civil War, the period discussed more broadly in the next chapter.

The forging of a bimetallic standard compatible with international practice and the dictates of the Constitution is a significant point, of course, but the extension of federal authority requires closer attention. Beyond the constitutional arguments, it is notable as well that the Bank of the United States, while providing a national paper money, devoid of legal tender standing, was organized beyond the direct control of the Congress.

The Bank of the United States, of course, was an early predecessor of the Federal Reserve System, this nation's central bank. The granting of a charter of incorporation to establish the Bank of the United States, despite no expressed power in the Constitution to charter corporations, actually preceded the coinage legislation, and it obviously sparked heated debate. The ultimate resolution of the constitutional issue in favor of Hamilton's position by the Supreme Court in *McCulloch* v. *Maryland* provides the legal undergirding of the constitutionality of the Federal Reserve System.

Hamilton's Plan for a National Bank

In December 1790 Treasury Secretary Hamilton submitted to the Congress his "Report on a National Bank." James Madison led the unsuccessful opposition to that legislation in the House of Representatives. In view of the controversy ignited by the bank issue, President Washington invited comments by his cabinet. Secretary of State Thomas Jefferson and Attorney General Edmund Randolph recommended a veto, and of course Hamilton presented a strong statement endorsing his proposal to establish a bank. Hamilton's arguments, as noted, provided the basis for Chief Justice John Marshall's opinion upholding in *McCulloch* v. *Maryland* (1819) the authority of the Congress to incorporate a bank, the second Bank of the United States in this case.

Hamilton's argument in support of the bank rested in part on the provision of capital conducive to economic development. Banks in good credit, he observed, can issue money in a multiple of two to three times their specie reserves. A national bank, moreover, could prove helpful in administering the government's financial affairs, providing credit, and collecting taxes. Hamilton commented at length on the charge that banks banish gold and silver from a country. He was not content with the response alone that "the intrinsic wealth of a nation is to be measured, not by the abundance of precious metals contained in it, but by the quantity of the production of its wealth and industry."[1] He contended that a "well-regulated paper credit, may more than compensate for the loss of a part of the gold and silver of a nation."[2] This compensation appears in the augmentation of economic activity leading to a larger volume of exports. Nonetheless, he supposed that the banishment of gold presents an extreme case, when a country faces a deficiency in circulating medium.

In rectifying this deficiency of money, Hamilton observed that emitting paper money "is wisely prohibited" to the states under the Constitution, and "the spirit of that prohibition ought not to be disregarded by the Government of the United States." Hamilton continued:

> they are of a nature so liable to abuse,—that the wisdom of the government will be shown in never trusting itself with the use of so seducing and dangerous expedient.[3]

Hamilton added that during times of tranquility paper money might be managed properly by the government, but during emergencies it is "almost a moral certainty" of becoming "mischievous." He continued:

> The stamping of paper is an operation so much easier than the laying of taxes, that a government in the practice of paper emissions would rarely fail, in any emergency, to indulge itself too far in the employment of that resource, to avoid, as much as possible, one less auspicious to present popularity. If it should not even be carried so far as to be rendered an absolute bubble, it would at least be likely to be extended, to a degree which would occasion an inflated and artificial state of things, incompatible with the regular and prosperous course of the political economy.[4]

While government paper is limited only by its own discretion, bank note emissions are limited by the possibility of the redemption. Besides note issues, Hamilton addressed the matter of public versus private control of the bank:

> Considerations of public advantage suggest a further wish, which is—that the bank could be established upon principles that would cause profits of it to redound to the immediate benefit of the State. This is contemplated by many who speak of a national bank, but the idea seems liable to insuperable objections. To attach full confidence to an institution of this nature, it appears to be an essential ingredient in its structure, that it shall be under a *private* not a *public* direction—under the guidance of *individual interest*, not of public policy; which would be supposed to be, and, in certain emergencies, under a feeble or too sanguine administration, would really be liable to being too much influenced

by *public necessity*. The suspicion of this would, most probably, be a canker that would continually corrode the vitals of the credit of the bank, and would be most likely to prove fatal in those situations in which the public good would require that they should be most sound and vigorous. It would, indeed, be little less than a miracle, should the credit of the bank be at the disposal of the government, if, in a long series of time, there was not experienced calamitous abuse of it. It is true, that it would be the real interest of the government not to abuse it; its genuine policy to husband and cherish it with the most guarded circumspection, as an inestimable treasure. But what government ever uniformly consulted its true interests in opposition to the temptations of momentary exigencies? What nation was ever blessed with a constant succession of upright and wise administrators?[5]

The government's best interests will be recognized, Hamilton continued, by a board composed of respectable and well-informed citizens. While the state may hold some of the stock in the bank, and share in its profits, it should not desire to participate in its governance, but be conducted by disinterested persons. Excluding "all pretension to control" policies, it should nonetheless be given a full accounting of the bank's financial condition.[6]

In the Senate, Hamilton's plan was referred to a four-member committee, consisting of three participants in the Constitutional Convention—Caleb Strong (Massachusetts), Robert Morris (Pennsylvania), and Pierce Butler (South Carolina), who were bank stockholders—and Hamilton's father-in-law, Philip Schuyler (New York). A bill favoring the bank was reported out of committee, and the Senate approved it on January 20, 1791. In the House, where a vote on February 8 of 39 to 20 favored the bank, the recorded debate dwelt on constitutional issues, and the vote was divided generally along geographical lines, with Northerners voting aye and Southerners voting nay. Support was found among the commercial and money classes (including creditors to the government), and opposition was concentrated among the agrarians who distrusted a strong central government.[7]

Constitutional Issues in Chartering the Bank

The proposal to charter the Bank of the United States raised a constitutional issue regarding the power of Congress to grant charters of incorporation, a power specifically rejected in the convention, and thus excluded from the enumerated powers and presumably left to the states by the Tenth Amendment. Madison and Jefferson assumed this position, along with other arguments, including a narrow interpretation of the "necessary and proper" clause. Hamilton marshaled the "implied powers" in a broadly based intellectual case that the bank was a natural means of carrying out a set of enumerated powers, while being consistent with the expression of sovereignty. These arguments are summarized as follows:

According to the records of the House of Representatives, Madison argued on February 2, 1791, that local institutions could more advantageously provide banking services. He maintained further that he had long held the view that the Congress was denied the power under the Constitution to establish banks. Moreover, he could not find that power in the clauses supposedly conveying it, e.g., that of laying taxes. The power could not be deduced from the right to borrow money, he added, for this was no such bill. He recognized that the Congress under the Articles of Confederation had, indeed, established a bank. Exigencies of government were such that it justified almost any infraction under the old Confederation, but Congress was still conscious that it did not possess all the powers for the complete establishment of a bank, so that it recommended that the individual states make appropriate regulations.[8]

Madison entertained, in his own estimation, a liberal interpretation of the "necessary and proper" clause; however:

> He averted to that clause in the Constitution which empowers Congress to pass all laws necessary to carry its powers into execution, and observing on the diffuse and ductile interpretation of these words, and the boundless latitude of construction given them by the friends of the bank, said that, by their construction, every possible power might be exercised.[9]

It was, therefore, dangerous to confer on Congress this power of incorporation. He denied the necessity of instituting a bank at this time, and considered it an infringement on the right of the states. He then referred to passages in state conventions, which were fully in favor of the idea that "the general government could not exceed the expressly-delegated powers," as now contained in the Tenth Amendment.[10] Despite Madison's arguments, the bill passed the House with a 39 to 20 vote margin and was sent to President Washington.

Jefferson, Randolph, and Hamilton responded to Washington's invitation for opinions on the bank bill. The opinions of Jefferson and Hamilton, who were more closely identified with the bank issue, are summarized here:

Jefferson's letter of February 15 was a tightly reasoned argument against incorporating a bank. He argued that the foundation of the Constitution rested on the Tenth Amendment—then known as the Twelfth Amendment, since it had yet to be ratified. To take a step beyond the boundaries thus specifically drawn, he continued, would open a boundless field of power. The incorporation of a bank, and the power assumed by the bill, have not been delegated to the United States by the Constitution. They are not found among the enumerated powers, e.g., the power to lay taxes, to borrow money, or to regulate commerce. Nor are they found within either of the general phrases "to provide for the general welfare of the United States," or "to make all laws necessary and proper for carrying into execution the enumerated powers." The powers so enumerated, moreover, can be carried into execution without a bank, so a bank is not necessary, and consequently not authorized by this phrase—a convenience does not constitute a necessary means. Jefferson further noted: "It is known that the very power now proposed as a means, was rejected as an end by the Convention which formed the Constitution."

Jefferson concluded by suggesting that a veto would be appropriate to protect against the invasions of the legislature, of the rights of the executive, of the judiciary, or of the states and state legislatures. This bill intrudes on a right remaining exclusively with the states, and should therefore be so protected. However, unless it is tolerably clear in the President's mind that it is unauthorized by the Constitution, a respect for the wisdom of the legislature would be appropriate.[11]

Hamilton's argument rested on the general principle that the government of the United States is sovereign in terms of the powers so granted to it by the Constitution, so that it could employ all the means necessary to attain the ends inherent in those powers, unless precluded by "restrictions and exceptions specified in the Constitution."[12] The erection of corporations is "unquestionably incident to sovereign power" in those areas where authority has been so granted.[13] Recognizing that there are "implied" as well as "express powers," which are also delegated equally, the power to erect a corporation "may as well be implied as any other thing," so that it may be "employed as an instrument or means of carrying into execution any of the specified powers, as any other instrument or means whatever."[14] The only question is whether or not its application relates to "the acknowledged objects or lawful ends of the government."[15] In terms of whether it is "necessary and proper" as a means, the purpose of that clause is not so restrictive as the secretary of state supposes, as if necessary were prefixed by "absolutely" or "indispensably."[16] Hamilton noted that there is no express power in any state constitution to erect corporations; necessity is not the determining factor but the criterion is constitutionality.[17] While the necessary and proper clause does not grant independent powers, it does give an "explicit sanction to the doctrine of implied powers, and is equivalent to an admission of the proposition that the government, as to its specified powers and objects, has plenary and sovereign authority, in some cases paramount to the States."[18] In determining what is constitutional, Hamilton concluded,

> the criterion is the end, to which the measure relates as a means.
> If the end be clearly comprehended within any of the specified
> powers, and if the measure has an obvious relation to that end,

and not forbidden by any particular provision of the Constitution, it may safely be deemed to come within the compass of the national authority.[19]

Also, if the proposed measure does not abridge a preexisting right of any state or any individual, there is a strong presumption in favor of its constitutionality.[20]

Hamilton observed that laws enacted by the federal government may alter state laws and not be considered to be unconstitutional. This bill "neither prohibits any State from erecting as many banks as they please, nor any number of individuals associating to carry on business, and consequently is free from the charge of establishing a monopoly."[21] As to the rejection by the convention to empower Congress to grant charters of incorporation, Hamilton argued, there are a variety of recollections so that no clear inference can be drawn from this rejection. Regardless of what the intentions of the framers may have been, the intention should be inferred from the instrument itself, not drawn from the circumstances at the convention.[22]

After this review of issues, Hamilton turned his attention to the matter of connecting the power to establish a bank with the enumerated powers. He stated that the power is derived from an aggregate of powers, including:

> the very general power of laying and collecting taxes, and appropriating their proceeds—that of borrowing money indefinitely—that of coining money, and regulating foreign coins—that of making all needful rules and regulations respecting the property of the United States. These powers combined, as well as the reason and nature of the thing speak strongly this language: that it is the manifest design and scope of the Constitution to vest in Congress all the powers requisite to the effectual administration of the finances of the United States.[23]

Thus,

> To suppose, then, that the government is precluded from the employment of so usual and so important an instrument for the administration of its finances as that of a bank, is to suppose what does not coincide with the general tenor and complexion of the Constitution,

and what is not agreeable to impressions that any new spectator would entertain concerning it.[24]

So that,

> Little less than a prohibitive clause can destroy the strong presumptions which result from the general aspect of the government.[25]

Hamilton alluded to the facts that the Congress had erected corporations in the form of governments in the western territories,[26] and that the state conventions expressed the view that Congress should not "erect any company with exclusive advantages in commerce."[27]

Supposing that the practices of mankind should carry great weight, Hamilton summarized the point:

> This other fact that banks are a usual engine in the administration of national finances, and an ordinary and most effectual instrument of loans, and one which, in this country, has been found essential, pleads strongly against the supposition that a government, clothed with most of the important prerogatives of sovereignty, in relation to its revenues, its debts, its credits, its defence, its trade, its intercourse with foreign nations, is forbidden to make use of that instrument, as an appendage of its own authority.[28]

President Washington, who had asked Madison to prepare a veto message, was apparently persuaded by his Treasury secretary's letter to sign the bill, which he did on February 25, 1791.

McCulloch v. Maryland

The Bank's charter lapsed in 1811, but the second Bank of the United States was chartered in 1816. The State of Maryland precipitated the constitutional test by imposing a tax on banks not chartered by the state and bringing suit against the Baltimore branch to collect the tax. The Maryland attorney general, Luther Martin, represented the state, and Daniel Webster was counsel for the Bank. Chief Justice John Marshall, as an incipient "supply-side" economist, observed that "the power to tax involves the power to destroy,"[29] and declared the tax to be an unconstitutional infringement of Congress's power to create a bank. Marshall, a staunch Federalist, also upheld in *McCulloch* v. *Maryland* (1819) the authority of the Congress to establish a bank:

> Among the enumerated powers, we do not find that of establishing a bank or creating a corporation. But there is no phrase in the instrument which, like the Articles of Confederation, excludes incidental or implied powers; and which requires that everything granted shall be expressly and minutely described. Even the 10th amendment, which was framed for the purpose of quieting the excessive jealousies which had been excited, omits the word "expressly, . . ." thus leaving the question, . . . to depend on a fair construction of the whole instrument. . . .

> Although, among the enumerated powers of government, we do not find the word "bank" or "incorporation," we find the great powers, to lay and collect taxes; to borrow money; to regulate commerce; to declare and conduct a war; and to raise and support armies and navies. The sword and the purse, all the external relations, and no inconsiderable portion of the industry of the nation, are intrusted to its government. . . . But it may with great reason be contended, that a government, . . . must also be intrusted with ample means for their execution. . . .

> It is not denied, that the powers given to the government imply the ordinary means of execution. . . .

> The creation of a corporation, it is said, appertains to sovereignty. This is admitted. But to what portion of sovereignty does it appertain? . . . The power of creating a corporation, though appertaining to sovereignty, is not, . . . a great substantive and independent power, which cannot be implied as incidental to other powers, or used as a means of executing them. It is never the end for which other powers are exercised, but a means by which other objects are accomplished. . . .

> But the Constitution of the United States has not left the right of Congress to employ the necessary means, for the execution of the powers conferred on the government, to general reasoning. To its enumeration of powers is added, that of making "all laws which shall

be necessary and proper, for carrying into execution the foregoing powers, . . ."

We admit, as all must admit, that the powers of the government are limited, and that its limits are not to be transcended. But we think the sound construction of the Constitution must allow to the national legislature that discretion, with respect to the means by which the powers it confers are to be carried into execution, which will enable that body to perform the high duties assigned to it, in the manner most beneficial to the people. Let the end be legitimate, let it be within the scope of the Constitution, and all means which are appropriate, which are plainly adapted to that end, which are not prohibited, but consistent with the letter and spirit of the Constitution, are constitutional.

After the most deliberate consideration, it is the unanimous and decided opinion of this court, that the Act to incorporate the Bank of the United States is a law made in pursuance of the Constitution, and is a part of the supreme law of the land. . . .[30]

Organization and Operations of the Bank

Using the Bank of England as a model (and his knowledge of the Bank of North America's charter), Alexander Hamilton prepared the charter for the Bank of the United States. The Bank was established on the basis of $10 million in capital, vastly exceeding the size of the four existing banks. Of the 25,000 shares, one-fifth were to be subscribed by the U.S. government and four-fifths by "any person, co-partnership, or body politic"—which finally included over one-third of the congressmen, Harvard College, the Massachusetts Bank, and the state of New York.[31] The government borrowed from the Bank an amount equal to its subscription, and the specie reserve was provided by other shareholders, who were to meet their subscriptions by paying one-fourth in gold and silver and three-fourths in Treasury debt obligations.

The U.S.-resident shareholders elected twenty-five directors, each serving a one-year term. Shareholder votes ranged from one to a maximum of thirty, depending on the number of shares held.

The Bank was located in Philadelphia, which was the financial center and the seat of the government for several years; eventually eight branches were established around the country.

The operations of the Bank were tightly restricted to banking, and its assets and liabilities were limited by its reserves—Hamilton having originated the legal concept of fractional reserve requirements.[32] The Bank served as the depository of public funds, and it collected public revenues. Beyond the initial subscription, the act prohibited the purchase of U.S. government debt obligations, and loan ceilings were set at $100,000 for the federal government and $50,000 for individual states. The Bank issued notes for general circulation and provided short-term loans and discounted paper at interest rates limited by law to 6 percent, while over time sharply reducing its holding of the public debt.[33]

The Bank of the United States was managed judiciously. It maintained substantial specie reserves, which in 1809, for example, amounted to 38 percent of its notes and deposits. It restricted the volume of state bank notes in circulation by presenting them for redemption, and thereby limited the extension of credit and the profitability of those state institutions while also operating as a competitor in the credit markets. As a result, the Bank aroused considerable hostility in large segments of the banking and business communities. When coupled with a continuing antipathy toward banking as such and the lingering opinion in some quarters that the Bank was unconstitutional, the effort to extend the charter failed, though by single-vote margins in the House and the Senate. In the Senate, being equally divided, the matter was decided by the president, George Clinton, who observed:

> The power to create corporations is not expressly granted; it is a high attribute of sovereignty, and in its nature not accessorial or derivative by implication, but primary and independent.[34]

The narrowest of margins in the votes defeating the Bank's rechartering reflected a change in sentiments by many identified as Republicans. The Bank was closely associated with northern business interests and the Federalists. Once in power, the agrarian interests within the Republican party were not so resolutely opposed to the Bank, recognizing its contribution to maintaining orderly financial conditions and administering the government's fiscal affairs. President Jefferson tolerated the Bank, deferring in fiscal matters to Treasury Secretary Albert Gallatin, who supported the Bank. Gallatin also served in that same capacity for several years under President Madison, who switched positions, favoring continuation of the Bank.[35]

The Second Bank

The War of 1812 revealed a need to conduct the nation's financial affairs in a more orderly fashion. In 1814, after considering the establishment of a national bank, proceedings in the House were suspended and the Committee of Ways and Means invited Treasury Secretary A. J. Dallas to suggest provisions to revive and maintain the public credit. In reply, Secretary Dallas recognized that the condition of the nation's currency was a "copious source of mischief and embarrassment." The exportation and hoarding of specie had depleted the supply of hard currency, and a large volume of paper currency was lost primarily through a suspension of payments in specie. He added that:

> Under favorable circumstances, and to a limited extent, an emission of treasury notes would, probably, afford relief; but treasury notes are an expensive and precarious substitute, either for coin or for bank notes, charged as they are with a growing interest, productive of no countervailing profit or emolument, and exposed to every breath of popular prejudice or alarm.[36]

Thus, he proposed a national bank with a capital of $50 million and governed by a board of fifteen directors, with five appointed annually by the President (one of whom would be designated as president of the bank).[37] After lengthy debate, a bill to charter the second Bank of the United States was defeated when the Speaker of the House, Langdon Cheves (South Carolina), cast the deciding vote—Cheves was later to serve as the president of the Bank of the United States. He felt that the bill would not serve its intended purposes.[38]

The House voted shortly thereafter to reconsider the bill. The bill passed both the House and the Senate in 1815, but it was vetoed by President Madison. After waiving the question of the constitutional authority of the Congress to establish a bank, Madison cited certain inadequacies of the proposed institution in providing a national currency, as the stock subscription with Treasury notes would reduce their volume and specie convertibility would limit the bank's capacity to issue notes during the war, and after the war, a substantial monopoly profit would accrue to the bank.[39]

President Madison, on December 5, 1815, advised the Congress to take steps to restore a uniform national currency. If the state banks cannot be depended upon to provide that currency, he argued, the establishment of a national bank should merit consideration. If neither could be deemed effective, he felt that attention should be given to the issuance of notes by the federal government to serve as a circulating medium.[40] Treasury Secretary Dallas expanded upon these points in a presentation to the Congress. In alluding to the monetary powers of the Congress, Dallas added that the "Congress is expressly vested with the power to coin money, . . . and (as a necessary implication from positive provisions) to emit bills of credit."[41] These sentiments were echoed by representatives John C. Calhoun (South Carolina) and Henry Clay (Kentucky). As Clay commented on the Congress's monetary powers:

> The plain inference is, that the subject of the general currency was intended to be submitted exclusively to the General Government.[42]

As an instrument to restore a national currency, Clay preferred an indirect remedy, in the form of a national bank. A bill to establish the Bank of the United States passed the House (80 to 71) and the Senate (22 to 12), and was signed by President Madison on April 10, 1816.[43]

Some years later, Madison explained his decision to sign the bill:

> The charge of inconsistency between my objections to the constitutionality of such a bank in 1791, and my assent in 1817, turns on the question, how far legislative precedent expounding the Constitution, ought to guide succeeding legislators, and to override individual opinions. . . .
>
> It was in conformity with the view here taken of the respect due to deliberate and reiterated precedent, that the Bank of the United States, though on the original question held to be unconstitutional, received the executive signature in the year 1817.[44]

Conformity to the express language of the Constitution commands respect, but precedent at some stage assumes a governing role in constitutional interpretation, according to Madison, so that the rules of conduct should be certain and known—a point well to be remembered in any current debate of constitutional interpretation.

The act provided for the establishment of a bank with $35 million in capital, again one-fifth of which was to be subscribed by the government and four-fifths by "any individual, company, corporation, or State." Subscriptions could be satisfied by the government with coin (U.S. or certain foreign coins) or its own obligations. Other shareholders were required to pay one-fourth in coin and three-fourths in coin or federal government debt instruments.

The Bank had twenty-five resident U.S. citizen directors. Five were appointed by the President with the advice and consent of the Senate, and twenty were elected by the shareholders, whose votes again ranged from one to thirty. The directors were empowered to elect the Bank's president from their number.

The Bank was authorized to issue notes up to the amount of its capital and to conduct other banking functions. It was the sole depository of federal funds unless the secretary of the Treasury directed otherwise. The Bank could establish branches—it had as many as twenty-five at one time. The charter was limited to twenty years, and for its privileges it paid the U.S. government $1.5 million in three annual installments.[45]

The Republican charter, therefore, provided specifically for minority-government representation on the board, for only U.S. citizens to serve on the board, and for part of the profits to be paid to the Treasury.

The Bank commenced operating in 1817 and soon overextended credit, and was subject to charges of mismanagement, speculation, and corruption. In 1819, Langdon Cheves was elected president, and he instituted austere measures, perhaps saving the institution but raising the ire of debtors, employees, and shareholders. Nicholas Biddle succeeded Cheves in 1823 and served with distinction during the "central bank period," 1823–30, but presided over the Bank as well when it was mired in political controversy for the remaining years of its charter. The charter expired in 1836, when the organization was granted a charter by Pennsylvania, only to fail in 1841.

President Jackson's Veto

In 1829 President Andrew Jackson announced his opposition to the Bank of the United States, being generally hostile toward banks and questioning the Bank's constitutionality. Jackson's position rallied the support of the state banks, of businessmen dissatisfied with credit restraint, and of Wall Street financiers who were determined to replace Chestnut Street (Philadelphia) as the country's financial center. Agrarian opponents to all banks and states' rights advocates also sided with Jackson.[46] In commemoration of Jackson's victory over the Bank, his portrait now adorns the $20 Federal Reserve note.

The Bank retained support in the Congress, and in 1832 a bill to recharter the Bank was passed. Jackson vetoed the bill, and the Senate failed to override the veto.[47] In his veto message, Jackson stated that he was "deeply impressed with the belief that some of the powers and privileges possessed by the existing bank are unauthorized by the Constitution."[48] He may, indeed, have been sympathetic toward an institution more strongly representing the public interest rather the "monied oligarchy."[49] Nonetheless, Jackson expanded on the argument that the Bank was a monopoly, which he valued at $17 million, but to be sold under the new charter for $3 million, while criticizing the absence of competition in the bidding for this monopoly. He charged that the Bank represented excessive foreign ownership of the stock, and that it generated an internal redistribution of wealth, flowing from the West to the East, with much of the flow proceeding on to Europe—this flow represented the geographical distribution of the shareholders. Jackson also claimed that the Bank was too large and that it infringed on the right of states to tax its private business activities. Among those assisting the President in preparing the veto message was Attorney General Roger B. Taney.[50]

Jackson's landslide victory in the election of 1832 fortified his resolve to withdraw the government's deposits from the Bank. The charter allowed the secretary of the Treasury to remove the government's deposits, but he had to explain to Congress the reason for that decision. The House rejected the idea, and two Treasury secretaries were replaced before Jackson found one who was willing to comply with his wishes. In 1833, Roger Taney was appointed to the post and immediately announced his plan to shift deposits to the "pet banks," allowing the government's deposits in the Bank of the United States to run off, thus effectively curtailing that institution's power to control the currency.[51] The disorderly banking conditions that soon followed were disrupted as well by the "specie circular," the strongest expression of Jackson's "hard money" sentiments, which directed land agents to accept only gold and silver in payment for public lands.

The state banking era in its purest form followed the demise of the Bank of the United States. It was in Taney's words that:

> perhaps no business which yields a profit so certain and liberal as the business of banking and exchange; and it is proper that it should be open so far as practicable, to the most free competition and its advantages shared by all classes of society.[52]

Hard Times Tokens

Hard times tokens encompass a series of tokens issued privately from 1832 to 1844. Many were politically inspired. Others were imitations of official coins, tradesmen's cards, and mulings of these issues, offering some relief from the coinage shortage associated with the panic of 1837. The politically oriented tokens bluntly expressed the controversies surrounding the Bank of the United States and the Independent Treasury System, a depository alternative to the government's dependence on the banking system.

One token depicts Andrew Jackson on the obverse, and presents on the reverse the inscription: "The Bank Must Perish. The Union Must and Shall be Preserved."[53] Opponents issued tokens with "Perish Credit. Perish Commerce," along with a bust of Jackson and the inscription: "My Substitute for the U.S. Bank." President Jackson was praised as "The Gallant, Successful Defender of N. Orleans."[54] While his friends boasted of Jackson's military record, his opponents satirically portrayed him in full uniform awkwardly brandishing a sword and grasping a money purse with the inscription: "A Plain System, Void of Pomp." The reverse shows a balking mule on which appears "LL.D.," with the words above, "Roman Firmness," and "Veto" below. The legend, "The Constitution as I understand it," was taken from Jackson's second inaugural address. The conferral in 1833 of an honorary Doctor of Laws degree by Harvard College was a special delight to Jackson's critics. The tyrannical seizure of the sword and purse in the same hands was seen as an alarming, constitutionally questionable concentration of power—an issue that can be traced back to the debates on the Constitution, and remains relevant today.[55]

Tokens celebrated the Whig party victory in 1834, declaring "For the Constitution Hurra."[56] Others bemoaned "Specie Payments Suspended, May Tenth 1837," while declaring the token to be a "Substitute for Shinplasters," a term applied to paper money of doubtful value.[57] Senator Daniel Webster (Massachusetts) was praised as a defender of the Constitution, favoring "Credit Currency," with a stable ship inscribed "Constitution." Depicted on the reverse is "Van Buren, Metallic Currency," with a ship in turbulent seas inscribed "Experiment."[58] President Martin Van Buren was celebrated as "The People's Choice," and the "Sub Treasury & Democracy" were linked together.[59] His opponents, in contrast, portrayed this "Executive Experiment" with a treasure chest moving slowly and insecurely on the back of a turtle as a "Fiscal Agent." The reverse quotes Van Buren's declaration in his inaugural address, "I follow in the steps of my illustrious predecessor," which represents him stepping in the footprints of a jackass.[60] Senator Thomas Hart Benton (Missouri) is also linked to the Sub-Treasury "Experiment."[61]

References to Benton and the Sub-Treasury appear on the reverse of a token depicting an ugly female head with a coronet inscribed "Loco Foco." The Loco Focos derived their name from a meeting in Tammany Hall in 1835, when their adversaries attempted to disrupt the meeting by turning off the gas lights, but they used loco-foco matches to light candles so that the meeting could proceed.[62] The Loco Focos, as members of the Equal Rights party, carried on the Jacksonian tradition. They asserted that state governments should be blocked from authorizing the issuance of bills of credit, in the form of state bank notes, in violation of the Constitution. In addition, they favored establishment of an independent Treasury (the Sub-Treasury, or Constitutional Treasury) that would accept only gold and silver coin.[63]

President Van Buren rejected the Whig party's proposal for a third Bank of the United States and objected to reliance on the state banks as government depositories, thus advocating independent depositories. The Independent Treasury Bill was introduced in 1837, but did not pass until 1840. In 1841, however, under President John Tyler, the law was repealed. Congress then passed a bill to establish the third Bank. Tyler vetoed the bill, charging that it was "unconstitutional to authorize branches in states without their consent."[64] A revised bill was again vetoed, prompting the immediate resignation of Tyler's entire cabinet, except for

Secretary of State Webster, who at the time was negotiating a treaty with Britain. In 1846, after the Democrats defeated the Whigs, the Sub-Treasury system was reenacted. The system was supported by antibank, hard-money advocates, such as Senator Benton. The Sub-Treasury system represented a victory for states' rights and a removal of federal control of banking and credit. After 1847, however, banks were used as depositories. Fluctuations in bank reserves caused by government receipts and expenditures were transmitted into the financial system, but in later years Treasury funds were managed in a manner to promote stability. The Sub-Treasury system was superseded in 1914 by the Federal Reserve System, although it existed in legal form until 1921.[65]

Conclusion

Constitutional issues are never resolved in any final sense, but it would seem unimaginable at this time to find the Supreme Court reversing the power of the Congress to establish a national bank. To claim that Madison's understanding of the Constitution, containing no such power, was in some way deficient seems a little shaky. Only precedent and practice, as Madison acknowledged, would seem reasonable to bridge the gap.

The matter of establishing a national bank was obviously a political issue provoking much contentious debate for decades. When established, the banks were clearly set apart from the direct control of the government. Beyond the governing role of market forces, in the supply of coins and bank notes, the management of the supply of paper money was placed under the regulatory authority of an "independent" national bank.

Notes

1. Henry Cabot Lodge, ed., *The Works of Alexander Hamilton*, vol. 3 (New York: G. P. Putnam's Sons, Knickerbocker Press, 1885), p. 141.

2. Ibid. This point clearly alludes to a function of the proposed bank to

regulate a paper credit, and the Bank issued and at times regulated the supply of paper money. Timberlake's contention is well taken, however, that the Bank was not in certain respects a central bank: it did not control the quantity of money, serve as a central depository, offer discount facilities for commercial banks, or serve as a lender of last resort. Timberlake further notes that its powers were not based on the monetary authority of the Congress and it did not supervise the few commercial banks operating at the time, but it did act as a fiscal agent for the government and served to facilitate certain national objectives. The Bank, of course, did at times assume a regulatory role, but it seems most appropriate to view that organization as a national bank, as Timberlake observes, rather than as a central bank as generally understood today. References in the text are qualified to the extent of suggesting that the Bank did perform certain functions of a central bank, and was in that sense a predecessor to the Federal Reserve. (Richard H. Timberlake, Jr., *The Origins of Central Banking in the United States* [Cambridge, MA: Harvard University Press, 1978], pp. 4–5).

3. Ibid., p. 149.

4. Ibid.

5. Ibid., pp. 162–63.

6. Ibid., p. 165.

7. Bray Hammond, *Banks and Politics in America: From the Revolution to the Civil War* (Princeton, NJ: Princeton University Press, 1957), pp. 115–19.

8. Jonathan Elliott, *Debates on the Adoption of the Federal Constitution,* vol. 4 (New York: Burt Franklin, 1964, from the edition of 1888), p. 413.

9. Ibid., p. 414.

10. Ibid., pp. 413–14.

11. Ibid., pp. 609–11.

12. Lodge, *The Works of Alexander Hamilton,* p. 181.

13. Ibid., p. 182.

14. Ibid., p. 184.

15. Ibid., p. 185.

16. Ibid., p. 188.

17. Ibid., p. 189.

18. Ibid., p. 191.

19. Ibid., p. 192.

20. Ibid.

21. Ibid., p. 195.

22. Ibid., pp. 196–97.

23. Ibid., p. 222.

24. Ibid.

25. Ibid.

26. Ibid., p. 206.

27. Ibid., p. 221.

28. Ibid., p. 223.

29. *McCulloch* v. *Maryland* (1819), 17 U.S. (4 Wheat.), 431.

30. Ibid., pp. 406–24.

31. Hammond, *Banks and Politics in America*, p. 123.

32. Ibid., p. 143.

33. Benjamin Haggott Beckhart, *Federal Reserve System* (New York: American Institute of Banking, 1972), pp. 5–7; "Acts to Charter the Bank of the United States, February 25; March 2, 1791," in Herman E. Krooss, *Documentary History of Banking and Currency in the United States*, vol. 1 (New York: Chelsea House, 1983), pp. 181–88.

34. M. St. Clair Clarke and D. A. Hall, *Legislative and Documentary History of the Bank of the United States Including the Original Bank of North America* (New York: Augustus M. Kelley, 1967), p. 446.

35. Hammond, *Banks and Politics in America*, pp. 208–22. The federal government sold 2,160 of its shares in the Bank during the Washington administration, 620 shares under Adams, and the remaining 2,220 shares under Jefferson—gaining a profit of $672,000 (or 30 percent), plus dividends of $1,100,000 (ibid., p. 207).

36. Clarke and Hall, *Legislative and Documentary History*, p. 481.

37. Ibid., pp. 481–82

38. Ibid., p. 571.

39. Ibid., pp. 594–95

40. Ibid., p. 609.

41. Ibid., p. 610.

42. Ibid., p. 672.

43. Ibid., p. 713.

44. Elliott, *Debates*, pp. 615–16. Madison approved the bill in 1816, but the date 1817 appears in the text from which the quotation was excerpted.

45. "Act to Charter the Second Bank of the United States," in Krooss, *Documentary History*, vol. 1, pp. 222–38.

46. Hammond, *Banks and Politics in America*, pp. 443–44.

47. State bank supporters apparently wielded sufficient influence in the Congress to defeat proposed charter amendments to relieve the Bank's president and cashier of the responsibility that they sign the Bank's notes, thus limiting the volume issued in favor of state bank notes (ibid., pp. 398–99).

48. "Message by President Andrew Jackson Vetoing the Bank Recharter, July 10, 1832," in Krooss, *Documentary History*, vol. 2, p. 21. Hacker, "Jackson's Veto of the Bank Bill, July 10, 1832," *Major Documents,* p. 55.

49. Hammond, *Banks and Politics in America*, pp. 408–9.

50. Hammond's comment on the veto message: "It is legalistic, demagogic, and full of sham" (ibid., p. 405).

51. Ibid, pp. 412–20, 438. In his statement on the removal of the government's deposits from the Bank, President Jackson summarized his position:

> It is the desire of the President that the control of the banks and the currency shall, as far as possible, be entirely separated from the political power of the country as well as wrested from an institution which has already attempted to subject the Government to its will. ("Statement by President Andrew Jackson on Removing Public Deposits from the Bank of the United States, September 18, 1833," in Krooss, *Documentary History*, vol. 2, p. 57)

Jackson maintained that this position was consonant with the Constitution, a view reiterated in his final state of the union message:

> It is apparent from the whole context of the Constitution, as well as the history of the times which gave birth to it, that it was the purpose of the Convention to establish a currency consisting of precious metals. ("President Andrew Jackson on Banking, State of the Union Message, December 5, 1836," ibid., p. 91)

52. Ibid., pp. 493–94.

53. Lyman Haynes Low, *Hard Times Tokens* (New York: Sanford J. Durst, Numismatic Publications, 1977), p. 16. Also see Hewitt Bros., *Hard Times Tokens* (Chicago: Hewitt Bros., n.d.); and Russell Rulau, *Hard Times Tokens* (Iola, WI: Krause Publications, 1980). Rulau also refers to certain politically motivated paper issues.

54. Low, *Hard Times Tokens*, p. 17.

55. Ibid., pp. 12, 18–19.

56. Ibid., p. 17.

57. Ibid., p. 29.

58. Ibid., p. 33.

59. Ibid., p. 32.

60. Ibid., pp. 21–22.

61. Ibid., p. 31.

62. Ibid.

63. Hammond, *Banks and Politics in America*, pp. 493–99.

64. A. Barton Hepburn, *A History of Currency in the United States* (New York: Augustus M. Kelley, 1967, reprint of 1924 edition), p. 151.

65. Beckhart, *Federal Reserve System*, pp. 14–15.

CHAPTER 7

Federal Coins and State Bank Notes

The monetary system from the adoption of the Constitution to the Civil War complied strictly with the express language of the Constitution, aside from the departure manifest in the establishments of the Bank of the United States. The federal government established a mint and promulgated coinage regulations. The regulations were modified frequently in an attempt to maintain a viable circulation of U.S. coins.

The Constitution was silent on banks and bank notes, which were to assume a major role in the financial system, although they were held in check at times by the operations of the Bank of the United States. The constitutionality of state bank notes was tested and found not to be the proscribed state-issued bills of credit.

The financial system was highly unstable, suffering periodic crises and specie payments suspensions. Financial crises were alleviated in part by private money issues and Treasury notes. The Treasury notes were issued ostensibly as debt instruments, but to a certain extent they were intended to circulate as currency without legal tender standing.

The money supply was competitively determined and rested ultimately on specie, a discipline that produced long-run stability in the level of prices. At the same time, the financial system was an integral part of an economy generating considerable short-run instability in money, prices, and business activity.

Coinage Plan

Opening the second session of the Congress on January 8, 1790, President Washington requested early action on coinage legislation:

> Uniformity in the currency, weights and measures of the United States, is an object of great importance and will, I am persuaded, be duly attended to.[1]

A week later, the House requested Secretary of State Jefferson to prepare a coinage plan, in which he urged the Congress to establish a mint:

> Coinage is peculiarly an Attribute of Sovereignty. To transfer its exercise into another Country, is to submit it to another sovereign.[2]

The House then directed Secretary of the Treasury Hamilton to prepare a report for establishing a mint.

Hamilton submitted his plan to the House on January 28, 1791. He agreed with Jefferson's observation, recognized the problem of reconciling the difference between the prevailing unit of account in British pounds and the general circulating currency in Spanish dollars, and proposed a bimetallic standard as a means to replicate current practice. An assay of the circulating Spanish dollars indicated a pure silver content of 371 grains, and the dollar was translated by merchants in terms of gold at 24¾ grains of pure gold. Given the market ratio of 15 to 1, Hamilton set the dollar at 371.25 grains. He recommended 11/12 fineness so that the mint could recoin European coins without refining the metal. Hamilton rejected Jefferson's proposal to link coinage with a uniform system of weights and measures, as might be inferred from the Constitution—Jefferson wanted to define the dollar in terms of the weight in silver of a cubic inch of rain water. Hamilton proposed a $10 eagle, a $1 gold piece, a silver dollar, a silver tenth, and a 1/100 and a 1/200 in copper—the latter small denomination being, as Robert Morris suggested, a way to restrain the minimum price of goods. A minimal 0.5 percent seigniorage was recommended along with heavy copper coins to discourage counterfeiting. The plan drew heavily on the proposals offered by Jefferson and the Grand Committee prior to the Constitution.[3]

Hamilton submitted his plan to the Senate on February 7, 1791, and it was received favorably. On March 3, 1791, the Congress resolved to establish a mint. A committee formed under Robert Morris drafted a bill, and Morris engaged artists to prepare patterns. When members of the House realized that a "monarchical" effigy of the President was being planned to appear on the coins, a storm of protest erupted, subsiding only after agreement was reached to portray on the coins "an impression emblematic of liberty," along with the inscription, "Liberty." President Washington apparently disapproved of the appearance of his own likeness on the coins.[4]

On October 20, 1791, President Washington assigned the mint to the office of the secretary of state, observing that the Post Office had been annexed to the Treasury so that a better balance of responsibilities could thus be achieved. In his last day in office, January 31, 1795, Hamilton reported to the President his dissatisfaction with the management of the mint and recommended that it be placed under the Treasury.[5] Instead, the mint was named an independent agency in 1799 and became part of the Department of the Treasury in 1873.[6]

Establishing the Mint

On April 2, 1792, the Congress passed an Act Establishing a Mint and Regulating the Coins of the United States. The act set forth regulations pertaining to the "denominations, values, and descriptions" of coins. The Mint Act established a bimetallic standard at a ratio of 15 to 1. The weight of the eagle was set at 270 grains standard, containing 247.5 grains of pure gold, thus translating into a gold dollar of 24.75 grains (or $19.39 per ounce of gold, i.e., 480/24.75 = 19.39). The weight of the silver dollar was set at 371.25 grains of pure silver, weighing 416 grains.[7] The eagle, half eagle, and quarter eagle were $1\frac{1}{12}$ fine (0.9167 fine or 91.67 percent gold). The silver dollar, half-dollar, quarter-dollar, disme, and half-disme were 1485/1664 fine (approximately 0.8924 or 89.24 percent silver). The cent was set at 264 grains of pure copper, and the half-cent at 132 grains, by an act of Congress on May 8, 1792. The coinage legislation corresponded closely with Hamilton's plan.

Only the gold and silver coins were granted legal tender status: copper coins were not legal tender. Bullion was coined free of charge, or a 0.5 percent charge was levied if an immediate exchange for coins was requested.[8] In 1793 the Congress conferred legal tender standing on a number of foreign gold and silver coins, including, of course, the Spanish milled dollar.[9]

Regulating Coins

Congress found it very difficult to maintain an acceptable supply of coins in circulation. Indeed, legislation was introduced in Congress to abolish the mint. Such a bill passed in the House in 1802 but failed in the Senate. Besides the lack of success in providing a circulating medium, there was a lingering sentiment that coinage was a manifestation of royalty. "Actually," observed numismatic historian Don Taxay, "there was little difference between the Federalists view of sovereignty and the Republican view of monarchy."[10]

The primary source of the coinage problem stemmed from variation in the world market value of gold relative to silver, which made pure bimetallism impractical. In addition, periodic financial crises prompted coin hoarding and the issuance of private tokens and scrip. The regulation of coins also reflected sensitivity to special interests, the accommodation of convenience in the public's use of coins, and profit to the Treasury.

The ratio in world markets soon rose above the 15 to 1 relationship chosen by Hamilton, thereby causing exportation of the undervalued gold coins. Although modest quantities of half eagles were struck in most years, coinage of eagles was suspended from 1805 to 1837, and coinage of quarter eagles was suspended from 1808 to 1820. Silver dollars were exported as well, being displaced in circulation by worn foreign dollar-size coins, so that their coinage was suspended from 1804 to 1835. Half-dollars were used extensively for sizable transactions and specie reserves. The Spanish dollar circulated widely, though, commanding a small premium, as Spanish coins constituted an estimated 22 percent of the coins in circulation in the early 1800s.[11]

Congress in 1834 set out to revise the 15 to 1 ratio, and a bill was written to fix it at 15.625 to 1. While this would be below the 15.8 to 1 ratio prevailing in Europe, it was deemed advisable to undervalue gold, since gold could be replaced with paper money and it would be best to maintain silver in circulation. In response to the interests of the gold-producing states, the bill was amended, and the ratio was raised to 16 to 1. Branch mints were also established in New Orleans, Charlotte, North Carolina, and Dahlonega, Georgia. The act, which passed both the House and the Senate with wide margins, was viewed as a victory over the Bank of the United States, with gold displacing paper money. Gold also tended to displace silver.[12]

The devaluation of the dollar in terms of gold reduced the gold content of the eagle to 232 grains, with the gold coin weighing 258 grains (or 0.8992 fine).[13] The gold dollar weighed 23.20 grains (or $20.69 per ounce). With certain interruptions, of course, the United States was de facto on the gold standard from 1834 to 1933. Secretary of the Treasury Levi Woodbury reported in 1837 that the devaluation increased the volume of gold in circulation immensely from $4 million in October 1833 to $28 million in December 1836. The specie in banks rose from $25 million to $45 million, and the paper money in circulation increased from $80 million to $120 million.[14]

The fineness of gold and silver coins was made uniform in 1837 at 0.900. The weight of the eagle was not changed, thereby increasing its gold content to 232.2 grains—the dollar, therefore, contained 23.22 grains of fine gold (or $20.67 an ounce). The weight of the standard silver dollar was reduced from 416 grains to 412.5 grains, such that the higher proportion of silver left its silver content unchanged at 371.25 grains.[15]

The California gold discovery in 1848 added to the list of gold coins and prompted the federal government to reduce the bullion content of fractional silver coins. The double eagle and the one-dollar gold piece were introduced in 1849; the three-dollar gold stella was authorized in 1853. Silver commanded a small premium in the 1830s, but increased production of gold was accompanied by further appreciation in the intrinsic value of silver coins. Gold coins tended to displace silver coins, which were exported in larger volumes, being replaced in part as well by more Mexican silver coins. When the postage rate was set at three cents, the Congress also provided in 1851 for the issuance of a subsidiary three-cent silver coin, with the silver content valued at 86 percent of its face value and its legal tender limited to thirty cents.

In 1853 the Congress made all fractional silver coins subsidiary by reducing their weight. Their free coinage was terminated and a ceiling on their legal tender was established. Reservations were expressed about the honesty of a fiduciary coinage and there was concern over the prospect of counterfeit coins. Profits from the coinage, of course, were transferred to the Treasury. Substantial quantities of subsidiary silver coins were produced, and for the first time in the nation's history fractional coins were in ample supply to meet transactions demand. In order to preserve bimetallism, however, the silver dollar's specifications remained unchanged, but its absence from circulation was expected.[16]

Congress in 1857 abolished the half-cent piece and reduced the size of the cent, while changing its design and metal composition as well. The one-cent coin, as well as the half-cent, was reduced from the size in the original act before the coin was struck, and again in 1796. The bulky one-cent piece remained unpopular, however, and "barely paid expenses" at the mint. The small cent was received with satisfaction by the public, and was used by a provision of the law to redeem small-denomination

Mexican coins—the value of these latter coins in circulation amounted to an estimated $3 million. The reckoning of payments in bits and other terms diminished, although it remains a practice on Wall Street to quote financial instruments in bits and fractions thereof. The legal tender status of the Spanish dollar was rescinded, and the legal tender provision for fractional coins was extended to the one-cent piece. Doubts were expressed, however, about whether indeed legal tender standing could be granted to copper coins.[17]

Private Gold Coins

The first private gold coinage under the Constitution was struck in 1830 by Templeton Reid in Georgia. The coins' gold content was worth less than the indicated face value, for which Reid was criticized by the press. Public confidence waned, and the mint closed the same year. (Reid struck coins from California gold in 1949 as well.)[18]

From 1830 to 1852 the Bechtler family operated a mint in Rutherfordton, North Carolina, which was the center of the principal gold-producing area in the United States from 1790 to 1840.[19] From 1831 to 1840, $3,625,840 worth of gold passed through the Bechtler operation, with $2,241,850.50 in gold coins struck—records for other years are not available. During the Civil War many contracts in the South specified payment in Bechtler gold. The Bechtler mint probably struck more gold coins than any other private venture.[20] Christopher Bechtler cited the advantages of coined gold:

> gold in a fluxed state of 22 and 23 carats is generally sold for 84 cents per dwt. in the bank, whereas its intrinsic value, if coined, is 90 or 94 cents, consequently an actual saving of 6 cents per dwt. will be made by having it coined after paying all expenses of coining, etc.[21]

Treasury officials did investigate the Bechtler operation in about 1834, but the government did not interfere with this private coinage business, finding the coins heavier than the official coins and that there was a need for specie in the Piedmont area.[22] A government assay report in 1851, however, indicated the coins were of a gold value slightly below their nominal value.[23] The Bechtlers managed their mint judiciously. When the secretary of the Treasury instructed the director of the mint to place the date "Aug. 1, 1834" on its coins to denote the reduction in weight, the Bechtlers reacted and placed the date on their coins; the government, however, introduced a new design instead.[24]

Private gold coins provided the dominant circulating medium in California from 1849 to 1855. Private mints were established in 1849 to meet the demand for coinage, and they continued to operate in competition with the U.S. Assay Office, which contracted for the issuance of official gold coins. The establishment of a branch mint at San Francisco in 1854 soon brought to an end the private coinage businesses, except for the small-denomination gold pieces, which were struck until 1882.[25]

The scarcity of metallic currency in California reflected the gold rush boom and the requirement that customs duties be paid in coined money. Imports from China, moreover, necessitated payment in silver. Premiums on coins resulted and brokerage businesses flourished. Raw gold traded at $16 an ounce. Although their coins were not accepted at the Customs House, private gold coinage enterprises were launched to meet the demand for an adequate circulating medium. The gold content of these issues fell short of their face value, however, and the state legislature in 1850 required their redemption. The legislature also established the Office of State Assayer, which stamped gold ingots. These acts were repealed in 1851, and Congress authorized the appointment of a United States Assayer. Moffat and Co., which had issued its own coins, obtained the federal contract. Production of private coins resumed. Even though they were refused by the banks, large quantities were issued for circulation. Coins were issued under the authority of the U.S. Assay Office from 1851 to 1853, and the San Francisco mint commenced operations in 1854, but large-denomination private coins were struck as late as 1855.[26]

A currency shortage in the Oregon Territory also led to private gold coinage. Responding to a petition by the citizens of the territory, the legislature in 1849 authorized the establishment of a territorial mint, with any profit to be used to pay the debt incurred for waging the Cayuse Indian War. The Territorial Governor (a post turned down by Abraham Lincoln) declared the act unconstitutional and refused to implement it. Eight "prominent merchants and men of affairs" proceeded to establish a private mint, the Oregon Exchange Company, striking $5 and $10 gold pieces. The beaver design on the reverse is the seal of the Oregon Territory, which apparently was taken from the North West Company token of 1820.[27]

Gold coins were also struck under the direction of Brigham Young in the Mormon Territory from 1849 to 1860,[28] and private gold coins were issued in 1860–61 in Colorado.[29] Clark, Gruber and Co., "conscious of some technical impropriety in their mint," supported the effort to establish a branch mint in Denver, coupled with the government's purchase of the company's properties. The plant was sold to the government, but because of the discovery of the Comstock Lode in Nevada, a branch mint was established in Carson City in 1870.[30] A branch mint was not opened in Denver until 1906.

The U.S. government exercised restraint for many years in the presence of private gold coinage. The Coinage Act of 1873 did impose penalties for making coins "in resemblance or similitude" to U.S. coins and foreign coins, whether the latter were by law "current" or were in "actual use and circulate[d] as money."[31] It was not until 1909 that a broad prohibition against private coinage was enacted:

> Whoever, except as authorized by law, shall make or cause to be made, or shall utter or pass, or attempt to utter or pass, any coins of gold or silver or other metal, or alloys of metals, intended for the use and purpose of current money, whether in the resemblance of coins of the United States or of foreign countries, or of original design, shall be fined not more than three thousand dollars, or imprisoned not more than five years, or both.[32]

Private Tokens

The circulation of privately issued tokens in the 1800s, according to Benjamin Wright, was "vital to the operation of everyday business," and the tokens "were an integral part of the monetary system of a community."[33] Tokens were especially prominent as a circulating medium when intrinsically valuable coins were hoarded under a suspension of specie payments by banks, most notably in the 1830s and during the Civil War. Few were issued between 1789 and 1820, and then the number gradually increased until the appearance in the 1830s of the Jackson or Hard Times tokens, when "millions of these pieces, satirical or commercial, came out, and were readily accepted in small change."[34]

The issuance of trade tokens was widespread by the 1850s.[35] Tokens issued until 1857, when the half-cent and the large cent were discontinued, tended to range in size between these two coins. Few large tokens were issued after 1857.[36] Nonetheless, their legal status must have been in doubt. As early as 1792, an "Act to provide for a Copper Coinage" stated:

> no copper coins or pieces whatsoever, except the said cents and half cents, shall pass current as money, or shall be paid, or offered to be paid or received in payment for any debt, demand, claim, matter or thing whatsoever; and all copper coins or pieces, except the said cents or half cents, which shall be paid or offered to be paid or received in payment contrary to the prohibition aforesaid, shall be forfeited, and every person by whom any of them shall have been so paid or offered to be paid or received in payment, shall also forfeit the sum of ten dollars, and the said forfeiture and penalty shall and may be recovered with costs of suit for the benefit of any person or persons by whom information of the incurring thereof shall have been given.[37]

State Bank Note Era

The state bank note era stands in importance as a piece of the fabric instituting the financial system that complies with the express language of the Constitution in the sense that these institutions existed when the Constitution was framed and ratified, were left unmentioned in the document and thus implicitly sanctioned. The state banks, of course, were regulated by the states, but also significant within this framework was the reliance on competitive markets, both in banking and in precious metals into which their notes were convertible, at least most of the time.

A substantial proportion of the nation's currency was supplied by state banks from the ratification of the Constitution to the Civil War. The Constitution provided a strong impetus to the formation of state-chartered institutions. The Bank of the United States did offer some restraint, however, as suggested by a boost in their number following the dissolution of the Bank in 1811. Between 1811 and 1815 the number of state banks increased from 88 to 246. A comparable discipline was administered by the second Bank of the United States, such that 330 state banks were operating in 1830, but their number grew to 1,601 by 1861.[38] Besides elimination of the Bank's restraint, "free banking" laws and economic development contributed to their growth.

The issuance of notes for circulation represented a money creation mechanism and essentially defined the function of banks in the early nineteenth century. In 1833, for example, the New York State Bank commissioner declared:

> The legitimate use of banks is not for the purpose of loaning capital, but for the purpose of furnishing currency to be used instead of specie.[39]

State bank notes were generally promissory notes issued by banks and payable to the bearer on demand in gold or silver. Notes were typically placed into circulation through business loans at interest rates from 6 to 10 percent for thirty days to six months.[40] Specie convertibility, charter provision, and the operation of the market in currencies limited their supply. State banking historian Davis Dewey observed:

banks in the Northern States, either through policy or compulsion,
rarely issued the legal maximum. Restriction by statute was opera-
tive upon the smaller banks, but was of little need in controlling the
larger institutions which had a legal capacity to supply far the greater
part of the circulating medium. These latter were effectively restricted by the rapidity with which the notes were turned back for
redemption.[41]

The larger banks, located in cities, had greater capital resources and relied more on deposits, in contrast to the small,
country banks, which issued proportionately more notes.[42] Some
notes circulated at a discount, depending on distance and the
reputation of the institution. Dealers in paper money set up operations soon after the establishment of commercial banks in the
1780s. They bought discounted notes with specie and presented
them for redemption. Bank note reports were published generally
from 1826 to 1858, listing the discounts on such "uncurrent bank
notes" and thus helping to facilitate operations that limited note
issues.[43] The existence of "wildcat banks" in some states, however, certainly dampened the effectiveness of this practice.

Periodic financial panics caused suspensions of specie payments, which occurred in 1814–15, 1837, 1857, and 1861. Specie was then hoarded by banks and individuals, and notes were
exchanged at varying rates among themselves and with specie.[44]
The U.S. government also issued Treasury notes with money
characteristics in 1812–15, 1837–43, 1846–47, 1857–60, and
1861.[45]

Unincorporated banks, companies, and individuals issued circulating notes during the era of state bank notes, a subject treated
below, but the states eventually passed laws forbidding this practice. Between the 1790s and the 1820s, the states assumed the
authority to limit note issues to those granted the authority to
issue them.[46] Charter provisions also imposed a ceiling on note
issues, initially based on bank capital and after the panic of 1837
limited by specie reserve requirements.[47] Specie reserve requirements generally ranged from 15 percent to 25 percent, but the
average ratio of paper money to gold reserves was apparently

around 2½ to 1.[48] This was also the era of "free banking," whereby individuals and associations could engage in banking by complying with the statutory requirements without obtaining a charter by a legislative act.[49] While failures abounded, the system worked sufficiently well in New York and Louisiana that they became the models for constructing the national banking system.[50] The supplying of convertible paper money by private, state-chartered banks seems to have worked better than the system that depended on the issuance of bills of credit by the colonial governments, and seems to have been vastly superior to the financial setting under the Articles of Confederation, when the states emitted their bills of credit. The economic settings were very different, however, and the financial system of course was still marked by considerable instability during the state bank note era.

State Bank Notes and Bills of Credit

The constitutionality of state bank notes was tested in *Craig* v. *Missouri* (1830), and the Court ruled that the notes in this case were indeed the proscribed "bills of credit." The "certificates" in question were emitted by the state government with the clear intention to provide a paper currency. Chief Justice Marshall concluded:

> Had they been termed "bills of credit," instead of "certificates," nothing would have been wanting to bring them within the prohibitory words of the constitution.[51]

In reference to bills of credit, Marshall also stated:

> Such a medium has been always liable to considerable fluctuation. Its value is continually changing; and these changes, often great and sudden, expose individuals to immense loss, are the sources of ruinous speculations, and destroy all confidence between man and man. To cut up this mischief by the roots, a mischief which was felt through the United States, and which deeply affected the interest and prosperity of all; the people declared in their constitution, that no state shall emit bills of credit.[52]

The Chief Justice further developed the argument that the attach-
ment of legal tender to these bills was not essential to satisfy the
definition. The Congress had not made its bills of credit a legal
tender, "perhaps could not," as this "power resided in the
states."[53]

In a dissenting opinion, Justice John McLean defined the relevant class of bills of credit as:

> Notes, which the government promised to pay at a future period
> specified, with or without interest, and which were made receivable
> in payment of taxes and all debts to the public.[54]

Prior to the Constitution, McLean continued, various statutes
were passed to sustain their value, and creditors were compelled
to receive the notes under the penalty of forfeiting their debt,
losing interest, or being denounced as enemies of the country,
even if they were not specifically made a legal tender. So that
under the Constitution, unlike the referenced certificates,

> to constitute a bill of credit, . . . it must be issued by a state, and its
> circulation as money enforced by statutory provisions. It must con-
> tain a promise of payment by the state generally, . . . and [be] circu-
> lated on the credit of the state.[55]

In 1837, after Chief Justice Marshall's death, the Court reversed this decision 8 to 1 in *Brisco* v. *Bank of Kentucky*
(1837). Justice McLean rejected Marshall's definition as too
sweeping—i.e., "bills of credit signify a paper medium, intended to circulate between individuals, and between government and individuals, for the ordinary purposes of society."[56]
McLean suggested instead the following definition:

> a paper issued by the sovereign power, containing a pledge of its
> faith, and designed to circulate as money.[57]

McLean argued that assuming a broad definition would imperil
the constitutionality of the state-chartered banks, which could
not have been the intention of the framers given the existence
of those institutions when the Constitution was composed.[58]

In his dissenting opinion, Justice Joseph Story denied any

assertion that the notes of all state-chartered banks (and the institutions themselves) were unconstitutional, but only the emissions by a state. However, he observed:

> The states may create banks, as well as other corporations, upon private capital; and so far as this prohibition is concerned, may rightfully authorize them to issue bill or notes as currency: subject always to the control of congress, whose powers extend to the entire regulation of the currency of the country.[59]

Justice Story's opinion, of course, even if prophetic, was shared by no other justice. In *Bank of Augusta* v. *Earle* (1839), moreover, Chief Justice Taney tied together the common law right of banking and the sovereign authority of the states.[60]

Marshall was no friend of paper money, it should be noted, which leaves some question about his view of paper money when issued as a legal tender. In *Sturges* v. *Crowninshield* (1819), he referred to the reason for the restrictions of the states' monetary authority:

> To relieve this distress [after the revolution], paper money was issued, worthless lands, and other property of no use to the creditor, were made a legal tender in payment of debts; and the time of payment, stipulated in the contract, was extended by law. These were the peculiar evils of the day. So much mischief was done, and so much more was apprehended, that general distrust prevailed, and all confidence between man and man was destroyed. . . .

> Was this general prohibition [to pass laws impairing the obligation of contracts] intended to prevent paper money? We are not allowed to say so, because it is expressly provided, that no state shall "emit bills of credit;" neither could these words be intended to restrain the states from enabling debtors to discharge their debts by the tender of property of no real value to the creditor, because for that subject also particular provision is made. Nothing but gold and silver coin can be made a tender in payment of debts.

> . . . The convention appears to have intended to establish a general principle, that contracts should be inviolable. The constitution, therefore, declares, that no state shall pass "any law impairing the obligation of contracts."[61]

It would seem that Marshall was averse to allowing such "mischief" to be carried out by the federal government, but a direct ruling on the matter obviously could have led to a conclusion very different from that which applied to the states.

Emergency Currency

The U.S. government issued paper money during wars and depressions in five periods prior to the Civil War. These notes, ostensibly debt instruments, generally paid interest, and some notes were issued in denominations small enough to serve as money. The notes were receivable for debts, taxes, and duties due the federal government, and they apparently circulated as paper money. Most of the issues consisted of large denominations, however, so that they served to facilitate government finances and to shore up the banking system, and were not intended as a general paper money medium. They were not legal tender for all debts, public and private. They were issued when the Bank of the United States was absent as a fiscal agent, and, although frequently issued, they were, as short-maturity instruments, temporary rather than permanent additions to the money stock.

The notes issued during the War of 1812 were initially issued in 1812 in $100 and $1,000 denominations, paying 5.4 percent interest. In the final emission in 1815, however, the smallest denomination was just $3 and it paid no interest. The volume authorized exceeded $36 million, but not all at one time.

The panic of 1837 prompted a series of notes issued from 1837 to 1843. The smallest denomination was apparently $50, and over $35 million were issued at interest rates up to 6 percent. The Mexican War brought a third set of notes, from 1846–47, again with the smallest at $50, and about $35 million were issued. The panic of 1857 brought an initial issue of some $20 million of notes, followed in 1860 with another series amounting to $15 million. Some of these notes, issued on a competitive basis, paid as high as 12 percent interest, as the Civil War approached. The final series of these generally interest-bearing notes of one to two years' maturities was authorized in 1861, amounting to $35 million at 6 percent interest, with denominations of $50 and larger.[62]

Private individuals and unincorporated associations issued notes along with banks prior to the general requirement around 1830 that limited this practice in nearly all states to incorporate banks. In the earlier period, a variety of notes circulated, especially during financial crises, as Dewey reported:

> It is stated that in Zanesville, in 1818, there were more than thirty kinds of paper passing from hand to hand; besides bank notes, there were shinplasters issued by bridge, turnpike, and manufacturing companies, city and borough authorities, tavern keepers, and shoeblacks, ranging from three cents to two dollars. With few exceptions, these notes were of little value.[63]

Some of these issues had the characteristics of bank notes rather than scrip, which, often as an "emergency currency," served as a temporary substitute for standard money, generally entitling the holder to lawful money or merchandise.[64] From about 1830 to the Civil War, private nonbank issues conform more closely to the definition of scrip. Many were of small denominations, "shinplasters," some of which took the value of Spanish coins down to one-half real, half-bit, or 6¼ cents. State banking laws did not prevent their issuance, as Dewey observed:

> Under the cover of suspension of specie payments and looser laws of the new Western States and the nonenforcement of the laws already in existence in the eastern section, a very considerable amount of fractional bills issued by individuals and business firms were at one time and another put into circulation, oftentimes for the purpose of supplying the want of small coin, due to the disappearance of silver after its undervaluation at the mint by the coinage act of 1834. A writer in *Merchant's Magazine* in 1853 stated that in the interior a large batch of private shinplasters had been issued, to the amount of between $1,000,000 and $2,000,000, which found a ready circulation.[65]

When specie payments were suspended, paper money tended to remain in circulation, but coins were hoarded, thus causing a shortage of small-denomination currency. During such times shinplasters were reportedly issued by

> banks, savings institutions, Savings Funds, boroughs, villages, cities, counties, States, merchants, turnpike companies, water companies, railroad companies, educational institutions, and various other organizations.[66]

Money, Prices, and Economic Activity

The market-oriented system, grounded on specie, reflected the distrust of the government's management of money implicit in the contemporary exercise of constitutional authority and generated a stability underlying an extraordinary incoherence in the money supply, as might be supposed from the above treatment of the subject. Long-run price stability and a respectable rate of economic expansion have been perhaps overshadowed by short-run instability in money, prices, and economic activity.

The panic of 1837 does not simply characterize the history from 1789 to 1861, even though instability no doubt marked the period. The tumultuous 1830s reflected Jacksonian policies as well as the inherent instability of the financial system. Friedman and Schwartz draw a parallel between that episode and the 1930s. The earlier experience also occurred within a worldwide crisis and was aggravated by the uncertainties related to the failure to renew the Bank of the United States' charter, and that organization's subsequent speculative ventures, as well as uncertainties related to the distribution of the government's surplus, the Specie Circular, and the Independent Treasury, such that a quarter of the banks closed and the money supply contracted by about one-third.[67]

The market-regulated supply of precious metals seemed to maintain long-run price stability, despite the financial system precariously built upon it, even though prices ascended and descended over periods extending beyond business-cycle durations. The wholesale price index was the same in 1861 as it was in 1789, and economic growth proceeded at a relatively high 4.4 percent rate.

The shorter subperiod, 1840–61, may be of more interest, however, since it has been characterized as an era of "free banking" and state bank notes. The de facto gold standard provided a 4.0 percent rate of increase in the world gold stock, and that was accompanied by a 4.7 percent growth rate in the money supply. Constant-dollar GNP expanded at a 4.1 percent rate and wholesale prices drifted lower at a 0.3 percent annual rate. The competitive determination of the money supply under the state-chartered banking system was obviously not inflationary.

The short-run behavior of the overall economic performance measures contrasts sharply with the long run, when compared with the period from 1960 to 1985. Money, prices, and economic activity were much more variable in the earlier period. The standard deviation of growth rates in the money supply for the years 1840 to 1861 was 9.0 percentage points, but just 2.3 percentage points from 1960 to 1985. This behavior appears in greater volatility in prices (7.2 to 5.2 percentage points) and wider fluctuations in general economic activity (6.2 to 2.5 percentage points for real GNP).[68]

Conclusion

The Congress established a mint "to coin money" and adopted legislation to "regulate the value thereof, and of foreign coin." Despite frequent revisions of the regulations, the Congress was unsuccessful for several decades in maintaining an acceptable circulation of coins. The government tolerated private coinage and formally recognized the circulation of certain foreign coins. Devaluation of the dollar in terms of gold, vast gold discoveries, and the relegation of fractional silver coins to a subsidiary status seemed finally to bring forth an ample supply of coins for transactions purposes.

The paper money supply was largely provided by state banks, although it was limited at times by the Bank of the United States. State bank notes were recognized as compatible with the Constitution. Periodic financial crises were accompanied by specie payments suspensions, and, in the absence of the Bank of the United States, Treasury notes without legal tender standing were issued by the federal government. Private tokens and scrip were most notably placed into circulation during such emergencies. The monetary system obviously lacked any real sense of "uniformity" of the currency.

The money supply was essentially competitively determined. The governing role of specie was consistent with the achievement of long-run price stability and an acceptable rate of economic growth. The financial system was highly unstable, however, transmitting considerable variability in money and prices and contributing to the amplitude of business fluctuations. The attendant economic risks inherent in this instability must have generated substantial redistributive flows of income and wealth.

Notes

1. Don Taxay, *The U.S. Mint and Coinage* (New York: Arco Publishing, 1966), p. 41.

2. Ibid., p. 42.

3. Ibid., pp. 44–50.

4. Ibid., pp. 51–62.

5. Ibid., pp. 73, 129.

6. Director of the Mint, *United States Mint: A Brief History* (Washington, DC: United States Mint, 1988), p. 5.

7. "The Mint Act, April 2, 1792," in *Documentary History of Banking and Currency in the United States*, vol. 1, ed. Herman E. Krooss (New York: McGraw-Hill, 1969), p. 203.

8. Taxay, *The U.S. Mint and Coinage*, p. 66.

9. Ibid., p. 67.

10. Ibid., p. 139.

11. Arthur J. Rolnick and Warren E. Weber, "Gresham's Law or Gresham's Fallacy?" *Quarterly Review*, Federal Reserve Bank of Minneapolis (Winter 1986), p. 18.

12. Taxay, *The U.S. Mint and Coinage*, pp. 195–200.

13. "Act of June 28, 1834," in Krooss, *Documentary History*, vol. 2, p. 1040.

14. Levi Woodbury, "Annual Treasury Report on the State of the Currency after the Devaluations of 1834 and 1837" in ibid., pp. 1050–52.

15. "Act of January 18, 1837," in ibid., pp. 1043–44.

16. Taxay, *The U.S. Mint and Coinage*, pp. 217–21; R. S. Yeoman, *A*

Guide Book on United States Coins, 1988, 42d ed. (Racine, WI: Western Publishing), pp. 9–10; and "Act to Devalue Silver Coinage, February 21, 1853," in Krooss, *Documentary History*, vol. 2, pp. 1243–44.

17. Taxay, *The U.S. Mint and Coinage*, p. 237; Yeoman, *United States Coins*, p. 83; "Act to End the Legal Tender Status of Foreign Coins, February 21, 1857," in Krooss, *Documentary History*, p. 1245.

18. Yeoman, *United States Coins*, pp. 220–21. More extensive treatment of private gold issues is contained in Donald H. Kagin, *Private Gold Coins and Patterns of the United States* (New York: Arco Publishing, 1981). The gold doubloon issued by Ephraim Brasher in 1787 can be considered as the first private gold piece struck in the United States, although it might have been intended as a pattern for a proposed copper coinage and it was struck prior to the adoption of the Constitution (ibid., p. 185).

19. Yeoman, *United States Coins*, pp. 221–24.

20. Clarence Griffin, "The Story of the Bechtler Gold Coinage," in American Numismatic Association, *Selections from the Numismatist* (Racine, WI: Whitman Publishing, 1960), pp. 32, 38, 39.

21. Ibid., p. 34.

22. Ibid., p. 38.

23. "Results of the Government Assay of a Number of Private Gold Coins," in *Selections from the Numismatist*, p. 50.

24. Yeoman, *United States Coins*, p. 222.

25. Ibid., pp. 224–38. Robert Friedberg includes companies in addition to those listed by Yeoman in *Gold Coins of the World* (New York: The Coin and Currency Institute, 1958), pp. 48–51.

26. A. Kosoff, "Private Gold Coinage in California," in *Selections from the Numismatist*, pp. 46–48; "Results of the Government Assay of a Number of Private Gold Coins," ibid., pp. 50–52.

27. G. A. Pipes, "The Story of the Beaver Coins of Oregon," ibid., pp. 41–44; Yeoman, *United States Coins*, pp. 237–38.

28. Ibid., pp. 239–40.

29. Ibid., pp. 240–42.

30. G. H. King, "The Clark Gruber & Co. Private Coinage," in *Selections from the Numismatist*, pp. 53–55.

31. "The Coinage Act of 1873, February 12, 1873," in Krooss, *Documentary History*, vol. 2, p. 1769.

32. "Selection 5461 as codified in section 167 of the Penal Code of the United States, March 4, 1909 (35 Stat. L., 1120)," in the National Monetary Commission, *Laws of the United States Concerning Money, Banking, and Loans, 1778–1909* (Washington, DC: Government Printing Office, 1910), p. 572.

33. Benjamin P. Wright, "Foreword," in *American Business Tokens* (Boston: Quarterman Publications, 1972).

34. T. L. Elder, "A Plea for American Token Collecting," in *Selections from the Numismatist*, p. 88.

35. Ibid., pp. 88–90.

36. Ibid., p. 90.

37. "Act to Provide for a Copper Coinage, May 8, 1792," in Krooss, *Documentary History*, vol. 1, p. 207.

38. "Statistics on the State of the Commercial Banks of the United States, 1811, 1815, 1816, 1819–30," ibid., vol. 2, pp. 1175–78; Eugene S. Klise, *Money and Banking* (Cincinnati, OH: South-Western Publishing, 1972), p. 183.

39. Margaret G. Myers, *The New York Money Market: Origins and Development*, vol. 1 (New York: Columbia University Press, 1931), p. 87.

40. D. C. Wismer, "Early Bank Notes Issued in the United States," in *Selections from the Numismatist*, p. 180.

41. Davis R. Dewey, *State Banking before the Civil War* (Washington, DC: Government Printing Office, 1910), p. 62.

42. Ibid., p. 58.

43. William H. Dillistin, *Bank Note Reporters and Counterfeit Detectors 1826–1866* (New York: American Numismatic Society, 1949), pp. 1–9, 41–58, 74–75, 80–82. Some paper money issues apparently circulated widely. The "dix" ($10) note issued by the Citizens Bank of Louisiana, for example, circulated extensively, and was apparently the derivation of the name "Dixie" for the South (W. A. Philpott, Jr., "Word 'Dixie' Derives from Old Bank Note," in *Selections from the Numismatist*, pp. 182–84).

44. Wismer, "Early Bank Notes," p. 181.

45. Chester L. Krause and Robert F. Lemke, *Standard Catalog of U.S. Paper Money*, 6th ed. (Iola, WI: Krause Publications, 1987), pp. 149–53.

46. Dewey, *State Banking*, pp. 143–51.

47. Ibid., pp. 11–22, 33, 41, 53–59, 73, 112, 120, 126, 217–24; Elgin Groseclose, *Money and Man: A Survey of Monetary Experience* (Norman, OK: University of Oklahoma Press, 1976), pp. 184–88.

48. Wismer, "Early Bank Notes," p. 181; Krooss, *Documentary History*, vol. 2, pp. 1050–52.

49. Groseclose, *Money and Man*, pp. 186–87.

50. Krooss, *Documentary History*, p. 1058.

51. *Craig* v. *Missouri* (1830), 29 U.S. (4 Peters), 433.

52. Ibid., p. 432.

53. Ibid., p. 435.

54. Ibid., p. 453.

55. Ibid., p. 454.

56. *Briscoe* v. *Bank of Kentucky* (1837), 36 U.S. (11 Peters), 313. The state of North Dakota currently owns and operates a commercial bank, the Bank of North Dakota (Richard Karp, "Hardnosed Socialism? The Bank of North Dakota Knows How to Make a Buck," *Barron's*, June 2, 1975, pp. 5, 18).

57. *Briscoe* v. *Bank of Kentucky*, p. 314.

58. Ibid., p. 317.

59. Ibid., p. 349.

60. *Bank of Augusta* v. *Earle* (1839), 38 U.S. (13 Peters), 595.

61. *Sturges* v. *Crowninshield* (1819), 204 U.S. (4 Wheat.), 204–5.

62. Krause and Lemke, *U.S. Paper Money*, pp. 149–53.

63. Dewey, *State Banking*, pp. 149–50.

64. V. L. Brown, "Emergency Currency or Scrip Issued in the United States, 1931–34," in *Selections from the Numismatist*, p. 191.

65. Dewey, *State Banking*, pp. 150–51.

66. J. A. Muscalus, "Use of 6¼ Cent and 12½ Cent Notes Prior to the 1860's," in *Selections from the Numismatist*, p. 185.

67. Friedman and Schwartz, *Monetary History*, pp. 299–300.

68. Thomas F. Wilson, "Institutional Change as a Source of Excessive Monetary Expansion," in *Inflation through the Ages: Economic, Social, Psychological and Historical Aspects*, ed. Nathan Schmukler and Edward Marcus (New York: Brooklyn College Press, 1983), pp. 79–93. Comparable statistical results were found by Michael David Bordo, "The Gold Standard: Myths and Realities," in *Money in Crisis*, ed. Barry N. Siegel (Cambridge, MA: Ballinger Publishing, 1984), pp. 197–237.

Some of the statistics have been updated since the author's earlier publication. Those sources include: for GNP, Thomas Senior Berry, *Revised Annual Estimates of American Gross National Product* (Richmond, VA: Bostwick Press, 1978), pp. 38, 41; and U.S. Department of Commerce, *Survey of Business*. For the wholesale price index, George F. Warren and Frank A Pearson, *Gold and Prices* (New York: John Wiley, 1935), pp. 12–14; and U.S. Department of Commerce, *Business Statistics* and *Survey of Current Business*. For the monetary base, Warren and Pearson, *Gold and Prices*, pp. 92, 151; Friedman and Schwartz, *Monetary History*, pp. 799–808; and Federal Reserve Bank of St. Louis. For the money supply, Warren and Pearson, *Gold and Prices*, p. 140; Friedman and Schwartz, *Monetary History*, pp. 705–22; and Board of Governors of the Federal Reserve System. The Berry work has been superseded by his later publication, *Production and Population since 1789: Revised GNP Series in Constant Dollars* (Richmond, VA: Bostwick Press, 1988). The revised numbers were used to compute the reported statistics.

James Hurst apparently holds a very different concept of money, as he argues that the government has never allowed money to be market-determined. This may be true in a very narrow, legal sense, but the money supply has always been determined in part by market forces (James Willard Hurst, *A Legal History of Money in the United States, 1774–1970* [Lincoln, NE: University of Nebraska Press, 1973], pp. 31, 211, 227).

A gold standard can constitute a highly inflationary (or deflationary) regime, as reported in the study by Dennis O. Flynn, "Sixteenth-Century Inflation from the Production Point of View," in Schmukler and Marcus, *Inflation through the Ages*. The postmortems on the gold standard differ widely. For a sampling of the recent literature, refer to Barry N. Siegel, *Money in Crisis: The Federal Reserve, the Economy, and Monetary Reform* (Cambridge, MA: Ballinger Publishing, 1984); Llewellyn H. Rockwell, Jr., ed., *The Gold Standard: An Austrian Perspective* (Lexington, MA: Lexington Books, 1985); and Michael D. Bordo and Anna J. Schwartz, eds., *A Retrospective on the Classical Gold Standard, 1821–1931* (Chicago: University of Chicago Press, 1984).

Federal "Bills of Credit"

Measures adopted to finance the Civil War ultimately enhanced the authority of the Congress to preside over the nation's currency, including federal "bills of credit" and a national banking system. The Legal Tender Act of 1862 provided for the issuance of the "greenbacks," the first legal tender paper money since ratification of the Constitution. This assertion of monetary authority by the Congress was eventually sanctioned by the Supreme Court, as a manifestation of sovereignty, but with considerable judicial conflict.

The Supreme Court was sharply divided in the resolution of the authority of Congress to make the government's paper money a legal tender in payment of private debts. Indeed, the Court initially ruled that the act of 1862 was unconstitutional, but after two new appointees joined the Court, the decision was reversed, again by the narrowest majority. Several years later the matter was more firmly decided, as this power of issuing legal tender paper money was deemed to be a political question to be determined by the Congress, not appropriately left to judicial scrutiny afterwards. In the aftermath of the Civil War, then, the courts recognized, as a matter of the national government's sovereignty, the power of the Congress to preside over a national currency.

Chief Justice Roger B. Taney

Congress enacted the Legal Tender Act on February 25, 1862, while Salmon P. Chase was serving as the secretary of the Treasury, and President Jackson's appointee, Roger B. Taney, was

presiding as chief justice of the Supreme Court. With the acqui-
escence of Chase, the "greenbacks" were declared a "legal tender
for all debts, public or private" (except for duties on imports and
interest on the public debt). The initial issue amounted to $150
million, but ultimately $432 million of "greenbacks" were au-
thorized for issuance by the Congress. Their constitutionality was
certainly in doubt. The Congress had rejected the use of legal
tender paper money during the War of 1812, and the Confederate
notes were not a legal tender—only gold and silver were recognized as legal tender in the Confederate Constitution, but state
notes were granted legal tender standing by the state legislatures.

Chief Justice Taney in an undelivered opinion branded the
legal tender issue unconstitutional. Taney's view was prompted
by a U.S. Supreme Court ruling in the case of *Roosevelt* v.
Meyer, which arose in the New York courts. A state court ruling
had denied Congress the right to issue paper money without adequate security. In another case, the Court of Errors and Appeals,
the state's highest court, reversed that ruling but the above-cited
case was appealed to the U.S. Supreme Court. In Taney's absence, because of ill health, the Court dismissed the case, claiming no jurisdiction on the matter. Historian David Silver observed
that the Court did not wish to interfere with a measure devised by
the Lincoln administration to aid the war effort. Yet the Court did
not choose to state that the legal tender notes were constitutional.
Thus, it "interpreted the Judiciary Act of 1789 narrowly and
gracefully side-stepped the broad issues involved."[1]

In response, Taney set forth his opinion in an essay, "On Paper
Money." He argued that a prohibition was unnecessary, since
Congress had only delegated powers. The framers were aware of
the temptation to issue paper money rather than impose taxes, so
no such power was granted to the Congress. Thus, Congress was
not given this power in express terms. It is not incidental to the
powers so conferred, according to Taney, nor is it a necessary
and proper device for carrying those powers into execution.
Moreover, Taney suggested, legal tender status should apply to
gold and silver coins,[2] an opinion with which Chief Justice Mar-

shall apparently concurred in *Sturges* v. *Crowninshield* (1819).[3]

Silver observed that fortunately for the administration no other cases on legal tender reached the Court during the war, inferring that "If the Court had had to rule directly upon the subject the administration rightfully could have feared an adverse decision."[4]

Chief Justice Salmon P. Chase

Upon the death of Chief Justice Taney in 1864, President Lincoln reportedly nominated Salmon P. Chase as Taney's successor after weighing the following factors:

> There are three reasons in favor of his appointment and one very strong reason against it. First, he occupies the largest place in the public mind in connection with the office, then we wish for a Chief Justice who will sustain what has been done in regard to emancipation and legal tenders. We cannot ask a man what he will do, and if we should, and he should answer us, we should despise him for it. Therefore we must take a man whose opinions are known. But there is one very strong reason against his appointment. He is a candidate for the Presidency, and if he does not give up that idea it will be very bad for him and very bad for me.[5]

Chase had not only served as secretary of the Treasury from 1861 to 1864, but his portrait appeared on the one-dollar note of 1862.[6] Nonetheless, defying "rational expectations," Chase declared with a 4 to 3 majority in *Hepburn* v. *Griswold* (1870) that the Legal Tender Act was unconstitutional. The decision excited strong opposition and spawned an effort to reverse the Court's ruling. Hope for a reversal of the decision hinged on two new appointments to the Supreme Court. The Court had been increased to ten members in 1863, but reduced to seven in 1866 to prevent President Andrew Johnson from filling any vacancies. Shortly after Ulysses S. Grant assumed office as President, the Congress expanded the Court to nine members, its traditional complement, and authorized the President to nominate an additional judge, as eight justices had heard the above-cited case but one had resigned (in accordance with an earlier commitment) so seven members rendered the decision—the retiring justice agreed with the majority.[7] With President Grant's two new appointees, the Court ruled the act valid by a vote of 5 to 4 in *Knox* v. *Lee* (1871) and *Parker* v. *Davis* (1871), with Chase then offering a minority opinion.[8]

Finally, in *Juilliard* v. *Greenman* (1884) the Supreme Court ruled that the Congress had the authority to make the notes of the government a legal tender in payment of private debts when it chose to do so. The Court resolved the matter of congressional authority to issue legal tender paper money by placing it among the powers belonging to sovereignty and not expressly withheld from the Congress.[9]

The legal tender status of the greenbacks was ultimately sanctioned, but the Supreme Court had held in *Bronson* v. *Rodes* (1869) that contracts specifying payment in gold or silver coin were constitutional.[10] In response to the "greenback inflation" and court rulings, gold clauses were inserted into contracts. Gold clauses were included in private and public bonds from 1879, when specie payments were resumed, until the 1930s, when they were declared unenforceable by the Supreme Court.[11]

Legal Tender I

In *Hepburn* v. *Griswold* (1870), Chief Justice Chase addressed the specific issue of whether the greenbacks were legal tender in the satisfaction of contracts made prior to the act of 1862. Thus, the question framed by Chase was whether or not Congress has the power to issue notes under its authority that are legal tender in the payment of debts that, when contracted, were payable by law in gold and silver coin. The Constitution provides, in Chase's reasoning, that the Congress has those powers implied by the condition of being "necessary and proper," but limited by the Tenth Amendment. The Constitution contains no express grant of "legislative power to make any description of credit currency a legal tender in payment of debts," Chase observed, so he proceeded to examine the Constitution's implied powers.[12]

Chase asserted that this power was not incidental to the power to coin money or to that of regulating coins, which is a power "to determine the weight, purity, form, impression, and denomination of the several coins."[13] He further claimed that the power to make notes a legal tender was distinct from the power to emit bills of credit:

> The old Congress, under the Articles of Confederation, was clothed by express grant with the power to emit bills of credit, which are in fact notes for circulation as currency; and yet that Congress was not clothed with the power to make these bills a legal tender in payment. And this court has recently held [*Veazie Bank* v. *Fenno* (1869)] that the Congress, under the Constitution, possesses, as incident to other powers, the same power as the old Congress to emit bills or notes; but it was expressly declared at the same time that this decision concluded nothing on the question of legal tender. Indeed, we are not aware that it has ever been claimed that the power to issue bills or notes has any identity with the power to make them a legal tender. On the contrary, the whole history of the country refutes that notion. The States have always been held to possess the power to authorize and regulate the issue of bills for circulation by banks and individuals, subject, as has been lately determined, to the control of Congress, . . . yet the States are expressly prohibited from making anything but gold and silver a legal tender.[14]

Chase inquired as to the existence of this power in that to carry on war, to regulate commerce, and to borrow money. He was not persuaded that the legal tender provision, for example, was "an appropriate and plainly adapted means for the execution of the power to declare and carry on war,"[15] or that it was implied by other powers. He felt, moreover, that it was not consistent with the spirit of the Constitution. Indeed, one might infer from the discussion in the Congress of the Northwest Ordinance and in the prohibition that "no State shall pass any law impairing the obligation of contracts," that "the spirit of this prohibition should pervade the entire body of legislation, and that the justice which the Constitution was ordained to establish was not thought by them to be compatible with legislation of an opposite tendency."[16] Moreover, the Fifth Amendment "ordains that private property shall not be taken for public use without compensation."[17] The act in question clearly deprives persons of property "without due process of law."[18]

Thus, Chase was led to conclude that:

> an act making mere promises to pay dollars a legal tender in payment of debts previously contracted, is not a means appropriate, plainly adapted, really calculated to carry into effect any express power vested in Congress; that such an act is inconsistent with the spirit of the Constitution; and that it is prohibited by the Constitution.[19]

In his dissenting opinion, Justice Samuel Miller observed that the Constitution removes the whole matter from the domain of state legislatures, but not the Congress:

> No such prohibition is placed upon the power of Congress on this subject, though there are, as I have already said, matters expressly forbidden to Congress; but neither this of legal tender, nor of the power to emit bills of credit, or to impair the obligation of contract, is among them. On the contrary, Congress is authorized to coin money and to regulate the value thereof, and of foreign coin, and to punish the counterfeiting, of such coin and of the securities of the United States. It has been strongly argued by many able jurists that these latter clauses, fairly construed, confer the power to make the securities of the United States a lawful tender in payment of debts.[20]

Legal Tender II

In the second round, the matter of legal tender was reversed, and the act was found to be constitutional for prior contracts and for contracts made after passage of the law. Newly appointed Justice William Strong rendered the opinion of the Court that the provision to make the Treasury notes a legal tender for all debts was not forbidden by the letter or spirit of the Constitution. He argued:

> To assert, then, that the clause enabling Congress to coin money and regulate its value tacitly implies a denial of all power over the currency of the nation, is an attempt to introduce a new rule of construction against the solemn decisions of this court. So far from its

containing a lurking prohibition, many have thought it was intended to confer upon Congress that general power over the currency which has always been an acknowledged attribute of sovereignty in every other civilized nation than our own, especially when considered in connection with the other clause which denies to the States the power to coin money, emit bills of credit, or make anything but gold and silver a tender in payment of debts.[21]

Justice Strong continued:

Whatever power there is over the currency is vested in Congress. If the power to declare what is money is not in Congress, it is annihilated. This may indeed have been intended. Some powers that usually belong to sovereignties were extinguished, but their extinguishment was not left to inference. . . . [I]t might be argued, we say, that the gift of power to coin money and regulate the value thereof, was understood as conveying general power over the currency, the power which had belonged to the States, and which they surrendered.[22]

Such provisions could scarcely be construed "as an implied prohibition to Congress against declaring treasury notes a legal tender."[23]

Turning to Chase's principal argument, that is, declaring the legal tender character to be prohibited by the spirit of the Constitution because the greenbacks indirectly impair the obligation of contracts, Strong insisted, first of all, that, excluding contracts specifying the form of payment, this cannot be claimed:

But the *obligation* of a contract to pay money is to pay that which the law shall recognize as money when the payment is to be made.[24]

Thus,

contracts for the payment of money are subject to the authority of Congress. . . . It cannot, therefore, be maintained that the legal tender acts impaired the obligation of contracts.[25]

Beyond that,

nor can it be truly asserted that Congress may not, by its action, indirectly impair the obligation of contracts. . . .[26]

moreover, is not applicable since it pertains to a direct appropriation of property, not one that is indirect.

Strong concluded:

> [W]ithout extending our remarks further, it will be seen that we hold
> the acts of Congress constitutional as applied to contracts made ei-
> ther before or after their passage. In so holding, we overrule much of
> what was decided in *Hepburn* v. *Griswold, as ruled the acts unwar-
> ranted by the Constitution so far as they apply to contracts made
> before the enactment.*[28]

In defending the Court's reversal, Strong noted that the earlier
decision was made by a divided Court, one having less than the
full number of judges that the law provided at the time, but the
full legal complement participated in this decision.

Justice Joseph P. Bradley, also just appointed by President
Grant, in concurring, observed that under the Constitution the
government of the United States possesses those necessary and
proper powers, so that, "As a government it was vested with all
the attributes of sovereignty."[29] Thus,

> The doctrine so long contended for, that the Federal Union was a
> mere compact of States . . . should be regarded as definitely and
> forever overthrown.[30]

It would seem to be, Bradley continued, a

> self-evident proposition that [the federal government] is vested with
> all those inherent and implied powers which, at the time of adopting
> the Constitution, were generally considered to belong to every gov-
> ernment as such, and as being essential to the exercise of its func-
> tions.[31]

The colonial bills were a legal tender, and Parliament in 1751
prohibited their issuance, which was a source of discontent cul-
minating in the revolution. During the war, Franklin deplored the
depreciation but noted one consolation, that the public debt is
proportionately diminished by their depreciation, as an impercepti-
ble tax. Moreover, Congress passed resolutions declaring that
they ought to pass current in all payments, and that a person

refusing to accept them ought to be deemed an enemy to the liberties of the United States. Thus,

> They established the *historical fact* that when the Constitution was adopted, the employment of bills of credit was deemed a legitimate means of meeting the exigencies of a regularly constituted government, and that the affixing of them of the quality of a legal tender was regarded as entirely discretionary with the legislature.[32]

While aware of Madison's report, the words "and emit bills" were struck out "with diverse views."[33] As it now stands,

> [W]ithout any words either of grant or restriction of power, . . . it is our duty to construe the instrument by its words, in light of history, of the general nature of government, and the incidents of sovereignty.[34]

Legal Tender III

The legal tender issue reached the Court once again in the case of *Juilliard* v. *Greenman* (1884), with the disputed issue being whether Congress could constitutionally make a paper money legal tender in times of both peace and war. Justice Horace Gray rendered the opinion of the Court, and Justice Stephen Field, who had been appointed by President Lincoln and had objected in the earlier legal tender cases, offered the lone dissenting opinion.

Justice Gray grounded the opinion of the Court on the view that under the Constitution a national government was established "with sovereign powers," and that in establishing a government and in "creating a national sovereignty," the Constitution should not be interpreted with the strictness of a private contract but with respect for the appropriate means of carrying the powers of government into execution. The Constitution contrasts with the Articles of Confederation, which declared that "each State retains its sovereignty, freedom, and independence, and every power, jurisdiction and right which is not by the confederation expressly delegated to the United States in Congress assembled."[35]

Justice Gray considered some of the opposing arguments. In reference to Marshall's opinion in *Sturges* v. *Crowninshield,* he maintained that the references to paper money and legal tender applied exclusively to the states, drawing no meaning for the national government. The debates in the convention related to striking the words "and emit bills" were, in his mind, "quite inconclusive." The opinion of Luther Martin, Gray declared, "who voted against the motion, and who declined to sign the Constitution, can hardly be accepted as satisfactory evidence of the reasons or the motives of the majority of the Convention."[36]

Justice Gray further observed that Madison's assertion that striking the power to emit bills would still leave the power to issue public notes was ambiguous, as Madison "has not explained why he thought that striking the words 'and emit bills' would leave the power to emit bills, and deny the power to make them a tender in payment of debts."[37] Finally, there is no way to know from the vote of the convention how many were influenced by Gorham's remark that he favored striking the clause, but opposed any prohibition, feeling that if the words stood, they might lead to the emission; and who later argued that the power, so far as it was safe, would be involved in that of borrowing.[38]

Thus:

> [T]he power to make the notes of the government a legal tender in payment of private debts being one of the powers belonging to sovereignty in other civilized nations, and not expressly withheld from Congress by the Constitution; we are irresistibly impelled to the conclusion that the impressing upon the treasury notes of the United States the quality of being legal tender in payment of private debts is an appropriate means, conducive and plainly adapted to the execution of the undoubted powers of Congress, consistent with the letter and spirit of the Constitution.[39]

Finally, in expressing a sentiment strongly held since then, the conditions for issuing legal tender notes are "a political question, to be determined by Congress, when the question of exigency arises, and not a judicial question, to be afterwards passed upon by the courts."[40]

In his dissent, Justice Field asserted:

> If there is anything in the history of the Constitution which can be established with moral certainty, it is that the framers of the instrument intended to prohibit the issue of legal tender notes both by the general government and by the States; and thus prevent interference with the contracts of private parties.[41]

Repeated references to "coin money" and "money" mean precisely that, and Congress has the power to alter the value of coins, but there is a "great trust devolved upon Congress, carrying with it the duty of creating and maintaining a uniform standard of value throughout the Union."[42] Beyond this, when the Constitution came before the conventions of the several states for adoption, a certain apprehension prevailed, so that the conventions in a number of states requested that further declaratory and restrictive clauses be added to prevent misconceptions or abuse of power. One such restrictive clause is the Tenth Amendment. Moreover, said Justice Field:

> The framers of the Constitution, as I have said, were profoundly impressed with the evils which had resulted from the vicious legislation of the States making notes a legal tender, and they determined that such a power should not exist any longer. They therefore prohibited the States from exercising it, and they refused to grant it to the new government which they created. Of what purpose is it then to refer to the exercise of the power by the absolute or the limited governments of Europe, or by the States previous to our Constitution. Congress can exercise no power by virtue of any supposed inherent sovereignty in the general government. . . . [T]here is no such thing as a power of inherent sovereignty in the government of the United States. It is a government of delegated powers, supreme within its prescribed sphere, but powerless outside of it. In this country sovereignty resides in the people, and Congress can exercise no power which they have not, by their Constitution, entrusted to it; all else is withheld. . . . The doctrine, that a power not expressly forbidden may be exercised, would, as I have observed, change the character of our government. If I read the Constitution aright, if there is any

weight to be given to the uniform teachings of our great jurists and of commentators previous to the late civil war, the true doctrine is the opposite of this. If the power is not in terms granted, and is not necessary and proper for the exercise of a power which is thus granted, it does not exist.[43]

Conclusion

President Grant appointed men to the Supreme Court whose views were predictable, where Lincoln failed. The narrow margins of the early legal tender decisions, however, would seem to reflect the importance of the matter at that time. The outcome, as expressed in the opinions, clearly rested on the matter of sovereignty, a matter seemingly settled by war. Beyond the matter of sovereignty, those who defended the authority of Congress to issue legal tender paper money interpreted the Constitution's monetary provisions and the proceedings of the convention in a manner that departs from a valid reading of history. Justice Field, in contrast, offers a more harmonious interpretation. The inference we should draw from the record, however, is that the Court ultimately saw no clear alternative but to declare that the Congress, as representative of the people, held a full complement of powers over the currency as an attribute of sovereignty in the absence of an express prohibition, and that the matter of legal tender was now settled as a precedent for the Court's decisions in the future.

Notes

1. David M. Silver, *Lincoln's Supreme Court* (Urbana, IL: University of Illinois Press, 1956), p. 145.
2. Ibid., p. 146.
3. *Sturges* v. *Crowninshield* (1819) 204 U.S. (4 Wheat.), 122.
4. Silver, *Lincoln's Supreme Court, p. 147.*
5. Ibid., pp. 207–8.
6. Robert Friedberg (with additions and revisions of Arthur L. and Ira S. Friedberg), *Paper Money of the United States* (Iola, WI: Krause Publications, 1978), p. 14. Chase's portrait also appeared on "legal tender," interest-bearing notes (ibid., pp. 34, 38, 43).
7. The decision could be considered as 5 to 3. Justice Robert C. Grier, who

concurred with the majority opinion, resigned on January 31, 1870, so he did not technically participate in the February 7, 1870, opinion (Gerald T. Dunne, *Monetary Decisions of the Supreme Court* [New Brunswick, NJ: Rutgers University Press, 1960], p. 72).

8. *Knox* v. *Lee* (1871), and *Parker* v. *Davis* (1871), *Legal Tender Cases*, 79 U.S. (12 Wall.), 457.

9. *Juilliard* v. *Greenman* (1884), 110 U.S., 421.

10. *Bronson* v. *Rodes* (1869), 74 U.S. (7 Wall.), 229; Dunne, *Monetary Decisions*, p. 71; and Henry G. Manne and Roger LeRoy Miller, eds., *Gold, Money and the Law* (Chicago: Aldine, 1975), p. 14n.

11. Manne and Miller, *Gold, Money and the Law*, pp. 2–3, 143–44.

12. *Hepburn* v. *Griswold* (1870), 75 U.S. (8 Wall.), 614.

13. Ibid., p. 616.

14. Ibid.

15. Ibid., p. 621.

16. Ibid., p. 623.

17. Ibid.

18. Ibid., p. 624.

19. Ibid., p. 625.

20. Ibid., p. 627.

21. *Knox* v. *Lee* and *Parker* v. *Davis* (1871), *Legal Tender Cases*, 79 U.S. (12 Wall.), 545.

22. Ibid., pp. 545–46.

23. Ibid., p. 547.

24. Ibid., p. 548.

25. Ibid., p. 549.

26. Ibid.

27. Ibid., p. 550.

28. Ibid., p. 553.

29. Ibid., p. 555.

30. Ibid.

31. Ibid., p. 556.

32. Ibid., p. 558.

33. Ibid., p. 559.

34. Ibid.

35. *Juilliard* v. *Greenman* (1884), *Legal Tender Cases*, 110 U.S., 440–42.

36. Ibid., p. 443.

37. Ibid.

38. Ibid.

39. Ibid., p. 450.

40. Ibid.

41. Ibid., p. 451.

42. Ibid., p. 465.

43. Ibid., pp. 467–68.

CHAPTER 9

National Currency System

The National Banking Act of 1863 created the national banking system with note issues based on government securities. In 1865, a prohibitive 10 percent tax was imposed on state bank notes and was upheld by the Supreme Court as an appropriate measure "to secure a sound and uniform currency." With the expansion of deposit banking, however, a dual banking system emerged. The banking system was to remain highly unstable and private money issues still appeared to shore up the financial system during financial crises.

The restoration of a monetary system grounded on gold was accomplished over the opposition of groups favoring more expansive policies. Between 1862 and 1879, the United States operated under a parallel fiduciary standard, issuing both greenbacks and gold, with the greenbacks trading at varying exchange rates with gold. Once the premium disappeared, the nation was effectively on the gold standard, and the price of gold was still set at the prewar price of $20.67 an ounce.

The Congress actively "regulated" the nation's currency, creating a variety of paper money issues and demonetizing silver. Bimetallism was formally terminated under the Coinage Act of 1873, "the Crime of '73." Opposition to the gold standard appeared in the form of the Greenback party and later the Populist party, the latter supporting "free silver."

The economy exhibited essentially the same performance characteristics that marked the state bank note era, as long-run price stability was maintained despite considerable short-run instability in money, prices, and business activity. The performance of the economy, reflecting the banking system, and the currency debate form the backdrop for the formation of the Federal Reserve System.

National Bank Notes

Congress, which had earlier incorporated one bank only after bitter debate, passed the National Banking Act of 1863 providing for the eventual incorporation of thousands of banks. The rationale for the legislation included the provision for uniformity of the currency and the capturing of seigniorage by the federal government, made secure in 1865 by a prohibitive tax on state bank notes; the immediate purpose, however, was of course to assist the government in financing the Civil War. The national banks, which were initially granted twenty-year charters, as the Bank of the United States, could issue notes up to 90 percent of the value of deposits with the Treasury of U.S. securities possessing the "circulation privilege."

These national bank note issues bore the name and charter number of the bank of issue, signatures of bank officials, and the seal of the state where the bank was located. The basic designs were the same, however, and they were identified as "national currency." The security legend read:

> This note is secured by bonds of the United States deposited with the U.S. Treasury in Washington.

The following statement was also printed on the notes:

> This note is receivable at par in all parts of the United States in payment of all taxes and excises and all other dues to the United States, except duties on imports, and also for all salaries and other debt and demands owing by the United States to individuals, corporations and associations within the United States, except interest on public debt.[1]

The notes were not granted full legal tender standing, and the banks' obligation stated, for example:

The Third National Bank of Pittsburgh, State of Pennsylvania, Will pay on Demand to Bearer ONE DOLLAR.

National bank notes were subject to a 1 percent tax per year when the yield on the underlying bonds exceeded 2 percent, otherwise the tax was 0.5 percent. The volume of national bank notes prior to 1900 was held down by a decline in the public debt and an accompanying decrease in bond yields, which reduced the profits to banks from their note issues. In 1900, the limit was raised to 100 percent of par value, and the public debt increased, while bond yields rose, thus generally spurring rapid growth in the issuance of the notes from then until 1913.[2] A currency shortage was associated with the panic of 1907, however, so that the security legend was amended by the Aldrich-Vreeland Act of 1908 to include "or other securities." This provision expired in 1915, but some notes were issued later with the legend.[3]

The hoarding of currency had periodically precipitated crises under the national banking system. The currency-issuing mechanism was clearly "inelastic." The strain on the system was exacerbated by the pyramiding set of reserve requirements. Cash reserves behind deposits were established at 15 percent for country banks (with a minimum of 40 percent in vault cash and the remainder held as deposits with city banks), 25 percent for reserve city banks (with a minimum of 50 percent in vault cash and the remainder in deposits with central reserve city banks), and 25 percent for central reserve city banks (with 100 percent held in vault cash).[4]

The banking system itself and the Treasury attempted to moderate the currency problem during banking crises, and the Aldrich-Vreeland Act of 1908 addressed the need for a more "elastic" supply of currency, as noted above. The act provided for currency expansion during emergencies and taxes on banks' currency issues to quicken a currency contraction after the crisis had passed—the Treasury, of course, had issued notes during banking crises prior to the Civil War. The emergency issuance of currency in 1914 set off by the outbreak of World War I probably averted a banking crisis.[5] In addition, Friedman and Schwartz have observed a "growing tendency on the part of the Treasury to intervene frequently and regularly in the money market. The central banking activities of the Treasury were being converted from emergency measures to a fairly regular and predictable operating function."[6] Thus, some progress toward stabilizing the financial system had been achieved prior to the advent of the Federal Reserve System, and these steps clearly influenced the thinking of those instrumental in forging that concept of a central bank.

The Tax on State Bank Notes

Secretary Chase favored the diversion of some seigniorage gain to the federal government in the Annual Treasury Report of 1861:

> The circulation of the banks of the United States, on the 1st day of January, 1861, was computed to be $202,000,767. Of this circulation, $150,000,000, in round numbers, was in States now loyal, including West Virginia, and $50,000,000 in the rebellious States. The whole of circulation constitutes a loan without interest from the people to the banks, costing them nothing except the expense of issue and the interest on the specie kept on hand for the latter purpose; and it deserves consideration whether sound policy does not require that the advantages of this loan be transferred, in part at least, from the banks, representing only the interests of the stockholders, to the government, representing the aggregate interests of the whole people.[7]

One would suppose, of course, that while indeed there was a gain generated by the issuance of the bank notes, competitive conditions would disperse the profit among the banking customers, depositors as well as borrowers, rather than stockholders. The extraction of some profit by a tax would shift that component to the federal government and the constituencies so represented.

Chase, a strong advocate of a national currency, later as Chief Justice offered the majority opinion in upholding the 10 percent tax on state bank notes in *Veazie Bank* v. *Fenno* (1869):

It cannot be doubted that under the Constitution the power to provide a circulation of coin is given to Congress. And it is settled by uniform practice of the government and by repeated decisions, that Congress may constitutionally authorize the emission of bills of credit. It is not important here, to decide whether the quality of legal tender, in payment of debts, can be constitutionally imparted to these bills; it is enough to say that there can be no question of the power of the government to emit them; to make them receivable in payment of debts to itself. . . . These powers, until recently, were only partially and occasionally exercised. Lately, however, they have been called into full activity, and Congress has undertaken to supply a currency for the entire country.

[This currency] now consists of coin, of United States notes, and of the notes of the National banks. Both descriptions of notes may be properly described as bills of credit, for both are furnished by the government. . . .

Having thus, in the exercise of undisputed constitutional powers, undertaken to provide a currency for the whole country, it cannot be questioned that Congress may, constitutionally, secure the benefit of it to the people by appropriate legislation. . . . Without this power, indeed, its attempts to secure a sound and uniform currency for the country would be futile.[8]

Chief Justice Chase ruled clearly that legislation securing the federal government's power to issue a national currency was appropriate, although he avoided the issue of legal tender, which did not apply in this case.

In a dissenting opinion, Justice Samuel Nelson alluded to the constitutional authority of the states to create banking institutions and to invest them with full banking powers. He argued that certain powers are reserved by the Tenth Amendment to the states, and the authority to create banks of issue was neither expressly nor by reasonable implication delegated to the federal government. The authority of the states was not questioned when the Bank of the United States was created, and Alexander Hamilton at that time made no reference to the constitutionality of state banks. Moreover, the legality and constitutionality of state banks were recognized in *McCulloch* v. *Maryland*. Indeed, when the Constitution was written, banks holding state charters existed, and:

> The framers of the Constitution were, therefore, familiar with these
> state banks, and the circulation of their paper as money; and were
> also familiar with the practice of the states, that was so common, to
> issue bills of credit, which were bills issued by the State, exclusively
> on its own credit, and intended to circulate as currency, redeemable
> at a future date. They guarded the people against the evils of this
> practice of the State governments. . . . As bills of credit were thus
> entirely abolished, the paper money of the State banks was the only
> currency or circulating medium to which this prohibition [of legal
> tender] could have had any application, and was the only currency,
> except gold and silver, left to the States. The prohibition took from
> this paper all coercive circulation, and left it to stand upon the credit
> of the banks.[9]

Thus, the power to incorporate banks was not surrendered to the
federal government but was reserved to the states, and so the
Constitution protects them from any encroachment upon this
right. A prohibitive tax, Nelson concluded, encroaches upon the
right of the states.[10]

The tax failed to achieve one intended objective—the elimination
of state-chartered institutions. The number of state banks did drop
sharply from 1,466 in 1863 to 325 in 1870, while, in contrast, national
banks grew in number from 66 to 1,612. Within twenty years,
however, the number of state banks exceeded the number of national
banks, 4,717 to 3,484, and their total assets were larger as well. The
tax on notes imparted accelerated growth to demand deposits—such
deposits were reportedly held by the Bank of North America as early
as 1786.[11] Arguments comparable to that advanced by Chase have
been applied to demand deposits (and other items with money
characteristics), but that position tends to fall victim to the ambiguity
in the concept of money.

Uniformity of the Currency

Uniformity of the currency generally applied to the authority
under which the currency was issued and, after the resumption of

specie payments, to the absence of the discounts closely associated with state bank notes, but there were a variety of currency issues associated with the Civil War and still others were introduced over the remainder of the century. The Congress continued to regulate the nation's coinage, largely as a reflection of the public debate on monetary policy.

The Civil War prompted issuance of the United States notes (the legal tender notes, or "greenbacks") and the national bank notes, as described above, but other series of paper money were inspired by the exigencies of the time.[12] Before the above issues, the government in 1861, following precedent, issued interest-bearing notes. The three-year issues were effectively debt instruments, perhaps doing some service as money. Interest was paid on a semiannual basis at a 7.30 percent rate, the so-called "7-30s." Five coupons were attached for that purpose, with the final interest payment scheduled at maturity. The notes were payable to order, rather than bearer, with a provision for the name of the purchaser and for a signature at maturity. Interest was paid in "lawful money," and the notes were convertible into U.S. bonds. Interest-bearing notes of one-year and two-year maturities were introduced in 1863, paying a lower interest rate and carrying the same legal tender inscription printed on the greenbacks.

The demand notes of 1861 were the original "greenbacks," and were known publicly as such, but they were not assigned legal tender standing for private debts. Prior to the suspension of specie payments on December 21, 1861, these notes were payable in gold, based on a circular issued by the secretary of the Treasury. The inscription read, for example:

> The United States promises to pay to the bearer Five Dollars on demand. . . . Payable by the Assistant Treasurer of the United States at Philadelphia. Receivable in payment of all public dues.

In 1863 the Treasury also introduced the compound interest Treasury notes, which bear in gold letters the surcharge, "Compound Interest Treasury Note." The notes were declared a "legal tender." Interest was paid at maturity in three years at a rate of 6 percent, as a means to sustain the value and circulation of the notes. Extensive counterfeiting, however, brought an early end to this series of notes.

Congress provided for the first issue of gold certificates in 1863, with the early emissions used primarily for the settlement of accounts among banks. Early issues bear the inscription, for example:

> It is hereby certified that Twenty Dollars have been deposited with the Assistant Treasurer of the U.S. in New York payable in Gold at his office to the bearer.

Some issues were payable to the order of ———— (for signature). These "yellowbacks," however, did not generate interest in the formation of a yellowback party to counteract the Greenback party.

The suspension of specie payments and the hoarding of coins during the Civil War brought a remedy in the form of fractional currency, first authorized in 1862. Issues of fractional currency were authorized as late as the 1870s, when provision was made for their redemption. Denominations from three cents to fifty cents were issued.

Following the Civil War, and prior to the formation of the Federal Reserve System, which has issued Federal Reserve Bank notes and the familiar Federal Reserve notes, Congress authorized additional forms of paper money. In 1870, Congress approved the issuance of national gold bank notes by nine California banks and the Kidder National Gold Bank of Boston (the Massachusetts bank never issued these notes; others circulated actively). The obligation to redeem these notes in gold coin rested with the bank of issue, not with the government.

Silver certificates were first authorized by the Congress in 1878. In 1879 interest-bearing refunding certificates were approved by the Congress. These notes paid 4 percent interest and were convertible into 4 percent U.S. bonds. The $10 denomination thus represented a savings vehicle, paying interest in perpetuity, but was rescinded in 1907, with the value fixed at $21.30. The Treasury or coin notes were introduced in 1890. The notes could be redeemed for gold or silver coin at the discretion of the secretary of the Treasury. The notes were a legal tender.

U.S. Coinage

Gold coins were struck each year during the greenback era, as were silver and copper coins. Larger quantities, of course, were struck after the resumption of specie payments. Coinage of one-dollar and three-dollar gold pieces was terminated in 1889. (The last quarter- and half-eagles were struck in 1929, and coinage of the eagle and double eagle was discontinued in 1933; bullion coins, of course, have been issued in recent years.)

A variety of minor coins were introduced during and shortly after the Civil War. The two-cent piece was issued from 1864 to 1873. The motto "In God We Trust" first appeared on this coin, reflecting the urging of Secretary Chase. Responding to the nickel interests, the three-cent nickel was first struck in 1865. Coinage of both the nickel and silver three-cent pieces continued until 1873, when the silver piece was last struck—the nickel coin was struck until 1889. The five-cent nickel appeared in 1866 and was issued along with the half-dime until coinage of the latter was discontinued in 1873. The twenty-cent piece was issued for a few years in the mid-1870s in order to facilitate equitable exchange in the West, where the Spanish "bit" circulated, but confusion with the quarter soon ended its coinage. The array of coins also included the copper one-cent piece and silver dimes, quarters, and half-dollars.

The silver dollar did not circulate widely, and coinage was suspended again in 1873, as noted above. The larger, trade dollar was authorized for transactions in the Orient, as a substitute for the peso, which commanded a substantial premium, but it was inadvertently given legal tender status domestically. This provision was soon rescinded. The official demonetization of silver, of course, was the focus of debate for the remainder of the century. To appease silver interests and other advocates of "free silver," production of the silver dollar was resumed in 1878, but not on a "free coinage" basis. (Coinage of the silver dollar was suspended again in 1904, resumed in 1921, discontinued in 1928, and struck again in 1934–35; the Eisenhower dollar was issued from 1971 to 1978, some as silver-clad coins, but most in copper-nickel, the same as the smaller Susan B. Anthony dollar, struck in 1979–81, and coinage of the large silver bullion "dollar" commenced in 1986.) The political strength of silver interests and greenback enthusiasts was clearly expressed in the nation's coinage and paper money during the latter decades of the nineteenth century, even though they ultimately failed at the time to institutionalize the more expansive monetary policies that they advocated.

Emergency Monies

The financial setting created by the Civil War spawned the issuance of private, emergency monies. In anticipation of a paper money inflation, all coins were hoarded, thus depriving the nation of small-denomination currency. Ordinary postage stamps were initially used as a substitute. In 1862 John Gault patented a brass encasement for stamps with a transparent mica window to make the stamps visible. The solid brass back was used by merchants as an advertising medium. The public-private currency circulated widely in denominations ranging from one cent to ninety cents. Since the cost of stamps equaled their exchange value, encased postage stamps were not competitive with other tokens.[13] The government (and private entrepreneurs) subsequently issued fractional paper money in three-cent to fifty-cent denominations,[14] and private tokens, generally of the size and weight of the U.S. cent, gained acceptance as a circulating medium.

The issuance of Civil War tokens "far exceeded 25,000,000 pieces," according to George and Melvin Fuld,[15] who go on to explain:

> They were commonly accepted as a medium of exchange for the value, which was usually one cent. It should be mentioned that mer-

chants could make a tidy profit using these coins, as the copper value in them was only 23/100ths of a cent.[16]

Civil War tokens consisted of two types. The patriot series, of which over 1,500 varieties are known, bore no merchants' advertisements. Tradesmen's tokens were issued in twenty-three states, and there are 8,500 known varieties.[17]

Tokens were also associated with the operations of post sutlers, post traders, and trading posts. Sutlers, appointed by the secretary of war, issued small-denomination tokens and scrip. Their appointments were discontinued in 1866 and were replaced by post trader appointments.[18] Post traders' tokens were issued from 1866 to 1893.[19] Tokens were then issued by traders and trading posts until about 1930.[20]

In 1862 the "Act to Authorize Payments in Stamps" referred specifically to tokens:

> That from and after the first day of August, eighteen hundred and sixty-two, no private corporation, banking association, firm, or individual shall make, issue, circulate or pay any note, check, memorandum, token, or other obligation, for less sum than one dollar, intended to circulate as money or to be received or used in lieu of lawful money of the United States; and every person so offending shall, on conviction thereof in any district or circuit court of the United States, be punished by fine not exceeding five hundred dollars, or by imprisonment not exceeding six months, or by both, at the option of the court.[21]

Large quantities of tokens, nonetheless, were issued in 1863. G. Hetrich suggests that the law authorizing the two-cent piece in 1864 actually "practically stopped" the issuance of these tokens.[22] That law stated:

> That if any person or persons shall make use of, pass, or cause to be made, issued or passed, any coin, card or token, or device whatsoever, in metal or its compounds, intended to pass or be passed for a one-cent piece or a two-cent piece, such person or persons shall be deemed guilty of a misdemeanor and shall, upon conviction thereof, be punished by a fine not exceeding one thousand dollars and by imprisonment for a term not exceeding five years.[23]

This law was apparently a response to such incidents as that involving a Mr. Lindenmueller, a New York City saloon keeper, who had issued by the spring of 1863 a million pieces of Lindenmueller currency. The Third Avenue Railroad of New York had accumulated a substantial number of his tokens and presented them for redemption, but Lindenmueller "laughingly refused" to redeem them.[24] The federal government was apparently reluctant to enforce such laws, especially under emergency conditions, when such tokens were undoubtedly a useful convenience to exchange. Tokens have been issued since 1864, with a number appearing during the Great Depression—"sales tax" tokens were initially issued by chambers of commerce and merchants associations, and later by states in denominations ranging from one mill to fifteen dollars.[25]

The Populist campaign for free silver in 1896 inspired issues of "Bryan Money," another manifestation of a spirited debate on monetary matters. These tokens were an expression of opposition to the free coinage of silver at a ratio of 16 to 1. Enlarged tokens conveyed the message of bulkiness in the prescribed standard. Others were more directly critical of William Jennings Bryan's monetary proposals.[26] One token depicts a donkey-headed goose with "POP" inscribed on a wing, and the legend, "In Bryan We Trust," all surrounded by "United Snakes of America." The reverse shows "Free Silver, 1896, One Dam." A few metals' firms also issued tokens. Tokens with devices similar to U.S. coins and the equipment for producing them were apparently seized, when found, by government officials.[27]

In the 1862 "Act to Authorize Payment in Stamps," cited above, the issuance of shinplasters was made illegal for banks as well as for individuals and nonbank associations; shortly thereafter the U.S. government commenced issuing shinplasters. The 10 percent tax on state bank notes also applied to scrip. Nonetheless, sizable quantities were issued periodically into the 1930s. V. L. Brown notes that "The scrip issued during this period [1931–34] was no doubt contrary to Government legislation and might have been subject to Federal taxation, but apparently, due to the emergency, nothing was done about it."[28]

Private scrip was associated with financial panics from the Civil War through the Great Depression. Emergency substitutes for official money were issued from the Civil War until the resumption of specie payments in 1879. The financial crises of 1884, 1890, and 1893 were accompanied by the issuance of scrip. These issues were placed into circulation by company stores and were paid to employees in lieu of cash. The crisis of 1893 prompted banks to restrict the conversion of deposits into currency, and for a short time currency sold at a premium to certified checks. The restriction of cash payments caused an enlarged demand for currency, which appeared as a shortage.[29] Clearinghouse certificates were placed into circulation, along with bank cashiers' checks, and in factory towns, pay checks, according to Farran Zerbe, "all did service as money and were the main factors in overcoming the currency stringency."[30] Elgin Groseclose reported that clearinghouse certificates and checks were issued for circulation in scores of communities, and railway companies and manufacturers issued them when arrangements could not be made with the banks.[31] J. DeWitt Warner estimated such currency issues at roughly $80 million (or 2 percent of the money supply).[32]

The Presiding Bishop of the Mormon Church in 1888 commenced issuing scrip to alleviate a currency shortage. Tithes were paid in kind at the Bishop's Storehouse, and scrip was used to pay half the wages of persons working on the Great Temple in Salt Lake City. Other payments were also made in scrip in denominations ranging from five cents to ten dollars. By 1908, when cash was more abundant, the issuance of scrip was terminated and slowly retired.[33]

Commercial banks in the 1850s commenced organizing clearinghouses, which during the national currency era issued clearinghouse certificates to alleviate liquidity pressures during financial panics, in addition to the restriction of deposit convertibility into currency. Clearinghouse certificates, as obligations of the clearinghouses themselves, were issued during the panic of 1873.[34] They were used more extensively during the panic of 1893.[35] The panic of 1907 was accompanied by the issuance of roughly $500 million of scrip (or 4.5 percent of the money supply). A. Piatt Andrew estimated that this total consisted of large clearinghouse certificates ($238 million), small clearinghouse certificates ($23 million), clearinghouse checks ($12 million), cashiers' checks ($14 million), manufacturers' pay checks ($47 million), and the remainder was composed of cashiers' checks and pay checks in cities where amounts were not reported.[36] A substantial portion of clearinghouse certificates (perhaps all of those reported as "large") was probably clearinghouse loan certificates, which were used instead of currency to settle balances among banks. In contrast, clearinghouse certificates were issued to the public for general circulation. The comptroller of the currency placed the amount of clearinghouse loan certificates at $256 million and other substitutes for cash at $250 million.[37] Again, the restriction of cash payments created a premium on currency over deposits, which reached as high as 4 percent.[38]

Clearinghouse certificates were issued in denominations ranging from twenty-five cents to one thousand dollars in over two hundred cities or localities in forty-one states.[39] In towns where there was no clearinghouse, Andrew explained, "they were issued under the auspices of temporary committees of the local banks, which accepted and held the collateral offered to guarantee their redemption."[40] Groseclose adds:

> In two-thirds of the cities of more than 25,000 population the banks suspended cash payments to one degree or another, and in at least half the larger cities resort was made to clearing-house checks, cashiers' checks only through the clearing-house, or other substitutes for legal money.[41]

Pay checks circulated as money in the form of checks drawn upon a bank by a customer and payable to bearer.[42]

Banking panics during the national currency era tended to magnify economic contractions rather than actually to cause them, and in this era, in the absence of formal central banking, the private market mechanism, as manifest in clearinghouse operations, was able to insulate the banking system from a more severe contraction.[43]

The Resumption of Specie Payments

The United States had effectively been on the gold standard prior to the Civil War, and a consensus favored restoration of gold to the prewar parity after the cessation of hostilities. Indeed, Secretary of the Treasury Hugh McCullough stated:

> The present legal tender acts were war measures, and, . . . ought not to remain in force one day longer than shall be necessary to enable the people to prepare for a return to the constitutional currency.[44]

The consensus disintegrated as business activity contracted and prices fell. Congress balked and the court decisions added to the disarray. Following another slump in business activity and a banking panic, the Congress under Republican leadership passed a bill in 1874 to expand the greenbacks, but this "Inflation Bill" was vetoed by President Grant on the ground that it was inconsistent with his pledge, and that of both political parties, to prepare for the redemption of notes in coin at the "earliest practicable period."[45] Many Republican candidates were defeated in the congressional elections of 1874 and the party lost control of the House. The "lame duck" Congress then passed the Resumption Act of January 14, 1875, declaring the intention to resume specie payments at the prewar parity on January 1, 1879.[46]

Passage of the Resumption Act stirred up considerable political opposition, represented formally by the organization of the Greenback party. Besides repeal of the Resumption Act, the party's platform called for monetary expansion and debt relief. While the party enjoyed little outright success, although it did win a few seats in the Congress, the issues addressed by the party generated broad support. In 1877 a bill to repeal the Resumption Act passed the House but was defeated in the Senate by a single-vote margin. The commitment to resume specie payments was effectively affirmed, although doubts remained whether that commitment would be honored.

Over the years prior to the resumption of specie payments, monetary growth was limited. Economic activity expanded substantially so that it was accompanied by a decline in the price level. The government accumulated specie reserves, buoying confidence that specie payments might indeed be restored. The greenbacks, which in 1864 had reached a price of $2.50 for a dollar's worth of gold at the old parity, gradually moved into alignment with gold, so that gold payments were resumed on schedule.[47]

Bimetallism

The controversy surrounding bimetallism emerged shortly after silver was demonetized by the Coinage Act of 1873,[48] and ran parallel to the greenback debate. By 1875, as the price of silver descended, it had become profitable to present silver bullion at the mint for coinage, but that was blocked by the 1873 act. Silver producers rallied around coinage at a ratio of 16 to 1. Farmers, debtors, and others favoring liberal monetary expansion joined the movement for "free coinage" or "free silver."

The silver crusade was led in the Congress by Representative Richard D. "Silver Dick" Bland (Missouri). The Bland-Allison Act of 1878 passed the Congress over the veto of President Rutherford B. Hayes, who objected to granting legal tender standing to silver at a value below its market value, thus impairing the obligation of contracts.[49] The act reflected a compromise, providing for a substantial volume of silver dollars (produced from purchases of $2 million to $4 million of bullion per month) but not "free silver." The silver dollars so coined failed to gain wide circulation, returning to the Treasury, where they were used as backing for the issuance of silver certificates. In recognition of this situation, President Grover Cleveland in 1885 favored repealing the Bland-Allison Act. He cited the inflationary implications of silver displacing gold, in the absence of an international agreement on silver coinage, and called for a suspension of silver coinage.[50] The same implications of the act persuaded President Benjamin Harrison in 1889 to recommend that bullion purchases be used to back the issuance of paper money, ceasing the silver dollar coinage.[51]

The Bland-Allison Act was repealed in 1890 and replaced by the Sherman Silver Purchase Act. This act provided for a larger volume of silver purchases (4.5 million ounces per month) using Treasury or coin notes, redeemable in gold or silver, thus providing a subsidy to silver producers. The coinage of silver dollars under the act was set at $2 million each month until 1 July, 1891, and thereafter as conditions required. The legislative response was still insufficient to placate those who favored a highly expansive monetary policy, even though some 570 million silver dollars were struck under the above acts. In 1893, President Cleveland recommended that the Sherman Act be repealed so that the government could "fulfill its pecuniary obligations in money universally recognized by all civilized countries."[52] The act was soon repealed, but on the condition that gold and silver would still be recognized as "standard money," and that efforts would be steadily directed toward the establishment of a "safe system of bimetallism."[53]

Several groups advocating the free coinage of silver formed the Populist party in 1892. The repeal in 1893 of the silver purchase clause in the Sherman Act further antagonized the Populists, and labor groups joined the controversy, seeking $500 million in legal tender notes. In 1894, a bill was introduced in the Congress requiring the coinage of seigniorage silver that was held in the Treasury, i.e., the uncoined silver representing the difference between its official monetary value ($1.29 an ounce) and the price paid for silver under the Sherman Act. The bill passed Congress, but was vetoed by President Cleveland. The broad base of the Populist party was obviously recognized by the major parties and a number of organizations were formed to further the cause of "free silver" or to study the establishment of bimetallism.

The party platforms shortly after the Civil War abhorred debt repudiation by the government and supported the resumption of specie payments. The parties' positions later incorporated references to bimetallism. The Democrats in 1884 favored the "gold and silver coinage of the Constitution," and the Republicans urged support of an international standard fixing the relative values of gold and silver. In 1892, besides favoring bimetallism, although less emphatically than the Populists, the Democratic party also recommended repeal of the 10 percent tax on state bank issues. A distinct polarization of the parties' positions developed in 1896. The Republican party opposed free silver, supporting an international conference to set a gold-silver parity, and supported the "sound money" provided by the gold standard. The Democrats adopted a free silver plank, noting that monometallism is a British policy, exacting servitude to London, and that the Constitution, though naming gold and silver together as money metals, made the silver dollar the monetary unit.[54] (Both parties in 1932 called for an international conference to consider the monetary role of silver.[55])

William Jennings Bryan gave the "Cross of Gold" speech at the Democratic national convention in 1896, to win the party's nomination over Bland by effectively articulating the dominant Populist attitudes and ideas. Bryan also ran as the candidate of the National Silver party and the Populist party; conservative Democrats nominated John M. Palmer. In his speech Bryan charged that the opposition grounded its policies on the concept that the prosperity of the well-to-do would (in an early version of the "trickle-down" theory) "leak through" to those below, and claimed that bimetallism would restore the money of the Constitution.[56] Bryan concluded:

> Having behind us the producing masses of this nation and the world, supported by the commercial interests, the laboring interests, and the toilers everywhere, we will answer their demand for a gold standard by saying to them: You shall not press down upon the brow of labor this crown of thorns, you shall not crucify mankind upon a cross of gold.[57]

Bryan, of course, lost the election of 1896 to William McKinley, who ran on a platform favoring gold until an international agreement could be negotiated for gold and silver coinage at a fixed ratio. McKinley's victory, the absence of success in adopting bimetallism on an international scale, and an increase in gold output paved the way for the Gold Standard Act of March 14, 1900.[58] The second defeat of Bryan in the presidential election of 1900 doomed bimetallism, but later, as President Woodrow Wilson's secretary of state, Bryan played an influential role on behalf of the administration in securing passage of the Federal Reserve Act of 1913.

Money, Prices, and Economic Activity

Major structural changes in the money supply mechanism had no enduring impact on the price level.[59] The inflation associated with the Civil War was offset by deflation, and the wholesale price index in 1889, a century after ratification of the Constitution, was essentially the same as its standings in 1861 and in 1789. Over the subsequent quarter-century, 1889–1914, the price level drifted upward at a moderate 0.8 percent annual rate. The national bank note era, we might say, may be compared with the state bank note era reviewed in chapter 7.

The period 1889–1914 corresponds very closely with the period 1840–61, despite the difference in the issuance of currency, apparently because of the underlying governance of gold and the "convertibility principle." The monetary base, consisting of national bank notes, as indirect obligations of the U.S. Treasury, and Treasury currency (including gold), i.e., currency held by the nonbank public and vault cash, expanded at a rate of 4.0 percent, the same as in the earlier period, and its annual variability was only marginally higher (4.2 percentage points, compared with 3.2 percentage points). The money supply expanded noticeably faster than it had earlier, however (6.3 percent, compared with 4.7 percent), as the expansion in deposit banking lifted the ratio of bank deposits to currency,[60] but its fluctuations were less extreme (5.7

percentage points compared with 9.0 percentage points). Under the national currency system, financial panics were apparently as prevalent as experienced under the preceding regime.[61] When compared with the 1960–85 period, however, both earlier periods exhibit slower monetary growth and greater variability in the monetary aggregates.

The national currency era, as indicated, was marked by a rising price level but less variability in the index than experienced earlier. The era of managed money (1960–85), of course, was characterized by a decidedly steeper rate of inflation, with only slightly greater variability than was experienced in the 1889–1914 period. The growth rate in constant-dollar GNP during the national bank note era fell somewhat below the rate achieved earlier, at 3.6 percent, but its fluctuations were nearly identical (6.0 percentage points compared with 6.2 percentage points). Lower growth and lower variability prevailed in the 1960–85 period.

The national currency era, then, looks more like the state bank note era than the recent period. Essential long-run price stability was accompanied by considerable short-run instability in money, prices, and economic activity.

Conclusion

The Congress created thousands of banks under national charters and an accompanying national currency. Once secure, the power to issue bills of credit was expressed in the issuance of several forms of paper money, along with continued regulation of the system of coinage, including the formal termination of bimetallism.

The monetary system's linkage to gold was restored in 1879, and that grounding produced long-run price stability along with a short-run instability in money, prices, and economic activity commensurate with that experienced under the preceding, state bank note era. Private money substitutes were issued during the Civil War and during the financial crises that punctuated the national currency era. The Treasury also responded to such crises, and later assumed certain central banking functions.

Notes

1. Robert Friedberg (with additions and revisions of Arthur L. and Ira S. Friedberg), *Paper Money of the United States* (Iola, WI: Krause Publications, 1978), p. 76.
2. Eugene S. Klise, *Money and Banking*, 5th ed. (Cincinnati, OH: South-Western Publishing, 1972), pp. 185–86; Benjamin Haggott Beckhart, *Federal Reserve System* (New York: American Institute of Banking, 1972), p. 21.
3. Friedberg, *Paper Money of the United States*, p. 75.
4. Harold Barger, *Money, Banking and Public Policy*, 2d ed. (Chicago: Rand McNally, 1968), pp. 148–49.
5. Milton Friedman and Anna Jacobson Schwartz, *A Monetary History of the United States, 1867–1960* (Princeton, NJ: Princeton University Press, 1963), pp. 162–72.
6. Ibid., p. 149.
7. "Annual Treasury Report, 1861," in *Documentary History of Banking and Currency in the United States*, vol. 2, ed. Herman E. Krooss (New York: McGraw-Hill, 1969), p. 1341.
8. *Veazie Bank* v. *Fenno* (1969), 75 U.S. (8 Wall.), 548–49.
9. Ibid., pp. 551–52.
10. Ibid., pp. 554–55.
11. Beckhart, *Federal Reserve System*, p. 20; Bray Hammond, *Banks and Politics in America: From the Revolution to the Civil War* (Princeton, NJ: Princeton University Press, 1957), p. 81.
12. On paper money, see Friedberg, *Paper Money of the United States*; and Chester L. Krause and Robert F. Lemke, *Standard Catalog of U.S. Paper Money*, 6th ed. (Iola, WI: Krause Publications, 1987).
13. George and Melvin Fuld, *Patriotic Civil War Tokens* (Racine, WI: Whitman Publishing, 1960), p. 3; Friedberg, *Paper Money of the United States*, pp. 203–5.
14. Matt Rothert, *A Guide Book to United States Fractional Currency* (Racine, WI: Whitman Publishing, 1963).
15. Fuld, *Patriotic Civil War Tokens*, p. 4.
16. Ibid.
17. Ibid.; George and Melvin Fuld, *A Guide Book to Civil War Store Card Tokens* (Racine, WI: Whitman Publishing, 1962).
18. James J. Curto, *Sutler Issues of the Civil War* (reprint from *The Numismatist*, 1959), p. 3.
19. James J. Curto, *Indian and Post Trader Tokens* (reprint from *The Numismatist*, 1962), p. 13.

20. J. J. Curto, *Our Frontier Coinage* (reprint from *The Numismatist*, 1956–57), p. 2.

21. "Act to Authorize Payments in Stamps, July 17, 1862," in Krooss, *Documentary History*, vol. 2, p. 1441.

22. G. Hetrich, "Civil War Tokens and Tradesmen's Currency," in American Numismatic Association, *Selections from the Numismatist* (Racine, WI: Whitman Publishing, 1960), p. 98.

23. Ibid.

24. Ibid., p. 101; George and Melvin Fuld, *Patriotic Civil War Tokens*, p. 4.

25. E. DiBello, "Sales Tax Tokens and Ohio Coupons," in *Selections from the Numismatist*, pp. 121–22.

26. Farran Zerbe, "Bryan Money: Tokens of the Presidential Campaigns of 1896 and 1900—Comparative and Satirical," *The Numismatist* 39, 7 (July 1926): 313–84.

27. Ibid., pp. 314, 331.

28. Brown, "Emergency Currency," in *Selections from the Numismatist*, p. 191.

29. Friedman and Schwartz, *Monetary History*, p. 110.

30. Farran Zerbe, "Emergency Currency, 1873–1914," in *Selections from the Numismatist*, p. 190.

31. Elgin Groseclose, *Money and Man: A Survey of Monetary Experience* (Norman, OK: University of Oklahoma Press, 1976), p. 212.

32. Friedman and Schwartz, *Monetary History*, p. 110; Gary Gorton, "Private Clearinghouses and the Origins of Central Banking," *Business Review*, Federal Reserve Bank of Philadelphia (January–February 1984), p. 8. Gorton shows $100 million.

33. Harvey L. Hansen, "Bishop's Money of Utah," in *Selections from the Numismatist*, p. 163.

34. Charles P. Kindleberger, *Manias, Panics, and Crashes: A History of Financial Crises* (New York: Basic Books, 1978), pp. 148–49.

35. Ellis Tallman, "Some Unanswered Questions about Bank Panics," *Economic Review*, Federal Reserve Bank of Atlanta (November/December 1988), pp. 18–19. Tallman notes that clearinghouse loan certificates and the restriction of payments were illegal, but faced little opposition by banks, courts, and depositors.

36. A. Barton Hepburn, *History of Currency in the United States*, revised ed. (New York: Macmillan, 1924), p. 393; Gorton, "Private Clearinghouses," p. 8.

37. Friedman and Schwartz, *Monetary History*, pp. 162–63.

38. Ibid., p. 161.

39. Zerbe, "Emergency Currency," p. 190.

40. Hepburn, *History of Currency*, p. 392.

41. Groseclose, *Money and Man*, p. 212.

42. Hepburn, *History of Currency*, p. 393.

43. Tallman, "Some Unanswered Questions about Bank Panics," pp. 6, 8, 17–18.

44. Friedman and Schwartz, *Monetary History*, p. 44. Quoted from "Annual Treasury Reports on Greenbacks and the Resumption of Specie Payments, 1865; 1867," in Krooss, *Documentary History*, vol. 2 (1983 edition), p. 380.

45. "Message of President Ulysses Grant Vetoing the Bill Providing for Additional Issuance of United States Notes, April 22, 1874," in *Documentary History of Banking and Currency in the United States*, vol. 3, ed. Herman E. Krooss (New York: Chelsea House, 1969), pp. 1673–76.

46. "The Resumption Act, January 14, 1875," in ibid., pp. 1683–84.

47. Friedman and Schwartz, *Monetary History*, pp. 44–50, 81–88.

48. "The Coinage Act of 1873 [The So-Called Crime of '73], February 12, 1873," in Krooss, *Documentary History*, vol. 3, pp. 1754–71.

49. "Message by President Rutherford B. Hayes Vetoing the Bland-Allison Act, February 28, 1878," in ibid., pp. 1920–22.

50. "President Grover Cleveland Calling for Repeal of the Bland-Allison Act, State of the Union Message, December 8, 1885," in ibid., pp. 1923–28.

51. "President Benjamin Harrison on the Silver Problem, State of the Union Message, December 3, 1889," in ibid., pp. 1930–31.

52. "Message by President Grover Cleveland Calling for Repeal of the Sherman Silver Purchase Act, August 8, 1893," in ibid., p. 1959.

53. "Repeal of the Sherman Act, November 1, 1893," in ibid., p. 1960.

54. "Banking and Currency Planks in Party Platforms, 1868–1896," in ibid., pp. 2055–61.

55. "Banking and Currency Planks in Party Platforms, 1932," in ibid., vol. 4, pp. 2692–93.

56. Harry R. Warfel, Ralph H. Gabriel, and Stanley T. Williams, eds., *The American Mind*, vol. 2 (New York: American Book Company, 1959), p. 948.

57. Ibid., pp. 948–49.

58. Friedman and Schwartz, *Monetary History*, pp. 113–19.

59. See note 68 in chapter 7 for references and data sources.

60. Friedman and Schwartz, *Monetary History*, pp. 799–808.

61. Tallman, "Some Unanswered Questions about Bank Panics," pp. 4–5. Six major banking panics occurred during the national currency era: 1873, 1884, 1890, 1893, 1907, and 1914. Severe panics were identified by Tallman in 1873, 1893, and 1907.

CHAPTER 10

Creation and Control of the Federal Reserve System

The Federal Reserve System was created according to this country's concept of a central bank, being "independent" of close supervision and control by the central government. The purpose of its creation was to check the destabilizing tendencies of the banking system. Failure to prevent massive bank failures, leading to the Great Depression, prompted steps to move the United States off the gold standard, tying our fortunes to the Federal Reserve's capacity to manage the nation's money supply grounded on "bills of credit."

Does the Federal Reserve Coin Money?

The Federal Reserve presides over a monopoly of the money supply issued by the government and private organizations. The legal status of the Federal Reserve has been questioned at times on the ground that the Federal Reserve banks are owned by the member banks. This ownership, although not a trivial matter, is nominal, however, but it reflects, along with the fourteen-year terms of the governors, the intention of the Congress to maintain a certain degree of "independence" of the central bank from political pressures. Questions also arise about its legitimacy—that is, about the constitutional basis for its powers, rather than just about its structure. Former Federal Reserve Board governor Sherman J. Maisel stated:

> Congress delegated its constitutional power to coin money and control its value to the Federal Reserve through the Federal Reserve Act of 1913, thus giving the Fed considerable freedom to manage the dollar.[1]

The Federal Reserve System, of course, does not encompass the United States Mint, nor does it regulate coins in any historical sense; that authority remains vested in the Congress. The Federal Reserve does issue paper currency; create bank reserves through open market purchases of securities and loans to financial institutions at the discount window; provide services to banks, foreign official institutions, and the U.S. Treasury; supervise banks; and administer certain government regulations. These functions are aligned reasonably closely with those proposed by Alexander Hamilton for the Bank of the United States, and upheld by Marshall in *McCulloch* v. *Maryland.* While several decades separate the Bank of the United States and the Federal Reserve System, many of the issues arising in the debate concluding with the establishment of the Federal Reserve extend back in time to the establishment of the Bank of the United States, with emphasis here on ownership and control, i.e., on the "independence" of the monetary authority.

National Monetary Commission

The panic of 1907 revealed once again the susceptibility of the banking system to periodic crises, disrupting financial affairs and destabilizing the economy. In response, the Congress passed the Aldrich-Vreeland Act of May 30, 1908, which provided certain palliative measures and the appointment of a National Monetary Commission. Senator Nelson W. Aldrich (Rhode Island) served as the commission's chairman, and the vice chairman was Representative Edward B. Vreeland (New York). The work of the commission produced extensive studies of U.S. and international banking practices, consuming much more time than had been needed for the creation of the Bank of the United States. The report of the commission in 1912, during the administration of Republican President William Howard Taft, recommended the establishment of a National Reserve Association, which laid the groundwork for the formation of the Federal Reserve System during the administration of Democratic President Woodrow Wilson.[2]

The Aldrich commission stated that the purpose of the suggested legislation was to provide "the means for a proper expansion of credit and the necessary enlargement of note issues in times of trouble" to be followed by a "healthy and legitimate contraction."[3] Among other things, the proposed National Reserve Association was to hold Treasury balances, mobilize reserves (by serving as a central depository of cash reserves for the banking system), issue circulating notes, reduce the unequal geographical distribution of credit, and control movements of gold and foreign exchange.

The Monetary Commission contemplated a distribution of power in the central bank comparable to our governmental structure. It was claimed that the association differed radically from the structure of the Bank of the United States and of the European central banks, since it was democratic in organization and not competitive with the commercial banks, but would represent them in an evolutionary step beyond the clearinghouse mechanism in the centralization of reserves and note-issuing authority based on gold reserves.[4] The National Reserve Association would consist of fifteen districts, each of which would have a branch. The directors of each branch would elect thirty-nine of the forty-six directors of the association (with fifteen representing nonbanking interests). The remaining seven directors would consist of the governor, two deputy governors, the secretary of the Treasury, the secretary of agriculture, the secretary of commerce and labor, and the comptroller of the currency. The governor would be appointed by the U.S. President to a ten-year term from among four nominees of the Board of Directors. The two deputy governors would be elected by the board for seven-year terms. Business would be conducted by an executive committee consisting of the governor, the two deputy governors, the comptroller of the currency, and five other members of the board.[5]

The commission responded to the complaint that the selection of the governor by the President and the *ex officio* members of the association's board might lead to "an attempt to control the organization for political purposes."[6] After alluding to the need to recognize the public interest in the management of the association, since the principal reason for its existence is found in its ability to sustain the public credit, and to its function as the principal fiscal agent of the government, the commission noted, on the other hand:

> As constituted under present proposals, however, neither the President nor any of the officials named could, from the inherent character of the organization, use any of its functions for personal or political purposes, but to give to the President the power to appoint all the directors of the reserve association, as has been suggested, would result in making the association a political machine, and appointments would be solicited and bestowed as a reward for political service.[7]

The commission also strived to prevent the possibility of its "control by any corporation or combination of corporations, banks or otherwise, by any individual or combination of individuals for selfish or sinister purposes."[8] While aware of the dominant position of New York in the financial markets, control of the organization would be dispersed nationally. The New York district, with 29 percent of the nation's banking resources, would have just 8 percent of the representation on the board.

The commission proposed giving the association the privilege of note issue, as the principal fiscal agent of the government, with all profits accruing to the U.S. Treasury, but with restrictions and limitations to make "undue inflation impossible." And, the commission added, "While it may be contended that the issue of money of any kind is a distinctive function of sovereign power, the exercise of this authority directly by Governments has, as shown by the experience of the world, inevitably led to disastrous results."[9] A 50 percent minimum in gold and other money of the United States would stand behind the association's liabilities (deposits and notes), and the outstanding note issue was capped at a $33\frac{1}{3}$ percent minimum reserve enforced by a tax. While the capacity to expand credit was essential to check financial panics, a dangerous inflation of the currency was limited by a progressive tax on reserve deficiencies.[10]

The commission envisioned a central bank largely controlled by the commercial banks, but with a muted voice for Wall Street. The role of the federal government was carefully circumscribed in order to restrict political influence and to block implanting the authority to print money directly under the government.

The Owen-Glass Bill

Opposition to the Monetary Commission's plan focused on the concentration of power in the banks at a time when public sentiment was aroused against the "money trust." The plan's association with Senator Aldrich, an old-guard Republican, doomed the legislation as the political tides shifted.

In early 1910 Senator Aldrich announced his intention to retire from active public life at the expiration of his term in 1913. The Aldrich Bill was introduced in the Senate on January 9, 1912, and in the House, won by the Democrats in the election of 1910, it was referred to the Banking and Currency Committee. The bill was never brought to a vote.

The Republican party, of course, was split in 1912. The Progressive party, under Theodore Roosevelt, adopted a platform declaring that:

> The issue of currency is fundamentally a government function and the system should have as basic principles soundness and elasticity. The control should be lodged with the government and should be protected from domination or manipulation by Wall Street or special interest.

> We are opposed to the so-called Aldrich Currency Bill because its provisions would place our currency and credit system in private hands, not subject to effective public control.[11]

The Taft wing of the party remained uncommitted to the Aldrich Plan, only supporting its conceptual foundation:

> In attaining these ends the independence of individual banks, whether organized under national or state charters, must be carefully protected, and our banking and currency system must be safeguarded from any possibility of domination by sectional, financial, or political interests.[12]

The Democrats gained control of the Congress and the presidency in the election of 1912. Reflecting its Jacksonian heritage, the party's platform declared its opposition to the "Aldrich Bill or a central bank." Some differences apparently arose regarding the proposed language in this plank of the party's platform. The understanding seemed to favor the word "for" instead of "or," but it was printed as "or." Democratic Representative Carter Glass (Virginia) was appointed chairman of the House Banking and Currency Committee, and he abided strictly by the printed language of the platform.[13]

Congressman Glass was instrumental in reformulating the Aldrich Plan to comply with the party's platform. Revisions in the plan reflected the work of H. Parker Willis, the committee's expert adviser, and the influence of Paul M. Warburg, who advised Senator Aldrich and was later appointed to the Federal Reserve Board by President Woodrow Wilson. Many others contributed significantly to the legislation's evolution toward becoming the Federal Reserve Act.

The Glass-Willis draft envisioned a regional concept—i.e., regional reserve banks tied together by a central board—in contrast to the Aldrich Plan's centralization of reserves with regional branches. The draft provided for a majority of the board appointed by the President, but with minority representation by the banks. Although the regional concept satisfied the Democrats in terms of their opposition to a "central bank," the matter of banker representation on the board failed to placate their fears of the system's domination by private banking interests.

Secretary of State William Jennings Bryan, who still commanded considerable influence in the party, and Democratic Senator Robert L. Owen (Oklahoma), who sponsored a companion bill, insisted on full government control of the board, excluding banker representation. President Wilson supported the Bryan-Owen proposal. In an effort to dissuade the President, Glass headed a delegation of prominent bankers in a meeting with President Wilson. The President was adamant, and, according to Glass, asked them: "Will one of you gentlemen tell me in what civilized country of the earth there are important government boards of control on which private interests are represented?" After painful silence from the group, Glass reported, Wilson inquired: "Which of you gentlemen thinks that the railroads should select members of the Interstate Commerce Commission?" With no convincing reply to either question forthcoming, and apparently no reference to central banks, the discussion turned to other matters. At the conference, however, the President did request that Glass include a provision in the legislation for the establishment of a Federal Advisory Council to be composed exclusively of bankers, which would meet periodically with the board in an advisory capacity.[14]

The Owen-Glass Bill providing for the establishment of the Federal Reserve System differed in certain critical respects from the Aldrich Bill, which provided for a National Reserve Association. The Federal Reserve Act provided for the creation of eight to twelve regional Federal Reserve banks to have minority government representation on their boards, and the Federal Reserve Board consisting entirely of government-appointed members. (The member banks of each district were to elect six directors, three bankers [Class A], and three representing other interests [Class B]; the three remaining directors [Class C] were to be appointed by the Federal Reserve Board.) The National Reserve Association had a centralized concept of reserves under a system of branches, and a board dominated by banking interests. The Aldrich Plan prescribed a minimum reserve of 50 percent behind notes and liabilities, and the notes were obligations of the National Reserve Association. The Owen-Glass Bill set minimum reserves at 40 percent against notes and 35 percent against deposits, but the notes were to be issued as obligations of the U.S. government. (The bill also provided for the issuance of notes by the Federal Reserve banks themselves on a basis comparable to the issuance of notes by the national banks, i.e., the Federal Reserve bank notes.) In terms of its functions as a central bank, however, the Federal Reserve System closely matches the Aldrich Plan as Warburg so ably demonstrated.[15]

Bryan hailed the Owen-Glass Bill as the "first triumph of the people in connection with currency legislation in a generation," and added another triumph in the control of money through a board of government officials, "without which the government issue of the money would be largely a barren victory."[16] Having satisfied the Bryan-Owen demands, the bill passed largely on the strength of the Democratic party votes over Republican opposition.[17] The bill's opponents stressed the fear that the nation's currency would be swamped by a fiat currency and that the system would be managed for political purposes. In opposition to the bill, Republican Senator Henry Cabot Lodge expressed the view that "I do not like to think that any law can be passed which will make it possible to submerge the gold standard in a flood of irredeemable paper currency"[18]—the opposition of Lodge and other Republicans was later to diminish. Lodge echoed the reservations of Warburg and Benjamin Strong, who was selected to serve as the first governor of the Federal Reserve Bank of New York. Warburg and Strong stressed their displeasure with the currency feature and the risk inherent in political control of the system.[19] The act specifically provided that no provisions therein should be construed to repeal the nation's commitment to the provisions of the Gold Standard Act of 1900.[20] Limitations were placed on Federal Reserve currency issuance, and Wilson seemed to support an organization free of close government control.[21] The Federal Reserve Act (the Owen-Glass Bill) was signed by President Wilson on December 23, 1913.

A Supreme Court of Finance

The resolution of the legislative debate in 1913 favoring an entirely government-appointed Federal Reserve Board, of course, did not completely close the matter of limiting the government's control of monetary policy. The Banking Act of 1935, indeed, represented an attempt to create what some called "a supreme court of finance."[22] Some years earlier, Senator Glass, now a U.S. senator and harsh critic of President Franklin D. Roosevelt's monetary policies, declared:

> While the Federal Reserve Board may never, if it should ever, become so detached and so completely independent of legislative and executive influence as to assume the status of the "Supreme Court of Banking," as many eminent bankers have desired, it is certainly to be devoutly wished that it may permanently hold such a high place of appreciation in the confidence and esteem of the country as to make it futile, if not positively dangerous, for political vandals to practice their arts against it. An intelligent and fearless performance of its functions involves as much of sanctity and of consequence to the American people as a like discharge of duty by the Supreme Court of the United States.[23]

A number of conditions are consistent with the view that the Federal Reserve System is, as is often maintained by Federal Reserve officials, "independent within the government not independent of the government." The attorney general of the United States on December 19, 1914, rendered an opinion, for example, that the Federal Reserve Board was an independent bureau, or establishment, of the government and as such did not fall under the jurisdiction of the Treasury Department.[24]

The framers of the Federal Reserve Act provided for the expenses of the board to be met by assessments of the Federal Reserve banks, thus blocking use of the appropriations process by the Congress to impose pressure on monetary policy. The precedent so avoided had been set by the Tariff Board, created by the Payne-Aldrich Tariff Act of 1909, but effectively terminated in 1912 when the Democrats in the House of Representatives refused to appropriate funds for its work.[25]

The Federal Reserve Board, as provided by the original Federal Reserve Act, continues to examine the books of the Federal Reserve banks. The expenditures of the board, but not the banks, were audited by the General Accounting Office until 1933, when the board was freed of that audit.[26] With the exception of monetary policy, on which the board reports directly to Congress twice each year, the Federal Reserve is now subject to audit by the General Accounting Office—the board is also audited by a private accounting firm.[27] The Federal Reserve, therefore, essentially remains beyond the easy reach of the Congress in terms of financial leverage, although the reporting requirement has expanded in recent years.

The formal ties with the executive branch have actually loosened since passage of the Federal Reserve Act. When established, the seven-member board included the secretary of the Treasury and the comptroller of the currency as *ex officio* members, and five others appointed by the President for ten-year terms with the advice and consent of the Senate. The President was to appoint no more than one member from each Federal Reserve district. Different interests were to be represented, but at least two appointed members were to be experienced in banking and finance. The secretary of the Treasury was to serve as *ex officio* chairman. One of the appointed members was to be designated by the President as governor, the active executive officer, and another as vice governor—it became customary to appoint each for a one-year term.

The number of appointive members was increased to six in 1922 so that President Warren G. Harding might appoint an "agriculturist," and the provision for two members experienced in banking and finance was rescinded. The Banking Act of 1933 increased the term of office to twelve years.

The Banking Act of 1935, in order to create "a supreme court of finance," as some called it, eliminated the *ex officio* positions on the board and increased the number of appointive members to seven, and their term of office to fourteen years. The President was granted the authority to appoint one member as chairman and one as vice chairman, each serving four-year terms. The purpose of the act was to enhance the independence and prestige of the board. Moreover, the secretary of the Treasury, Senator Glass asserted, had always rendered a pernicious influence—Glass himself had served in that capacity from 1918 to 1920.[28]

The effort to insulate the Federal Reserve from political pressure has continually faced the opposing view, favoring subordination of the central bank to the Treasury. Monetary policy, of course, was subordinated to Treasury debt financing for several years prior to the Treasury–Federal Reserve Accord in 1951. Congressman Wright Patman in the 1960s introduced legislation to place the Federal Reserve under the control of the Treasury, restoring the chairmanship to the secretary, while granting the power to the President to appoint the other members (eleven under Patman's plan) for four-year terms, as well as explicit power to remove them from office. Recently proposed legislation, the Hamilton-Dorgan Bill, among other features, contains a provision restoring the secretary of the Treasury to the Federal Open Market Committee (FOMC). The private Commission on Money and Credit recommended a smaller, five-member board, serving ten-year terms, with no geographical qualifications. The four-year terms of the chairman and vice chairman, selected from among the governors, would be coterminous with the President's term.[29]

Milton Friedman has maintained for some time that the Federal Reserve should be converted into a bureau of the Treasury Department. While Friedman recognizes that the central bank has not been fully independent, monetary policy, he contends, should be conducted with the same accountability to the public as fiscal policy. The historical record, in Friedman's view, suggests that congressional committees, indeed, may have produced a more stable policy than the Federal Reserve actually implemented. An independent central bank, according to Friedman, tends to disperse responsibility, to make policy dependent on personalities, and to give undue emphasis to the perspective of banks. Beyond that, he questions the appropriateness in a democracy to concentrate so much power in a body free from any kind of political control.[30] The allusion to "a supreme court of finance," of course, is supposed to suggest objectivity free of close political scrutiny, projecting the image of the U.S. Supreme Court that might otherwise be composed of members appointed by the President for four-year terms and chaired by the attorney general.

Centralization of Policy Making

The regional reserve banks under the original Federal Reserve Act were presumably autonomous units, but with a supervisory role for the board. Regional autonomy emphasized the control wielded by the privately elected directors of the Federal Reserve banks. The private character of the regional banks, of course, stood in contrast to the government-appointed board. Centralization eventually shifted the locus of power, however, to the publicly-controlled board, but in the early years the leadership role devolved to the Federal Reserve Bank of New York.

The Federal Reserve banks initially exercised those powers granted to them in conducting monetary policy within the framework of regional independence, including open market operations. Inadequacy of earnings prompted the regional banks to engage in open market purchases of government securities. The uncoordinated purchases of securities by the banks disrupted the securities markets, and the earnings impact was being offset by member banks paying down their rediscounts. The banks recognized, however, that such open market operations affected credit conditions. In order to coordinate policies, the Governors' Conference in 1922 created the Committee on Centralized Execution of Purchases and Sales of Government Securities by the Federal Reserve Banks. As a result, transactions were coordinated and conducted at the Federal Reserve Bank of New York. The recognized need for policy coordination was soon brought under the supervision of the board, as the board in 1923 dissolved the above committee and formed the Open Market Investment Committee (OMIC), thus removing this expression of regional autonomy, even though the individual banks could decline to follow the committee's recommendations. Open market operations became the primary monetary policy instrument, while the setting of discount rates became secondary in policy implementation, as public control strengthened relative to private control.

The strength of the Federal Reserve banks within the System emerged in World War I, when cooperation in managing war finances drew together the Treasury and the Federal Reserve Bank of New York. The leadership role of the latter institution in the 1920s reflected the banking acumen and personality of Benjamin Strong, the governor of the Federal Reserve Bank of New York, the concentration of financial power in New York, and the Treasury's support for lodging the effective authority with that bank.[31] With respect to relations with the Treasury, Congress was critical of the Federal Reserve after the war for not breaking away from the Treasury earlier.[32] The Federal Reserve operated autonomously under the Republican administrations in the 1920s, a period that Friedman and Schwartz characterize as "the high tide of the Federal Reserve,"[33] and Strong effectively presided over the System's policies, such that in London, for example, the Federal Reserve Bank of New York was considered this country's "central bank," which prompted a reaction by Glass:

> Benjamin is a man of such unusual ability, whose usefulness to the Federal Reserve System can scarcely be overestimated, and I like him so much, that I hesitate to say anything to him which would seem critical; but I have a notion to talk with him on this point.[34]

Strong's death in October 1928 left a vacuum in the leadership of the Federal Reserve at what was obviously a critical point in U.S. monetary history.

The banking legislation of the 1930s shifted the locus of power to the board in Washington. OMIC was renamed the Open Market Policy Conference in 1930, and, in turn, it was given statutory recognition under the Banking Act of 1933 and renamed the Federal Open Market Committee (FOMC). Representatives of the reserve banks constituted the committee. Open market transactions were permitted only with the board's approval, but the banks could still decline to engage in those operations. Viewing this as unworkable, proposals were considered to reconstitute the committee. It was initially proposed that the board be represented by three members, and the banks' representatives be cut to two. The board, led by Chairman Marriner Eccles, opposed this arrangement, proposing instead that the policy-making power be vested exclusively with the board, with an advisory committee composed of five reserve bank representatives. The House favored control by the board, but the Senate rejected this arrangement, reflecting Senator Glass's preference for no change in the committee's composition.

A compromise was reached in restructuring the committee under the Banking Act of 1935. The twelve voting members of the committee under the act, as it now stands, consist of the seven governors, thus constituting a majority, and five of the Federal Reserve bank presidents, serving on a rotational basis. The legislation also changed the name of the central board from the Federal Reserve Board to the Board of Governors of the Federal Reserve System. The title "governor" now applied to all the members of the board, no longer just the operating executive. This elevation of status was accompanied by demotions of the banks' governors to positions of presidents. The law also gave the FOMC decisional rather than advisory power. Congressman Henry B. Steagall (Alabama), chairman of the House Banking and Currency Committee, seemed satisfied with this structure, given the board's approval of reserve bank presidents and the striking of the provision that two of the seven governors must be experienced in banking. In 1942, an amendment required that the committee's elected representatives be the reserve banks' president or first vice president, and revised the rotational groupings (giving the Federal Reserve Bank of New York a permanent seat).

Congress felt that the FOMC, as a committee, would not be so easily controlled by the Congress itself or the President, as would policies set by the chairman. The FOMC was established as an agency of the government, and open market operations would be executed by the Federal Reserve Bank of New York. The chairman would report to the Congress, however. While less likely to be dominated by the executive branch, accountability to the Congress was enhanced.

The composition of the FOMC has remained a matter of political contention since 1935, but the Congress has been reluctant to make substantive changes. Congressman Patman offered several proposals to change the committee, as an expression of his opinion that the reserve banks do not represent the people. Congressman Henry S. Reuss (Wisconsin) introduced the Federal Reserve Reform Act of 1976, which provided for the Federal Reserve bank presidents to be appointed by the President and confirmed by the Senate, but that provision was struck from the bill. The congressional debate on that issue raised no question on the constitutional infirmity of the FOMC's structure. Several proposals have been introduced in recent years that would alter the composition of the FOMC, but the supporters of this legislation have been unable to persuade their colleagues to adopt their positions.

Congressman Reuss and Senator Donald W. Riegle (Michigan) in separate actions attempted to persuade the courts to restructure the FOMC. Congressman Reuss in the 1970s brought legal action against the Federal Reserve claiming injury by the defendants, who exercised governmental authority affecting his property without having been appointed in conformity with the Constitution's appointments clause, and thereby violating his right to due process. The appointments clause states:

> [The President] shall nominate, and by and with the advice and consent of the Senate, shall appoint ambassadors, and other public ministers and consuls, judges of the Supreme Court, and all other officers of the United States, whose appointments are not herein otherwise provided for, and which shall be established by law; but the Congress may by law vest the appointment of such inferior officers, as they think proper, in the President alone, in the courts of law, or in the heads of departments. (Article II, Section 2)

In *Reuss* v. *Balles* (1978), the court dismissed the case on the ground that the alleged economic loss was merely conjectural.

Senator Riegle brought legal action against the FOMC, claiming violation of the senator's rights under the appointments clause. In *Riegle* v. *Federal Open Market Committee* (1981), the court held that "equitable discretion" required dismissal, because "judicial action would improperly interfere with the legislative process." The court suggested, however, that several classes of private plaintiffs might have standing, and that the absence of private plaintiffs would be reason to hear the suit. Based on *Riegle*, a variety of individuals claimed that they were injured by high interest rates and that those rates were caused by an undemocratic composition of the FOMC. In this action, *Committee for Monetary Reform* v. *Board of Governors of the Federal Reserve System* (1985), the court ruled that the plaintiffs' alleged connection between high interest rates and the composition of the FOMC was too tenuous to support standing.

Senator John Melcher (Montana), prior to the latter case, challenged the legitimacy of the FOMC in *Melcher* v. *Federal Open Market Committee* (1984). The District Court ruled that since no plaintiff is available to enforce the appointments clause, equitable discretion is no longer an appropriate basis for dismissal of Melcher's complaint, so the District Court heard the case. The court, nonetheless, held for the defendants, ruling that the reserve bank representatives on the FOMC need not be officers of the United States, so that they need not be appointed in conformity with the appointments clause. The manner of selecting the reserve bank members does not violate the appointments clause, the court reasoned, as "the lessons of history" fully support the Congress's decision to include them, observing that the nation's monetary system has always been "governed by a subtle and conscious blend of public and private elements." Few issues have been so thoroughly considered as central banking and the regulation of the money supply, the court continued, and private participation in these areas has been prescribed by Congress, and the court is reluctant "to upset this delicate time-honored balance." The court concluded that the "plaintiff has failed to offer any cogent reason why Congress may not establish or continue a partnership of public and private control over [open market] functions in lieu of execution of these responsibilities exclusively by government officials."

Senator Melcher subsequently filed an appeal with the United States Court of Appeals for the District of Columbia. On December 18, 1987, the court invoked the doctrine of "equitable discretion," as in *Riegle*, and ruled that equitable discretion does not depend upon the ability of a private plaintiff to bring suit, thus disagreeing with the opinion of the District Court. The court held that judicial action would interfere with the legislative process, in a dispute properly within the domain of the legislative branch. The court appreciated that the decision could render a constitutional question unreviewable, but that should not constrain the court's exercise of equitable discretion. While this ruling places in tension the vindication of meritorious claims grounded on the Constitution, the courts "are not at liberty to embark upon a broad, undifferentiated mission of vindicating constitutional rights; after all, Article II specifically limits the judicial power of the United States to the resolution of actual cases or controversies."[35]

Federal Reserve System and the Treasury

The secretary of the Treasury under the emergency legislation of the 1930s was granted considerable power in the management of monetary affairs, and the Federal Reserve cooperated with the executive branch in the implementation of policy. The cost to the government of financing the public debt during the 1930s was a source of conflict between the Federal Reserve and the Treasury, which objected to policies that might erode the price of government bonds. Beyond that, Secretary of the Treasury Henry Morgenthal, Jr., thought that the government, through the Treasury, should control monetary policy, rather than the Federal Reserve banks, which were privately owned and dominated by banker-minded people. In this conflict, Morgenthal in one instance attended an FOMC meeting, and President Roosevelt wondered whether the Federal Reserve realized that its independence was at stake. The Federal Reserve complied with the President's wishes. The President did listen to the chairman, and did not always side with the Treasury.[36] The chairman conferred with the President and the heads of executive agencies, perhaps as a matter of "self-preservation" of the System's independence, but this set a precedent for continued political influence of the Federal Reserve.[37]

The Federal Reserve's independence was limited further during World War II in cooperating with the Treasury in financing the war. The Federal Reserve maintained an orderly market in government securities and a structure of interest rates designed to keep interest costs low for the government, to encourage private investors to place funds in government debt instruments, and to prevent any rise in profits for the banks. There was a lingering concern that the Treasury might envelop the Federal Reserve, and perhaps the banking system as well.[38]

Immediately following World War II, the Federal Reserve stepped tentatively toward restoring its earlier independence. In an agreement with the Treasury in 1947, a slight increase in interest rates was allowed in exchange for turning over 90 percent of the Federal Reserve's profits to the Treasury.[39] In the late 1940s, while still subject to pressures from the Treasury to maintain a pegged-price policy toward government securities, the Federal Reserve edged toward a more "flexible" policy. The Federal Reserve remained cautious, however, still cognizant of the threat to its status in the government, and the central bank was not eager to combat the ongoing inflation by tightening policy, fearing, as did many others, that a more serious danger was posed by a postwar depression.[40]

The inflationary surge associated with the outbreak of hostilities in Korea tipped the perceived policy balance toward restraint. The Federal Reserve sought to shift policy toward providing orderly markets rather than a fixed pattern of interest rates. The Treasury resisted, and President Harry S. Truman sided with the Treasury. Indeed, on January 31, 1951, President Truman met with the FOMC and requested full support by the Federal Reserve for the Treasury's debt financing. The President was later surprised by the absence of such support, and the White

House announced its understanding that monetary policy would support the market in Treasury securities. The FOMC informed the President by letter of its intentions to maintain confidence in the market, but did not commit itself to a fixed rate pattern. The Federal Reserve under Chairman Thomas B. McCabe asserted its independence, and support was found in the press and in the Congress, where Senator Paul Douglas observed that the Federal Reserve had been intimidated by the threat of its nationalization, and suggested that Treasury financing should be subordinated to the Federal Reserve's policies. A joint resolution of the Congress maintained that monetary policy should be the domain of the Federal Reserve, the Treasury should coordinate its debt financing with the Federal Reserve, and the Federal Reserve should take precedence in the conflict with the Treasury. The independence of the Federal Reserve in conducting monetary policy was then formally recognized in the Treasury–Federal Reserve Accord of March 4, 1951.[41]

The 1951 accord was interpreted as an agreement to cease pegging the price of Treasury obligations, but to maintain orderly markets in a spirit of cooperation with the Treasury. The support of the Congress was critical in strengthening the position of the Federal Reserve. In this connection, some concern was expressed in the Congress when, after the resignations of McCabe and Eccles, who had remained on the board after being replaced as chairman, William McChesney Martin, Jr., and J. L. Robertson, both former Treasury officials, were appointed to the board. That concern diminished, however, as the Federal Reserve moved to consolidate its position. The Federal Reserve instituted a "bills only" policy in order to appear less preoccupied with fixing the rates on Treasury securities, and it changed the procedure for setting open market policy, abolishing an executive committee, which gave much discretion to the Federal Reserve Bank of New York, and concentrated authority in the FOMC, which established a more specific policy than earlier to be carried out by the manager of the open market account under its "directive."[42]

Postaccord Independence

In his 1952 presidential campaign, Dwight D. Eisenhower supported "a Federal Reserve exercising its functions in the money and credit system without pressure for political purposes from the Treasury or the White House."[43] The statement presumably allowed some latitude for nonpolitical pressures, and the Treasury and the Council of Economic Advisers were at times at odds with the posture of monetary policy, but Eisenhower apparently maintained a position congenial with an independent central bank, in contrast to the two Democratic administrations that preceded him. The rising pattern of interest rates no doubt was an irritant to the Congress, and Senator Douglas remained critical of the Federal Reserve's sensitivity to the interests of the Treasury and the banking community. Chairman Martin seemed to shield the Federal Reserve effectively from undue pressures, however.[44]

The prestige of the Federal Reserve and its independence were clearly enhanced by the tenure of Chairman Martin, which spanned the Eisenhower, Kennedy, and Johnson administrations. Martin insisted that the Federal Reserve was "independent within the government." He was willing to defy President Lyndon B. Johnson by raising the discount rate in 1965, ushering in a restrictive policy. The President later reappointed the chairman based on his calculation that Martin was worth $1 billion in gold—i.e., the value of the gold that might be exported should confidence in the dollar be shaken by a failure to reappoint the Chairman.

It is perhaps a reflection of the extent to which Martin achieved a position of independence that Arthur F. Burns, closely identified with President Richard M. Nixon, has been charged with complicity with the political interests of that administration. The charges against Burns focus chiefly on the conduct of monetary policy during the presidential campaign of 1972 and the culpability of the Federal Reserve in underwriting the escalation of inflation in the 1970s. There is no doubt that Burns was the target at times of intense pressure from the White House during the Nixon administration.[45] On the surface, this suggests that Burns was not simply compliant. The rapid rate of monetary expansion in 1972 has been offered as evidence of Burns's political sensitivities, although a concurrent rise in the federal funds rate would seem to qualify the existence of such a reelection strategy. In Burns's defense, Paul W. McCracken, who served as chairman of the Council of Economic Advisers under President Nixon, stated:

> [E]ven though President Nixon appointed Arthur Burns to the Federal Reserve Board, Mr. Burns showed no reluctance (if I may be permitted an "insider's comment") about standing firm on occasion against urgent efforts by the president to persuade him otherwise.[46]

Perhaps the key words are "on occasion," but in McCracken's opinion, the charge of political motivation leaves unanswered the obvious fact that Burns was only one vote on the board and the FOMC, albeit a persuasive one. The other members apparently do not subscribe to the claim of political manipulation by the chairman as well. Beyond that, monetary growth rates were extraordinarily high in 1972 on an international scale, which McCracken links to the breakdown of the Bretton Woods international monetary system.[47]

In "The Anguish of Central Banking," Arthur F. Burns offers a rationale for the policies during his tenure as chairman of the Federal Reserve Board in the 1970s.[48] Reflecting on his experience, Burns addresses the question of why, despite the antipathy of central bankers to inflation and the powerful weapons they wield, they have failed so utterly in their mission. The paradox, to Burns, seems representative of other industrial countries, as well as the United States. The failure of central bankers to confront this inflation, in Burns's view, can be traced to the philosophical and political currents, beginning in the 1930s, that imparted an inflationary bias in the economy. The New Deal measures laid the foundation for an activist government, providing relief, but raising expectations as well as assuming responsibilities, displacing the precept of self-reliance. Management of aggregate demand was coupled with an extended range of regulatory activities and market interventions. The process was cumulative, as the government was increasingly called upon to address a widening array of social and economic problems. While much of this was wholesome, in Burns's view, it generated a secular inflation.

The Federal Reserve had the power to abort that inflation, Burns concedes, but, "It did not do so because the Federal Reserve was itself caught up in the philosophic and political currents that were transforming American life and culture."[49] Burns further notes that "the Federal Reserve had themselves been touched by the allurements of the New Economics." As such, the Federal Reserve felt compelled to accommodate the upward pressures on prices, and "Not only that, the Federal Reserve would be frustrating the will of the Congress, to which it was responsible."[50] As a result, policy came to be governed by the principle of undernourishing the inflationary process, as was the case for other central banks operating in a similar political environment. Even so, the Federal Reserve,

> evoked violent criticism from both the Executive Branch and the Congress and therefore had to devote much of its energy to warding off legislation that could destroy any hope of ending inflation. This testing process necessarily involved political judgments, and the Federal Reserve may at times have overestimated the risks attaching to additional monetary restraint.[51]

Aside from any errors of political judgment, the Federal Reserve, Burns admits, committed errors of economic or financial judgment. Economic statistics were misinterpreted, and changes in financial practices expanded the opportunities for misjudgment under an inflation where central banking lost its moorings.

Burns concludes that central banks retain the capacity to check inflation, but they are limited by political forces. In this connection, he sees hopeful signs that "the inflationary bias that has been sapping the economic and moral vitality of the democracies can be finally routed."[52] Federal Reserve Board chairman Paul A. Volcker accepted this challenge, and, upon returning from hearing Burns's speech in Yugoslavia, held a special meeting of the FOMC on October 6, 1979, at which a more austere policy in undernourishing the inflationary process was adopted.

The tenure of Paul Volcker restored respect for the office, as Volcker orchestrated a successful deceleration of inflation. The orthodox policy of monetary stringency forced interest rates steeply higher, and economic activity contracted severely, exposing serious liquidity problems, but the wage-price spiral receded, generally much more quickly than had been anticipated. While a certain ambivalence pervaded the administration of President Jimmy Carter, as the inflationary undercurrent frustrated his policies, President Ronald Reagan seemed willing to accept the apparent necessity of curtailing monetary expansion in order to reduce inflation. The absence of a focal point for policies outside the Federal Reserve seems as well to have helped preserve its autonomy. Volcker's successor, Alan Greenspan, inherited a position carrying considerable independence, at least within the context of a moderate rate of inflation. The monetary powers executed by the Federal Reserve now seem to be well shielded from political abuse, but, under the administration of President George Bush, pressure on the central bank to lower interest rates seems unrelenting, and, no doubt, further testing of the Federal Reserve's "independence" will be administered in the future.

Conclusion

The Federal Reserve was founded in a way to mesh the interests of the banking community with the public interest represented by a "capstone" board in Washington. The board was to consist entirely of government appointees, including two *ex officio* members, but the thinking was that it would not be subservient to the executive branch, nor closely monitored by the Congress. Legislative provisions were consistent with this "independent" identity.

Banking interests were more clearly represented in the Federal Reserve banks, as those organizations mobilized reserves and served as a source of credit. The Federal Advisory Council provided the bankers a formal communications linkage with the board. Reflecting the Democratic party's Jacksonian heritage, the "central bank" was purposely decentralized to diffuse political and economic power. Moreover, the gold standard, confirmed in the Federal Reserve Act, was to serve as the ultimate determinant of the money supply.

The locus of power shifted over time from the Federal Reserve Bank of New York to the Treasury, then to the board (and the FOMC), with extended periods of uneasiness in that movement. The demise of the gold standard in a meaningful way within the domestic monetary system left the Federal Reserve System with powers not generally contemplated, although feared by Senator Lodge and cheered by Secretary Bryan, at the time of its formation. Thus, an "independent" monetary authority became the reservoir of control over money that had been left earlier to the determination of markets.

The resulting concentration of monetary powers was nonetheless congenial with the tradition of distrust of lodging those powers directly in the hands of the government. That institutional structure, moreover, complies with the organization of government in a federal system with a separation of powers. While seemingly solidly entrenched, the notion of an "independent" monetary authority, then, fits both those qualities in adapting to the Constitution, even though the Constitution as interpreted has been informally amended by the Supreme Court to accommodate departures engineered by the Congress from its original strictures.

Notes

1. Sherman J. Maisel, *Managing the Dollar* (New York: W. W. Norton, 1973), p. 24. Paul Meek, an officer at the Federal Reserve Bank of New York, offered the same opinion:

The Federal Reserve System derives this power to create bank reserves from the Congress, which has been given the power by the Constitution to "coin money [and] regulate the value thereof" (Article I, Section 8). (Paul Meek, *Open-Market Operations* [Federal Reserve Bank of New York, 1973], p. 7)

2. Milton Friedman and Anna Jacobson Schwartz, *A Monetary History of the United States, 1867–1960* (Princeton, NJ: Princeton University Press, 1963), p. 170.

3. National Monetary Commission, *Report of the Monetary Commission*, Senate Documents, vol. 7, 620, Congress, 2d Session, Document No. 243, January 9, 1912 (Washington, DC: Government Printing Office, 1912), p. 12.

4. Ibid., pp. 15–16.

5. Ibid., pp. 12–13, 56.

6. Ibid., p. 14.

7. Ibid., pp. 14–15.

8. Ibid., p. 32.

9. Ibid., p. 18.

10. Ibid., p. 36.

11. Quoted from Paul M. Warburg, *The Federal Reserve System: Its Origins and Growth* (New York: Macmillan, 1930), p. 78.

12. A. Jerome Clifford, *The Independence of the Federal Reserve System* (Philadelphia: University of Pennsylvania Press, 1965), p. 57.

13. Warburg, *The Federal Reserve System*, p. 79; and Carter Glass, *An Adventure in Constructive Finance* (New York: Doubleday, 1927), pp. 31–34.

14. Glass, *An Adventure in Constructive Finance*, pp. 115–16. The idea of an advisory council had been suggested to President Wilson shortly before this meeting on June 24, 1913, by Louis D. Brandeis in a letter dated June 12, 1913 (Gabriel Kolko, *The Triumph of Conservatism: A Reinterpretation of American History, 1900–1916* [New York: The Free Press of Glencoe, 1963], p. 232).

15. Warburg challenged Senator Glass's claim that the Federal Reserve Act differed substantially from the Aldrich Plan, presenting a detailed comparison of the legislative proposals along with a history of the legislative process. See especially, Warburg, *The Federal Reserve System*, pp. 178–406, and Glass, *An Adventure in Constructive Finance*.

16. Warburg, *The Federal Reserve System*, pp. 484, 754. Warburg was highly critical of the Bryan "triumphs," fearing political control of the Federal Reserve.

17. The significance of Bryan was acknowledged by Warburg and Glass (Warburg, *The Federal Reserve System*, p. 754, and Glass, *An Adventure in Constructive Finance*, pp. 160–61). Bryan's role is also described in his memoirs. William Jennings Bryan and Mary Baird Bryan, *The Memoirs of William Jennings Bryan* (New York: Haskell House Publishers, 1971), pp. 367–74.

18. Glass, *An Adventure in Constructive Finance*, pp. 221–22. In reference to Lodge, Glass commented:

He could, in this connection, have clearly recalled by contrast that the only "fiat" paper money ever issued in the history of the Republic was that issued under a party administration of Mr. Lodge's own faith and, contrary to the teaching of Hamilton and Gallatin, validated by a "readjustment" of the Supreme Court of the United States. (pp. 223–24)

19. Warburg opposed a political board and notes issued as obligations of the government (*The Federal Reserve System*, p. 127). He later observed:

A study of four years from within the System and of almost four years without, leads me to think that its gravest danger lies in the gradual ascendency of political influence. . . .

Unless the Federal Reserve Board is raised to a position of the greatest possible dignity, and men of real strength, independence, and knowledge are found to serve on it in the future, it is to be feared that the System will become the football of politics. A splendid instrument of protection might thus become an element of dangerous disturbance. (Ibid., vol. 2, pp. 774, 777)

Among his criticisms, Strong objected to the "provisional return to the heresies of Greenbackism and fiat money" and supervisory power vested in "a body of political appointees and government officials" (Lester V. Chandler, *Benjamin Strong, Central Banker* [Washington, DC: The Brookings Institution, 1958], p. 35).

20. "The Federal Reserve Act, December 23, 1913," in *Documentary History of Banking and Currency in the United States*, vol. 4, ed. Herman E. Krooss (New York: Chelsea House, 1969), p. 2468.

21. Clifford quotes Wilson as saying that the board was "to feel perfectly free to pursue its course within the law without a particle of constraint or restraint from the Executive" (*The Independence of the Federal Reserve System*, p. 92).

22. Benjamin Haggott Beckhart, *Federal Reserve System* (New York: American Institute of Banking, 1972), p. 33.

23. Glass, *An Adventure in Constructive Finance*, p. 250.

24. Beckhart, *Federal Reserve System*, p. 31.

25. Ibid., p. 32.

26. Ibid., p. 31.

27. Board of Governors of the Federal Reserve System, *Annual Report, 1984*, p. 205.

28. Beckhart, *Federal Reserve System*, pp. 33–34.

29. Ibid., pp. 34–35; and the Commission on Money and Credit, *Money and Credit: Their Influence on Jobs, Prices, and Growth—The Report of the Commission on Money and Credit* (Englewood Cliffs, NJ: Prentice-Hall, 1961), pp. 87–88.

30. Friedman and Schwartz, *Monetary History*, p. 8.

31. Clifford, *The Independence of the Federal Reserve System*, pp. 98–103. Warburg's German background seriously undercut his leadership potential during World War I, and he left the board in 1918 when his term expired.

32. Ibid., p. 116.

33. Friedman and Schwartz, *Monetary History*, p. 240f.

34. Chandler, *Benjamin Strong*, p. 450.

35. *Melcher* v. *Federal Open Market Committee* 836 F.2d 561, 266 U.S.App.D.C. 397, 1987. Briefs filed on behalf of Senator Melcher and the FOMC were obtained from the Federal Reserve Board. Those briefs contain references to the aforementioned cases. For further discussion of the Melcher case, see the author's paper entitled, "Senator Melcher's Challenge to the FOMC's Legitimacy," proceedings of the Allied Social Science Associations annual meetings, Atlanta, GA, 1989.

36. Clifford, *The Independence of the Federal Reserve System*, pp. 151–57.

37. Ibid., pp. 160–61.

38. Ibid., pp. 168–95.

39. Ibid., p. 204; Friedman and Schwartz, *Monetary History*, p. 578.

40. Clifford, *The Independence of the Federal Reserve System*, 198–217.

41. Ibid., pp. 229–53. Friedman and Schwartz contend that dwelling on the conflict between the Federal Reserve and the Treasury misrepresents the situation in the sense that the Federal Reserve favored the bond support program, being in favor of low interest rates, and to prevent presumed deflationary tendencies, thus seeking a more flexible policy setting, not complete abandonment of the prevailing policy (*Monetary History*, pp. 625–26).

42. Clifford, *The Independence of the Federal Reserve System*, pp. 261–89.

43. Ibid., p. 301.

44. Ibid., pp. 302–60.

45. Charles Colson, in *Born Again* (Falls Church, VA: Conservative Press, 1983, pp. 62–63, 185–87), relates his role in passing along to the press a false charge against Burns, and his subsequent apology to the chairman.

46. Paul W. McCracken, "Reflections of an Economic Policy Maker: A Review Article," *Journal of Economic Literature*, vol. 23 (June 1980): 582.

47. Ibid., pp. 582–83. William Greider in *Secrets of the Temple: How the Federal Reserve Runs the Country* (New York: Simon & Schuster, 1987) offers a harsher view of Burns's tenure, blaming the chairman for the high, accelerating rate of inflation in the 1970s and, in so doing, serving as a puppet of the Nixon administration. The charge is presumably that of duplicity, acting on behalf of the administration, or for personal gain, while asserting that policy was forged independent of partisan political influence. Likewise, the related charge is that the chairman in public was resolutely opposed to inflationary policies, but in private or within policy-making circles, was an advocate of inflationary policies. Thus, without documentation, Greider claims that "high-level officials" considered Burns to be an "arrogant fraud" (ibid., p. 66).

Greider, of course, does not consider Burns as forward-looking in setting policies to comply with the dictates of the presiding administration, which is precisely what he advises. Indeed, Greider suggests that the Federal Reserve be "directly responsive to the wishes of the President" (ibid., p. 534), as the central bank would be converted into an agency of the Treasury. The Federal Reserve, then, would be accountable to the executive branch and subject to congressional oversight (ibid., p. 757), in a government exercising selective credit controls and setting interest-rate ceilings (ibid., p. 755), thus suggesting that monetary policy could then be as stabilizing as fiscal policy!

Greider quotes President Nixon that Burns was expected to conclude as chairman that Nixon's "views are the ones that should be followed" (ibid., p. 341). Greider then asserts that Burns "delivered promptly." "Two weeks later," Burns, according to Greider, argued forcefully in favor of the easing in policy "that the President wanted" (ibid.). Greider neglects to mention that the economy was sinking in a recession. Moreover, former governor Maisel recounts the episode very differently. Maisel observes that Nixon's jokes left Burns and Martin "extremely uncomfortable," and that both men knew that the Federal Reserve "had acted to ease credit and lower interest rates several weeks earlier" (Sherman J. Maisel, *Managing the Dollar* [New York: W. W. Norton, 1973], p. 107).

Despite the observations of former governor Andrew F. Brimmer that Burns was not motivated by a reelect-Nixon strategy (Greider, *Secrets of the Temple*, pp. 749–50), Greider asserts otherwise: "The majority [of the FOMC] did not wish to tempt collision with Richard Nixon's reelection strategy" (ibid., p. 344). Beyond that, an anonymous "former aide" to the chairman supposedly remarked that:

> The word "sordid" is probably too strong, but what Burns did immediately after Jimmy Carter's election in terms of monetary policy can be documented. There was a rapid shift in monetary policy and it was designed to ingratiate Burns with Carter so he would be reappointed chairman. (Ibid., p. 346)

A staff aide moreover supposedly advised the chairman that "Carter can be seduced," and suggested that Burns should "reassure the President that you won't criticize him publicly every six months" (Ibid., p. 346).

Maxwell Newton, financial editor of the *New York Post*, also employs the scholarly arts as practiced in the journalism profession in *The Fed: Inside the Federal Reserve, the Secret Power Center that Controls the American Economy* (New York: Times Books, 1983). In an allegedly "monetarist approach," he also castigates Burns, and concludes that we would be better off without the Federal Reserve. He favors subordination of the central bank to the Treasury, or even zero growth of the money supply (pp. 323–23).

48. Arthur F. Burns, "The Anguish of Central Banking," *Federal Reserve Bulletin* 73, 9 (September 1987): 687–98. This article is a reprint of the sixteenth Per Jacobsson Lecture delivered by Dr. Burns in Belgrade, Yugoslavia, on September 30, 1979.

49. Ibid., p. 692.

50. Ibid.

51. Ibid., p. 693.

52. Ibid., p. 698.

CHAPTER 11

Managing an "Elastic"
Supply of "Bills of Credit"

The Federal Reserve System was supposed to manage an "elastic" currency in order to avert financial panics. Failure to check massive bank closings, leading to the Great Depression, prompted steps to move the United States off the gold standard—private money issues emerged once again in order to arrest the degenerative process, but appeared to be largely a sign of debility. The abandonment of the gold standard encompassed the nationalization of private gold holdings and the abrogation of gold clauses in contracts. The Supreme Court upheld these bold assertions of monetary authority, thus tying our fortunes to the Federal Reserve's capacity to manage the nation's money supply grounded on "bills of credit." The results in recent decades have not been satisfactory, as chronic inflation has replaced a regime providing long-run price stability, but the trade-off appears to be markedly less short-run instability than was experienced under the earlier institutional arrangements.

An "Elastic" Currency

> *Under this system, as I have indicated, there will never again be a financial panic.*
>
> —*Carter Glass*[1]

Senator Glass's prediction in 1923 came among other optimistic appraisals for world peace and prosperity, only to ring hollow in the 1930s. It was, of course, a return to the drawing boards for the senator in formulating new banking legislation to correct the perceived deficiencies in a financial system still vulnerable to financial panics.

The Federal Reserve Act of 1913, in response to the panic of 1907, constructed a monetary system designed to overcome the disadvantages of the national banking system, chiefly inelasticity of paper currency and pyramiding of bank reserves, by organizing a central bank that could also serve as a "lender of last resort." The Federal Reserve clearly was not sufficiently responsive to check massive bank failures at the outset of the Great Depression. Between 1929 and 1933, more than 9,000 banks failed, and the money supply contracted by one-third. As Milton Friedman and Anna Schwartz conclude:

> The drastic decline in the stock of money and the occurrence of a banking panic of unprecedented severity did not reflect the absence of power on the part of the Federal Reserve to prevent them. Throughout the contraction, the System had ample powers to cut short the tragic process of monetary deflation and banking collapse. . . . Such measures were not taken, partly, we conjecture, because of the fortuitous shift of power within the System from New York to other Federal Reserve Banks and the weakness of the Federal Reserve Board in Washington, partly because of the assignment—by the community at large as well as the Reserve System—of higher priority to external than to internal stability.[2]

High-powered money, consisting of currency held by the public, vault cash, and deposits with the Federal Reserve banks, did not expand sufficiently through monetary policy actions to meet currency hoarding by the public, an asset adjustment that provided protection from bank failure and a high real return when prices were falling, and to satisfy the demand for "excess" reserves as a cushion for banks, without causing a succession of contractions in a fractional-reserve banking system. Friedman and Schwartz describe it as follows:

> If deterioration in credit quality or bad banking was the trigger, which it may to some extent have been, the damaging bullet it discharged was the inability of the banking system to acquire additional

high-powered money to meet the resulting demands of depositors for currency, without a multiple contraction of deposits. That inability was responsible alike for the extent and importance of bank failures and for the indirect effect bank failures had on the stock of money.[3]

Federal deposit insurance in 1934 probably succeeded, where the Federal Reserve failed, in preventing severe contractions in the money supply induced by banking panics.[4] Since the 1930s, however, the Federal Reserve has exhibited sensitivity to the onset of a crisis, supplying liquidity and serving as a lender of last resort so that deposit insurance has not been the only check to financial panics.[5]

Eliminating Gold from the Monetary System

Besides the banking legislation reviewed in chapter 10, the government devalued the dollar in terms of gold and prohibited private ownership of monetary gold. While permitting a more expansive monetary policy, these steps raised constitutional issues pertaining to gold clauses in contracts and the presumed legal tender status of gold. The administration devalued the dollar in order to reflate the price level and confiscated private gold holdings earlier to prevent private individuals and organizations from reaping profits from the devaluation—the devaluation generated a profit of about $2.8 billion for the Treasury.[6]

The inauguration of Franklin D. Roosevelt as President on March 4, 1933, was followed two days later by the declaration of a "bank holiday." The action taken to close the banks temporarily was based on the authority conferred by the Act of October 6, 1917. The President supposed that heavy withdrawals of gold and currency for the purpose of hoarding posed a threat to the banking system and that speculation abroad in foreign exchange could cause a severe drain on the nation's gold stock. Payments in gold from the Treasury were restricted to those issued a license by the secretary.[7]

Congress passed the Emergency Banking Act on March 9, 1933, confirming the actions taken by the executive branch under the 1917 legislation. The act also amended the Federal Reserve

Act, authorizing the secretary of the Treasury to require all persons to deliver to the Treasury all gold coin, gold bullion, and gold certificates, in exchange for an equivalent amount of other U.S. currency, valuing bullion at the legal price of $20.67 per fine ounce. An executive order on April 5 required all persons (and banks) to deliver to the Federal Reserve banks their gold coins, bullion, and certificates on or before May 1, 1933, with the equivalent of other currency received in exchange—exceptions to the nationalization of gold included rare coins, reasonable inventories for use in industry and the arts, and $100 per person in gold coin or certificates. By order of the secretary of the Treasury on December 28, 1933, the requirement for delivery of all gold coin, gold bullion, and gold certificates was tightened, excluding only rare coins and a few minor items.[8]

The Thomas Amendment to the Agricultural Adjustment Act of May 12, 1933, provided the President with the authority to fix the weights of the gold and silver dollars in a manner that would stabilize domestic prices and adjust for adverse effects of foreign currency depreciation. Any devaluation of the dollar was limited to 50 percent of the prevailing legal standard. (The dollar immediately commenced depreciating against gold, as the price of gold soon reached $30 an ounce, then fluctuated in a range between $27 and $35 an ounce.) The bill also authorized the President, under certain circumstances, to direct the secretary of the Treasury to enter into agreements with the Federal Reserve for open market operations and for the purchase of an additional $3 billion of bills directly from the Treasury. Senator Elmer Thomas (Oklahoma), in the Bryan tradition, also inserted in the act the powers, unused by the President, to restore bimetallism and issue up to $3 billion of greenbacks, and the act provided that:

> Such notes and all other coins and currencies heretofore or hereafter coined or issued by or under the authority of the United States shall be legal tender for all debts public and private.[9]

The joint resolution of June 5, 1933, declared that obligations providing for the payment in gold obstructed the power of the

Congress to regulate the value of money and were inconsistent with the stated policy of Congress to maintain the equal, uniform value of every dollar issued in the United States. Therefore, Congress resolved:

> That (a) every provision contained in or made with respect to any obligation which purports to give the obligee a right to require payment in gold or a particular kind of coin or currency, or in an amount in money of the United States measured thereby, is declared to be against public policy; and no such provision shall be contained in or made with respect to any obligation hereafter incurred. Every obligation, heretofore or hereafter incurred, whether or not any such provision is contained therein or made with respect thereto, shall be discharged upon payment, dollar for dollar, in any coin or currency which at the time of payment is legal tender for public or private debts. Any such provision contained in any law authorizing obligations to be issued by or under authority of the United States, is hereby repealed, but the repeal of any such provision shall not invalidate any other provision or authority contained in such law.[10]

The declaration that private protective measures were "against public policy" is reminiscent of similar pronouncements during the Revolutionary War. The Congress also declared that the term obligation applies to U.S. government obligations, excluding currency, and that all coins and currencies of the United States, specifically "including Federal Reserve notes and circulating notes of the Federal Reserve banks and national banking associations"[11] shall be legal tender for all debts, public and private. The joint resolution was followed by additional executive orders.

Congress passed the Gold Reserve Act on January 30, 1934, confirming the actions of the President and the secretary of the Treasury under earlier acts, but set a ceiling of 60 percent for setting the gold value of the dollar, so that the gold value could be fixed between 50 percent and 60 percent of the prevailing legal standard. On January 31, the President issued a proclamation fixing the gold dollar at 15 and $\frac{5}{21}$ grains, nine-tenths fine, or down 59.06 percent from the earlier standard of 25.8 grains, nine-tenths fine—the gold content of the dollar was therefore reduced from 23.22 grains to 13.714 grains. Gold was now valued at $35 an ounce, up from $20.67.

The act also provided for the transfer of gold held by the Federal Reserve banks to the Treasury, which issued gold certificates in exchange to be held as reserves. Federal Reserve notes were no longer convertible into gold, but they could be redeemed for "lawful money." A $2 billion fund was established for the Treasury to use in stabilizing foreign exchange rates. The devaluation of the dollar in terms of gold raised the Treasury's holdings to almost $7 billion.

The removal of gold from circulation was followed by successive steps to reduce its restrictive role in the conduct of expansive monetary policies. The gold requirements behind Federal Reserve deposits and notes were cut in 1945, eliminated for deposits in 1965, and then removed entirely in 1968. The dollar was formally devalued in 1971, with the official price of gold raised to $38 per ounce, and dollar convertibility into gold by foreign official institutions was suspended, and again in 1973, when the official price was boosted to $42.22 an ounce. Since the collapse of the Bretton Woods system of fixed exchange rates, the dollar has fluctuated in foreign exchange value under a system of "managed" float. Gold has gyrated in price vis-à-vis the dollar, but the dollar has implicitly exhibited further devaluation, despite the absence of change in the legal value.

After the practical ties with gold were all virtually severed, the legal right of private ownership of gold was restored on December 31, 1974, gold (or other value-maintenance) clauses were legalized in 1977, and the Gold Bullion Act of 1985 authorized the striking of gold coins, chiefly as a competitive alternative to foreign bullion coins. The issuance of nine-tenths fine silver coins was terminated in the 1960s, when the market value of the silver in the coins exceeded their face value—the silver coins were not nationalized, but instead prominent speculators were rescued when the bubble later burst. Although several special coins have been struck recently as profit-seeking ventures, including a commemorative coin to honor the Congress (but no companion coins honoring the executive or judicial branches), gold and silver have become items of inflation-hedging speculation, and the government has tied the nation's monetary system to its "bills of credit."

Gold Clause Cases

The four *Gold Clause Cases* were decided by the Supreme Court in 1935 on the basis of a 5 to 4 decision.[12] Two cases involved corporate obligations containing gold clauses. The Court ruled that the clauses were effectively nullified by the joint resolution. The third case related to a United States Fourth Liberty Bond Loan of 1918, which promised to pay "in United States gold coin of the present standard of value." The Court rejected the argument that the joint resolution broke the agreement, but since the holding of gold was unlawful, no appreciable damage resulted when payment on an equivalent basis was denied. The final case involved gold certificates. The Court ruled that if payment in gold had been made, the recipient would have been required to return this to the Treasury, so that he sustained no actual damages.[13]

Chief Justice Charles Evans Hughes delivered the opinion of the Court. He observed, first of all, that the rulings upholding gold clauses—e.g., *Bronson* v. *Rodes* (1869)—were made when gold was still in circulation and no act of Congress had prohibited the enforcement of those clauses.[14] In those cases, the distinction was made between gold, specie, or money. In contrast, wrote Hughes, "We are of the opinion that the gold clauses now before us were not contracts for payment in gold coin as a commodity, or in bullion, but were contracts for the payment of money."[15] Those contracts, Hughes continued, were presumably made in this form to protect against a depreciation of the currency, and at a time when they were not repugnant to any act of Congress. Thus, we should now consider the power and implications of the Congress to establish a monetary system, the power of Congress to invalidate existing contracts, and whether the clauses in question do in fact constitute such an interference with the power of Congress.

Hughes cited Marshall's view that the Constitution formed "A national government with sovereign powers," conferring to Congress an "aggregate" of powers over financial matters with a provision to make all laws "necessary and proper for carrying into execution" the enumerated powers. The Constitution was designed to provide for a uniform currency, and whatever power there is over the currency is vested in the Congress.[16]

Congress may invalidate existing contract provisions that interfere with the exercise of its constitutional authority:

> Contracts, however express, cannot fetter the constitutional authority of the Congress. . . . Parties cannot remove their transactions from the reach of dominant constitutional power by making contracts about them.[17]

Moreover, according to Hughes, the gold clauses do interfere with the monetary policy of the Congress. They are incompatible with the public interest to check the hoarding of gold and the exporting of capital, running counter to the Treasury's need to conserve its gold reserves.[18]

In conclusion, Hughes wrote:

> We are concerned with the constitutional power of the Congress over the monetary system of the country and its attempted frustration. Exercising that power, the Congress has undertaken to establish a uniform currency, and parity between kinds of currency, and to make that currency, dollar for dollar, legal tender for the payment of debts. In the light of abundant experience, the Congress was entitled to choose such a uniform monetary system, and to reject a dual system, with respect to all obligations within the range of the exercise of its constitutional authority. The contention that those gold clauses are valid contracts and cannot be struck down proceeds upon the assumption that private parties, and States and municipalities, may make and enforce contracts which may limit that authority. Dismissing that untenable assumption, the facts must be faced. We think that it is clearly shown that these clauses interfere with the exertion of the power granted to the Congress and certainly it is not established that the

Congress arbitrarily or capriciously decided that such an interference existed.[19]

In *Perry* v. *United States* (1935), the Court addressed the matter of gold clauses in obligations of the Treasury, as the Congress exercised its power to borrow money on the credit of the United States. Citing *Ling Su Fan* v. *United States* (1910), Hughes noted that despite the ownership of coins, there are attached limitations that public policy may require as a result of their qualities as a legal tender and medium of exchange. Public law gives to such coinage a value beyond their intrinsic value, and the impression of the sovereign power fixes their value and authorizes their use in exchange. The holder of a Treasury obligation, however, has no better case than the holder of gold coins.[20] The claim that the plaintiff is entitled to one dollar and sixty-nine cents in present currency for every dollar promised is simply untenable.[21]

In concurring, Justice Harlan Fiske Stone concluded:

> I therefore do not join in so much of the opinion as may be taken to suggest that the exercise of the sovereign power to borrow on credit, which does not override the sovereign immunity of suit, may nevertheless preclude or impede the exercise of another sovereign power, to regulate the value of money; or to suggest that although there is and can be no present cause of action upon the repudiated gold clause, its obligation is nevertheless, in some manner and to some extent, not stated, superior to the power to regulate the currency which we now hold to be superior to the obligation of the bond.[22]

The Court ruled, then, that the obligations of the United States could not be repudiated as such by legislation, but there were no proven damages as Congress has the power to regulate the value of the nation's money.

Dissenting Opinion

Justice James C. McReynolds wrote the dissenting opinion on the four *Gold Clause Cases* on behalf of the "Four Horsemen," including himself, who steadfastly resisted the New Deal legislation. That minority was usually joined by another colleague (typically Justice Owen J. Roberts) in rejecting those measures, which helped to precipitate the President's plan to "pack" the Court. The attack on the "institutional integrity of the Court" provoked a strong reaction against the plan but the crisis subsided when in the same year Justice Roberts aligned his opinions with those supportive of New Deal reforms.[23] The *Gold Clause Cases*, of course, were decided before the Court-packing episode, and the decision upheld the administration's initiatives.

Justice McReynolds concluded that "enactments here challenged will bring about confiscation of property rights, and repudiation of national obligations"[24]—McReynolds's commentary on his opinion was published in the *Wall Street Journal*.[25] He prefaced his remarks, however, with a statement that he was not about to challenge the power of Congress to adopt a proper monetary policy. While alluding to the *Legal Tender Cases*, decided with a "strong dissent," he suggested that to reopen "any abstract discussion of Congressional power over money would only tend to befog the real issue."[26]

McReynolds saw no constitutional basis for the destruction of gold clauses:

> Just men regard repudiation and spoliation of citizens by their sovereign with abhorrence; but we are asked to affirm that the Constitution has granted power to accomplish both. No definite delegation of such a power exists; and we cannot believe the farseeing framers, who labored with hope of establishing justice and securing the blessings of liberty, intended that the expected government should have authority to annihilate its own obligations and destroy the very rights which they were endeavoring to protect. Not only is there no permission for such actions; they are inhibited. And no plenitude of words can conform them to our charter.[27]

McReynolds alluded to the employment of the clauses for more than one hundred years, the sale of bonds for billions of dollars to support World War I, the issuance of bonds as late as May 2, 1933, with the solemn promise to pay in standard gold coin, and interpretations of the Permanent Court of International Justice upholding gold clauses.

The doctrine applied by the minority of the Court was drawn from an earlier case, where the clauses were understood to protect against currency depreciation against the standard gold coin containing 25.8 grains to the dollar or the currency value of that number of grains, which could be easily calculated on the basis of the devalued dollar.

McReynolds observed:

> The fundamental problem now presented is whether recent statutes passed by Congress in respect of money and credits, were designed to attain a legitimate end. Or whether, under the guise of pursuing a monetary policy, Congress really has inaugurated a plan primarily designed to destroy private obligations, repudiate national debts and drive into the Treasury all gold within the country, in exchange for inconvertible promises to pay, of much less value.

> Considering all the circumstances, we must conclude they show that the plan disclosed is of the latter description and its enforcement would deprive the parties before us of their rights under the Constitution. Consequently, the Court should do what it can to afford adequate relief.[28]

In reciting the history of U.S. currency, McReynolds referred to the 6 percent devaluation of 1834, to balance the exchange values between gold and silver, which generated no apparent profit to the Treasury and no injury to creditors, and to the legal tender issues under a "great emergency," when a return to specie payments was expected and no attempt was made to make "paper a standard of value." But despite Fifth Amendment protection:

> We are dealing here with a debased standard, adopted with the definite purpose to destroy obligations. Such arbitrary and oppressive action is not within any congressional power heretofore recognized. . . .[29]

> Under the challenged statutes it is said the United States have realized profits amounting to $2,800,000,000. But this assumes that gain may be generated by legislative fiat. To such counterfeit profits there would be no limit; with each new debasement of the dollar they

would expand. Two billion might be ballooned indefinitely—to twenty, thirty, or what you will.[30]

McReynolds seems to have identified the administration's motives and the injustice in its repudiation of the government's own obligations. While confirming the power of the Congress to manage money in an arbitrary fashion, the blocking of windfall gains in order to prevent politically undesirable redistributive effects did little to engender confidence in the administration's management of the economy and monetary affairs.

Emergency Currency

The Great Depression was also accompanied by an enormous increase in the demand for currency, which provided liquidity, a high implicit return, when commodities prices were falling, and safety, with massive bank failures and defaults on debt obligations. The ingenuity of the public was expressed in the issuance of about $1 billion in scrip.[31] While the issuance of scrip exemplifies the failure of public policies, it underscores the point that the power of the Congress over money is limited, in this case by the public's willingness to conduct business with substitutes for the official medium of exchange, despite the government's claims of authority and the concurring opinions of the Supreme Court.

Scrip was issued by "unemployed groups, municipalities, merchants associations, chambers of commerce, companies, boards of education, and others."[32] Clearinghouse certificates did not play as significant a role as they had earlier with roughly $34 million actually issued. While some $660 million had been authorized, most of the certificates were withheld from use because of legislation creating an emergency government issue of currency, the Federal Reserve bank notes, of which $209 million were issued.

Some early scrip issues were barter and trade certificates of organizations for unemployed persons. In January 1933 there were an estimated 140 such organizations with over one million persons using barter and scrip. The National Development Association of Salt Lake City, Utah, operated eighteen branches in six states. Persons provided services or commodities in exchange for scrip. The association also provided educational, social, and recreational activities for its members. Another successful effort was managed by Organized Unemployed, Inc., of Minneapolis, Minnesota. Vernon L. Brown offers the following description of its operations:

> In order to carry on the activities of the group, scrip was issued which was backed by the property of the organization. With the use of scrip it operated a retail store, shoemaker store, restaurant, wood-cutting projects, clothing factory, and canned thousands of quarts of fruits and vegetables to feed its members. . . . The organization was practically self-supporting and furnished employment for over 300 persons. The group was in existence for three years, 1932–35, and during this period over $150,000 worth of scrip was placed in circulation. Of this amount $16,000 was never presented for redemption, as the final issue was called as of June 30, 1935. It ceased operations because its activities had been curtailed, due to the inflow of Federal funds, its members securing work on W.P.A. and C.W.A. projects.[33]

Much of the scrip can be dated with the "bank holiday" of March 1933. When the banks were closed, many companies issued scrip in the form of checks or promissory notes to their employees. The scrip was accepted by businesses and it was generally redeemable in three to ten days A.B.H., "After Bank Holiday." Before the closing of the banks, many local governments fell under financial stress because of bank failures, ebbing revenues, and weakened borrowing capacity. In response they issued their own scrip. After the bank holiday, most of their scrip was tax anticipation notes, some of which were interest bearing.[34]

Two types of scrip were designed to quicken the velocity of money. "Prosperity checks" were issued by the Pajaro Valley National Bank of Watsonville, California, apparently in response to President Herbert Hoover's appeal to the nation to stop hoarding money. The checks measured 7 by 15 inches and had seventy spaces for endorsements. The check was supposed to be used for purchases within twenty-four hours. It could be presented for redemption after accumulating seventy signatures. A more important innovation was stamped scrip, which was issued in about one hundred communities.[35]

Stamped money attracted illustrious supporters, but it was only introduced by small communities as a type of scrip. John Maynard Keynes, who was sympathetic to the notion of stamped money, reviewed briefly in *The General Theory* the work of Silvio Gesell and alluded to Gesell's stamped money proposal[36]— that is, the requirement that stamps be purchased and affixed periodically to paper currency in order for it to retain its value in exchange. This represents what Irving Fisher has described as "a sort of ambulatory tax."[37]

Fisher had sufficient confidence in stamped money to assert that "There is one measure little known as yet, but which, I believe, is destined soon to command nation-wide attention, which might bring us substantially out of the depression, if properly applied, in a few weeks."[38] Fisher reviews the history, nature, and prospects for stamped money in his book *Stamp Scrip*. The first issue of stamped scrip in the United States was apparently in Hawarden, Iowa, in October 1932. Fisher visited Hawarden and describes in his book several other known experiments.[39] A proposal for the issuance of $1 billion of legal tender, stamped scrip was contained in the Bankhead-Pettengill Bill, but no such currency was issued by the U.S. government.[40]

Private currency issues again served a supportive function during a financial emergency, reflecting the ingenuity of the public and the distress of the times. While the private sector exercised its power to issue currency, it seems baffling that public policies in supplying currency were so tentative, unresponsive, or insensitive to those financial conditions. The federal government did tolerate the private ventures, and wisely so, and they illustrate again the public's receptivity to private money issues and provide evidence of the parallel circulation of monies of varying origin. Under inflation, we have seen some gold bullion coins of private mintage, but the hedges have been primarily conventional.

Inflation Overview

Under the Constitution the Congress regulated the value of gold coins and maintained the fundamental position of gold within the financial system for nearly 150 years. The money supply ultimately depended on the supply of gold, and the price level adjusted accordingly. The money supply and prices fluctuated widely in the short run, as private money creation and private and government departures from gold periodically interrupted the governing role of the gold market. While recurring episodes of inflation and deflation punctuated those years, the price level was remarkably stable over extended periods of time. Once the linkage with gold was severed, the ensuing fiduciary standard has sustained inflation over the past half-century, with the consumer price index increasing by a factor of eight (a 4.2 percent annual rate).

This price record requires further elaboration, however. The wholesale price index in early 1933, indeed, stood at the same level as recorded in the late 1780s.[41] The index was also at roughly that level prior to World War I, but the immediate postwar correction was incomplete, and prices fluctuated narrowly during the remainder of the 1920s. As economic activity contracted from 1929 to 1933, prices fell steeply, effectively completing the correction for World War I. The attempt to restore prewar gold parities may have been instrumental in deepening the depression. The severity of the contraction in the early 1930s may very well have been alleviated, as Friedman and Schwartz contend,[42] but the price level probably would not have declined, at least not so dramatically.

Devaluation of the dollar in 1934 was followed by a price "reflation," and the price index reached the 1929 level early in World War II. The upswing in prices associated with World War

II was less dramatic compared to earlier wars, and there was essentially no postwar correction, or a depression, as the price level resumed its upward course. A similar pattern surrounded the Korean conflict, and inflation was very mild for several years after the war. In retrospect, one would be hard-pressed to fault this record as excessively inflationary without considering the escape from a severe deflationary fallout. The focal point of criticism, of course, has been the role of the Federal Reserve in fomenting the "great contraction."

The removal of constraints imposed by gold reserves on monetary expansion, stepping beyond the earlier devaluation, nonetheless may have provided the latitude for policy to underwrite the inflationary spiral that emerged in the 1960s, as Arthur Burns contended. The "great inflation" eroded confidence in the government's resolve to maintain reasonable price stability, thus destroying the historic expectation of long-run stabilization of the price level.

Money and the Monetary Base

The historical evidence suggests that a stable price level in the long run depends on a slow, steady rate of growth in the monetary base, in agreement with Milton Friedman's constitutional prescription. The institutional transmission of its growth into growth in the money supply in general under the gold standard did not permit an enduring departure in those rates, and, concomitantly, in that for the price level. In a cyclical setting, in contrast, the institutional structure allowed considerable variance in the growth rates, as the volume of money built on the monetary base was subject to sizable fluctuations, and the monetary base varied cyclically as well. Institutional arrangements governed those rates of change, and they reflected a competing mixture of government controls and market forces.[43]

The money supply depends upon the behavior of market forces and institutional constraints imposed by laws and regulations. Under the gold standard, market forces largely determined the monetary base and the money supply, as the government, according to a "convertibility principle,"[44] set the legal price of gold and more or less abided by the "rules of the game." Under a fiduciary monetary regime, the government controls the monetary aggregates, but market forces often override regulations, limiting the government's control of the money supply.

The significance of the latter phenomenon is clearly illustrated by the recent U.S. monetary experience. Control of deposit ceilings and other regulations have been accompanied by market adjustments (and market-induced regulatory adjustments) to high, inflation-bloated interest rates, which have created new forms of money that display sensitivity to interest rates. As a result, such adjustments alter the relationship between the monetary base and the money supply, and between the money supply and GNP. Still, from the historical record one might suppose a tendency toward long-run stabilization; however, should government regulations and private innovations continue to change the institutional framework, the above linkage would remain loose. As a result, monetary rules, such as the Friedman prescription, could soon prove to be unreliable as a stabilizing performance standard. Had a monetary rule been adopted twenty years ago, many of those changes in the monetary system would not have occurred, but the technology of payments practices would still have altered the institutional setting.

Between 1914 and 1960, the period studied by Friedman and Schwartz, the monetary base (now including Federal Reserve notes and deposits as well as Treasury currency) expanded at a 5.9 percent rate, identical to the growth in nominal GNP. This fidelity agrees with the close tracking of these two measures in earlier periods. In the subsequent period, 1960–85, in contrast, GNP expanded at a rate (8.5 percent) some 1.8 percentage points faster than the monetary base (6.7 percent). The M2 concept of the money supply grew in both periods at rates comparable to GNP, and the M1 concept of the money supply expanded at rates comparable to the monetary base. The differentials in growth rates observed for the most recent period reflect the institutional changes alluded to earlier, as the "velocities" of the monetary base and M1 incorporate the effects of new money forms having lower (or essentially no) reserve requirements. Such institutional changes imply a revision of the appropriate concept of the money, as they undermine the reliability of the monetary base as a stabilizing, intermediate policy target.

The banking system was vastly overextended on its reserve base in 1929, even if we suppose that the Federal Reserve took steps to precipitate a one-third contraction in the money supply.[45] The monetary base actually increased from 1929 to 1933,[46] which coincides with the earlier experience as well. That is, changes in the size of the monetary base corresponded little to cyclical variability in the money supply and in real GNP over the history prior to the advent of the Federal Reserve System.

Money, Prices, and Economic Activity

The Federal Reserve, in contrast to the immediately preceding market-oriented regime, has carried out policies consistent with long-run inflation.[47] Between 1914 and 1960, faster monetary expansion was accompanied by inflation, with the wholesale price index climbing at a 2.2 percent rate, but economic growth proceeded at a moderate, 3.2 percent rate. The internal consistency of the various growth rates, cited here and above, seems remarkable in a period spanning World War I, the Great Depression, World War II, and the Korean War, along with dramatic changes in the monetary standard and banking practices. Nonetheless, this period would seem to be at best a weak test of the Federal Reserve's effectiveness in managing monetary policy. While this is certainly not to dismiss the central bank's complicity in deepening the depression in the 1930s, the other developments cited above, the lack of clear "independence" of the monetary authority, and the observation above that the results could have been worse suggest that the appropriate test would apply to more recent history.

From 1960 to 1985 the Federal Reserve conducted policies

compatible with substantially higher inflation than had been experienced earlier. The monetary base and the money supply expanded at highly inflationary rates, while real GNP slowed to a 3.1 percent rate. The wholesale price index advanced at a 4.8 percent rate (5.3 percent for the consumer price index). The economy was subjected to inflation sufficiently high that restraint in managing the monetary base would no doubt have moderated its tempo. Another dimension in the analysis, however, is the variability of the measures of economic performance.

The 1960–85 period might be characterized as the Federal Reserve note era, in contrasting performance, as in earlier chapters, with the periods 1840–61, the state bank note era, and 1889–1914, the national bank note era. The Federal Reserve presided over a serious acceleration of inflation, of course, in contrast to earlier periods of essential long-run price stability, as monetary growth was much higher. In terms of variability, however, the money supply and GNP (both real and nominal) fluctuated much less. Prices exhibited about the same variability.

Variations in the monetary base under the gold standard exceeded decidedly those experienced under the Federal Reserve System. For those earlier years, however, the money supply and the monetary base were not significantly correlated. During the 1960–85 period, the monetary base fluctuated a moderate 1.9 percentage points, but year-to-year variations in the two monetary aggregates were relatively highly correlated when the monetary base was assigned a one-year lag.

The state bank note era, as expected, produced substantial variability in the money supply. Fluctuations in the money supply were markedly less from 1889 to 1914. Under generally accelerating inflation since 1960, the Federal Reserve has conducted policies compatible with moderate year-to-year variations in monetary growth. Nonetheless, a clear procyclical pattern is evident, with a lead of roughly a year at cyclical peaks, for both the money supply and the monetary base, as both supported steepening inflation.

The linkage between the monetary base and current-dollar

GNP was essentially absent during the earlier periods; that is, variations in the monetary base were sufficiently irregular that they were not transmitted to GNP on a year-to-year basis. While the monetary base has not fluctuated so much in recent years, its variations do correlate with GNP. These results agree with the observed procyclical pattern for the monetary base and the contention that discretionary powers exercised in the management of the monetary base have been employed to contain cyclical swings in interest rates. Perfectly stable growth in the monetary base, of course, would not be correlated with year-to-year changes in GNP.

The correlation of GNP and the money supply produces more striking results. The results are nearly the same for each period, although—perhaps reflecting the loosening of the linkage attributable to institutional change—they are slightly lower for the recent period. They were significant for very different reasons. The banking system must have accommodated expanding demand for credit and therefore enhanced the cyclical amplitude of economic activity during both the 1840–61 and the 1889–1914 periods. For the 1960–85 period, in contrast, the banking system, or even more broadly the private financial system, and the Federal Reserve, given the correlation of the money supply and the monetary base, jointly accommodated cyclical fluctuations in economic activity.

Beginning in October 1979 the Federal Reserve instituted an orthodox anti-inflationary policy by sharply decelerating the rate of monetary expansion. Two successive recessions, with the second terminating in November 1982, as the deepest since World War II, created sufficient slack in the economy to decelerate the pace of inflation.[48] The U.S. monetary policy, moreover, was coordinated with monetary stringency maintained by other major industrial countries and accompanied by growth-retarding debt burdens of the less developed countries. Now, however, the Federal Reserve is being subjected to intense political pressure to accommodate the nation's debt overhang by implementing policies that could once again accelerate the rate of inflation.

The stability of the banking system since the 1930s—although that quality is being severely tested—probably reflects in part deposit insurance in checking the susceptibility of fractional reserve banking to financial panics. "Lender of last resort" rescue efforts for tottering corporations have limited destabilizing credit crunches as well—with special efforts undertaken to rescue silver speculators. Beyond that, demand management policies have sustained a reasonably high level of economic activity by shifting abruptly in an expansive direction once the economy begins to falter seriously. Given the absence of impediments, expansive policies have not been offset by generalized deflation, thus generating chronic inflation. Thus, long-run price stability has been sacrificed in order to achieve less short-run instability. The record has been unsatisfactory, but the trade-off is generally considered to be an improvement over the earlier monetary regimes. Reduced economic instability, of course, could reflect factors other than monetary policy, and it could have been achieved with a lower growth rate; however, these conditions clearly do not consider the muffled impact of the banking system on the economy.

Conclusion

The Federal Reserve in the early 1930s clearly failed miserably in carrying out its mission to check financial panics. Instead of dismantling the central bank, the gold standard, as a governing force on the level of prices, was dismantled. In a set of emergency measures asserting the government's monetary authority, the Congress acquiesced to the administration's plan to "reflate" the price level. The government nationalized private gold holdings, renounced its gold contractual commitments, and nullified private gold-clause contracts. The cutting of the monetary linkages with gold was upheld in a Scottish orphan's defense by the Supreme Court by a one-vote margin. In the process, however, the Court recognized that the nation's monetary authority rested fully in the hands of the Congress.

Private money again partially filled the void left by the severe contraction in the money supply, as an expression of market ingenuity and the receptivity of the public to private money.

In the absence of market restraints on the issuance of money, the Federal Reserve has underwritten chronic inflation, but in recent years money and economic activity have experienced less instability. The performance record remains unsatisfactory, yet the proposals for improving on the record scarcely seem to promise any better results, as described in the next chapter.

Notes

1. "The Federal Reserve System: An Address by United States Senator Carter Glass before the Democratic Women's Luncheon Club of Philadelphia," April 12, 1923, p. 10.

2. Milton Friedman and Anna Jacobson Schwartz, *A Monetary History of the United States, 1867–1960* (Princeton, NJ: Princeton University Press, 1963), p. 11.

3. Ibid., p. 356.

4. Ibid., p. 11.

5. Hyman P. Minsky, *Can "It" Happen Again?: Essays on Instability and Finance* (Armonk, NY: M. E. Sharpe, 1982), pp. xiv–xvi.

6. Henry G. Manne and Roger LeRoy Miller, *Gold, Money and the Law* (Chicago: Aldine, 1975), pp. 23, 137, 145; and Eugene S. Klise, *Money and Banking*, 5th ed. (Cincinnati, OH: South-Western Publishing, 1972), pp. 76–84.

7. A banking crisis of enormous proportions was unfolding in the final days of the Hoover administration. Bank holidays were declared by governors in seventeen states and banks were closing in other states. Issues of scrip were widespread and emergency measures were being considered by the administration under the 1917 legislation. See William Manchester, "Excerpts from 'The Great Bank Holiday,' " in *Standard Catalog of Depression Scrip of the United States: The 1930s, Including Canada and Mexico*, ed. Ralph A. Mitchell and Neil Shafer (Iola, WI: Krause Publications, 1984), pp. 314–16. While the dimensions of the crisis are described by Manchester in terms of scrip and the policy response, the perspective from the Federal Reserve Bank of New York is given by its president, George L. Harrison:

> We shall never forget the first three days of March in the Federal Reserve Bank of New York. On Wednesday, March 1, in the bank alone, we paid out $51,000,000 of currency to our member banks; on March 2 it was $80,000,000; on March 3 it was $176,000,000. On the last day, March 3, we also lost $78,000,000 through gold exports and earmarking. In addition, the public

crowded into our bank corridors to withdraw gold. In those three days, they carried off in bags, in suitcases, and in their pockets over $100,000,000 in gold coin and certificates. ("Some Essentials of Monetary Stability," *Quarterly Review/Special Issue: 75th Anniversary* [May 1989], Federal Reserve Bank of New York, p. 18)

The banking holiday in the estimation of Friedman and Schwartz (*Monetary History*, p. 330) was a "cure" worse than the disease, and the crisis stemmed in part from the uncertainties spawned by the change in administrations. They conclude:

One would be hard put to it indeed to find a more dramatic example of how far the resul: of legislation can deviate from intention than the contrast between the earlier restrictions of payments [in U.S. financial history] and the banking holiday under the Federal Reserve System, set up largely to prevent their repetition.

8. Apparently about 50 percent of gold coin and 25 percent of gold certificate holdings of the public were not turned in to the Treasury by the January 17, 1934, deadline (Friedman and Schwartz, *Monetary History*, p. 464n). Private estimates still place the value of gold coins outstanding at $300 million (at the old parity). Much of the private holdings of gold certificates was apparently turned in after the January 1934 deadline. One future governor of the Federal Reserve Board retained possession of his 1889-s double eagle, and the volume of gold coins on the market in the early 1960s seems consistent with the Friedman-Schwartz analysis.

9. "The Thomas Amendment to the Agricultural Adjustment Act, May 12, 1933," in *Documentary History of Banking and Currency in the United States*, vol. 4, ed. Herman E. Krooss (New York: Chelsea House Publishers, 1969), p. 2718.

10. Louis M. Hacker, ed., *Major Documents in American Economic History*, vol. 2 (New York: D. Van Nostrand, 1961), p. 71.

11. Ibid., p. 72.

12. *Norman* v. *Baltimore & Ohio R. Co.* and *United States* v. *Bankers Trust Co.* (1935), 294 U.S., 240; *Nortz* v. *United States* (1935), 294 U.S., 317; and *Perry* v. *United States* (1935), 294 U.S., 330 (hereafter these four cases may be cited as *Gold Clause Cases*).

13. This summary reflects the opinion of Justice McReynolds (ibid., p. 369).

14. Ibid., p. 300.

15. Ibid., p. 302.

16. Ibid., p. 305.

17. Ibid., pp. 307–8.

18. Ibid., pp. 312–13.

19. Ibid., p. 316.

20. Ibid., p. 356.

21. Ibid., p. 358.

22. Ibid.

23. G. Edward White, *The American Judicial Tradition: Profiles of Leading American Judges* (Oxford: Oxford University Press, 1976), pp. 178–99.

24. *Gold Clause Cases*, p. 361.

25. *The Wall Street Journal,* February 23, 1935, pp. 1–2.

26. *Gold Clause Cases*, p. 369.

27. Ibid., p. 362.

28. Ibid., pp. 369–70.

29. Ibid., p. 372.

30. Ibid., p. 381.

31. H. Parker Willis and John M. Chapman, *The Banking Situation* (New York: Columbia University Press, 1934), p. 15.

32. Ralph A. Mitchell and Charles V. Kappan, "Depression Scrip of the U.S.: A Catalog, Period of the 30s," *Calcoin News 12, 2 (March 1958): 33–36; and Mitchell and Shafer, Standard Catalog of Depression Scrip.* An issue of stamped scrip by the Franklin Chamber of Commerce in Franklin, Indiana, depicts a border of swastikas, as illustrated on p. 78 in the latter publication.

V. L. Brown reports that:

> In the Chase Bank's Collection there are over 2,000 specimens of scrip issued during the years 1931 to 1934. It is believed to be one of the most complete collections of recent-day emergency currency ever brought together, as there is scrip from over 500 communities, representing 48 States, the District of Columbia, and the Territory of Hawaii. In the collection are about 600 different varieties, including scrip printed on wood, sheepskin, buckskin, leather, fishskin, aluminum, and clam shell. (V. L. Brown, "Emergency Currency," in American Numismatic Association, *Selections from the Numismatist: United States Paper Money, Tokens, Medals, and Miscellaneous* [Racine, WI: Whitman Publishing, 1960], p. 192)

33. Brown, "Emergency Currency," p. 194.

34. Ibid., pp. 191–92.

35. Ibid., pp. 192–93.

36. John Maynard Keynes, *The General Theory of Employment, Interest and Money* (New York: Harcourt, Brace & World, 1936), pp. 353–58. Keynes viewed stamped money as a device to reduce the return on money and concomitantly to serve as an escape route from a liquidity trap:

> According to my theory [the cost of stamps] should be roughly equal to the excess of the money-rate of interest (apart from the stamps) over the marginal efficiency of capital corresponding to a rate of new investment compatible with full employment. (P. 357)

Keynes qualified his enthusiasm for stamped money, however:

> The idea behind stamped money is sound. It is, indeed, possible that means might be found to apply it in practice on a modest scale. But there are many difficulties which Gesell did not face. In particular, he was unaware that money was not unique in having a liquidity-premium attached to it, but differed only in degree from many other articles, deriving its importance from having a *greater* liquidity premium than any other article. Thus if currency notes were to be deprived of their liquidity-premium by the stamping system, a

long series of substitutes would step into their shoes—bank money, debts at call, foreign money, jewelery and the precious metals generally, and so forth. (Pp. 357–58)

Keynes was apparently unaware of the actual experiments with stamped scrip on a modest scale.

Gesell, writing before the Great Depression, advanced his stamped money proposal to check massive currency hoarding, which he supposed was the cause of severe contractions in economic activity (see *The Natural Economic Order: Money Part* [San Antonio, TX: Free-Economy Publishing, 1934]). Gesell observed that money (i.e., currency) served as a medium of saving, because it is "indestructible" while goods deteriorate in value, and as a medium of exchange (pp. 8–9, 136). He sought to nullify the former function. The state, he reasoned, could temporarily stimulate the economy with an infusion of new money, but interest rates would fall. A decline in interest paid by savings banks would cause currency holdings to increase, thus depriving the economy of money required to support economic activity. Increases in the money supply are consequently offset by decreases in velocity through hoarding in a type of "liquidity trap" (pp. 116–17).

Gesell argued that one component of interest, "basic interest," arises from the hoardable quality of money. Basic interest, then, is the charge levied by owners of money for its use in exchange, and it is limited by the differential in efficiency between money and the substitutes for money. Stamped money, according to Gesell, would transform money into a pure medium of exchange, thus eliminating basic interest and creating "Free-Money."

Gesell served in 1919 as Minister of Finance in a short-lived socialist government of Bavaria, where the stamped money plan was soon launched as a private venture. Stamped scrip gained attention in 1931 when it was placed into circulation in Schwanenkirchen, Bavaria, but, due to a fear of inflation, its issuance was shortly prohibited by the government of Germany. Stamped scrip was used in Woergl, Austria, in 1932 (Irving Fisher, *Stamp Scrip* [New York: Adelphi, 1933], pp. 17–29).

37. Ibid., p. 11.

38. Irving Fisher, "The Stamp Scrip Plan," *The New Republic* 73 (December 21, 1932): 163.

39. Fisher, *Stamp Scrip*, pp. 30–34; Mitchell and Kappan, "Depression Scrip," *Calcoin News* 12, 2 (March 1958) to *Calcoin News* 15, 4 (February 1961).

40. Fisher, *Stamp Scrip*, pp. 79–83. The $1,000,000,000 of legal tender stamped money certificates proposed in the Bankhead-Pettengill Bill were to be issued in $1 denomination with a provision for fifty-two two-cent stamps to be affixed to each certificate (one each week). The bill provided for discontinuation of the program when the wholesale price index reached 80 percent of its average standing in 1926 ("H.R. 14757," in Mitchell and Shafer, *Depression Scrip of the United States*, p. 311).

41. George F. Warren and Frank A. Pearson, *Gold and Prices* (New York: John Wiley, 1935), pp. 12–14.

42. Friedman and Schwartz, *Monetary History*, pp. 299–419.

43. For references and data sources, refer to chapter 7, note 68.

44. Axel Leijonhufvud, "Constitutional Constraints on the Monetary Powers of Government," in *The Search for Stable Money: Essays on Monetary Reform*, ed. James A. Dorn and Anna J. Schwartz (Chicago: University of Chicago Press, 1987), p. 136.

45. Friedman and Schwartz, *Monetary History*, pp. 712–14.

46. Ibid., pp. 803–4.

47. The British experience essentially coincides with the American record. From the establishment of the Bank of England in 1694 until the beginning of the Napoleonic Wars in 1793, when the government usurped control of the money supply, the average annual rate of inflation was a mere 0.01 percent. In 1821, the government returned control of the money supply to the Bank, and the Bank established an official gold standard. Between 1822 and 1913, the privately controlled Bank presided over a rate of inflation of 0.42 percent that was again statistically indistinguishable from zero. By 1931, the government had once again seized control of the money supply. Since then, the annual inflation rate has run at 6.47 percent—6.87 percent from 1946 to 1982, excluding the depression and World War II (G. J. Santoni, "A Private Central Bank: Some Olde English Lessons," *Review*, Federal Reserve Bank of St. Louis, 66, 4 [April 1984]: 19).

48. Martin Spechler's historical study of severe inflations concludes that neither a gradual winding down of inflation, aided by incomes policy, nor supply enhancements work to calm inflation, but that an orthodox, determined monetary shock seems necessary to set the economy on a disinflationary track. Such orthodox treatment will be accompanied by increased unemployment and by an effective confiscation of financial assets through this process. The redistributive effects are also consistent with another theme running through this book, as severe inflations also bring a spontaneous replacement of the national currency by gold-backed, commodity, or token money (Martin C. Spechler, "Ending Big Inflations: Lessons from Comparative European Economic History," paper presented at the Allied Social Science Associations meeting, New York City, December 1985, pp. 30–33).

CHAPTER 12

A Supreme Court of Finance

Conceptualization of the Federal Reserve Board as a Supreme Court of Finance is an obvious allusion to the U.S. Supreme Court and its independent status as a branch within the federal government. Appointment of the governors of the Federal Reserve System to fourteen-year terms clearly provides a certain independence in setting monetary policy, approaching comparability to the life appointment of the Supreme Court justices. Many decry the power wielded by the unelected board, and some of the same sentiments are expressed in the lack of democratic sensitivities of the Court. Given its constitutional standing, few seem prepared to argue that the Court should be subordinated to the Justice Department. The Court's independent status, of course, is solidly institutionalized, but few commentators seem aware of the long tradition of an independent monetary authority, running from Alexander Hamilton to Carter Glass in the formation of U.S. central banks, as developed in the preceding chapters, and its institutional character now recognized in the independent status of the Federal Reserve. The Federal Reserve is very different, however, because it operates within the boundary of the laws passed by Congress, while the Supreme Court decides if the acts of Congress are consonant with the Constitution.[1]

The constitutional interpretation of the monetary powers has evolved from a restricted role for the federal government provided by the express language of the document to a lifting of monetary powers to a plenary status. Within this setting, an independent monetary authority represents a historical compromise between full assumption of the monetary powers by the Congress and a concern that such authority risks serious inflation and politicization of the policy process. A certain tension has existed as well between assuming those powers and allowing market determination of money, income, and the level of prices. Congress has circumscribed the role of markets, but a preference for some market determination has prevailed along with independence of the monetary authority. Indeed, the extent to which the Congress should rely on market processes largely characterizes the policy debate today on regulation/deregulation of the financial services industry.

We might suppose that Congress envisions a structure of the monetary system that fits into our nation's concept of a representative democracy, despite any prerogatives of sovereignty. Self-restraint exercised by the Congress does not suppose that in some way the legislature fails to meet its obligations by preferring to maintain independence of the Federal Reserve System or by allowing banks to create money. Irving Fisher argued, for example, that absolute control of the money supply is a "prerogative of government," and that "Virtually, if not literally, every checking bank coins money, and the banks, as a whole, regulate, control, or influence the volume of money."[2] To Fisher, such private power encroached on the constitutional power of the Congress. The Congress, however, may choose to employ its powers to allow such private practices, recognizing a reasonable zone of authority in its exercise of self-restraint.

This chapter summarizes the foregoing chapters, focusing on the exercise of self-restraint by the Congress, in particular the independence of the Federal Reserve System, and the transition in constitutional interpretation, so that the Congress presumably holds the sovereign powers to control the nation's money supply. This chapter also serves as a point of convergence, where the power of the Congress to establish a central bank, defined earlier in the nation's history under the Constitution, and the power to control a fiduciary currency, defined by the *Legal Tender Cases* and solidified by the *Gold Clause Cases*, come together in the form of the Federal Reserve System.

Transition in Constitutional Interpretation

The emergence of sovereignty as a rationale for the expansive interpretation of the Constitution's monetary powers, despite the history and language of the relevant provisions, raises questions regarding the reason for this interpretive mode and what might be considered a broadly grounded basis for this transition in constitutional interpretation. The prerogatives of sovereignty were mentioned in decisions along with an aggregate of expressly delegated powers, in addition to the enabling "necessary and proper" clause, in sanctioning the exercise of monetary powers by the Congress. It would seem that in general the Court was willing to defer to the Congress on monetary matters in recognition of the public sentiment represented by the Congress itself. The exigencies to which the Congress responded made it difficult for the Court to unwind established practices, upon which precedent allowed further steps beyond the express language of the Constitution. The ballot box and market ingenuity serve, then, as enforcement mechanisms in governing self-restraint by the Congress within, we would trust, the confines of a society governed as a representative democracy.

The legitimacy of the current exercise of monetary powers by the Congress cannot be found in the express language of the Constitution; that legitimacy is simply a recognition of years of practice under Congress as representative of the people. The Civil War, with the advent of legal tender paper money, was no doubt a critical factor in drawing broader implications from the Constitution, as the courts sanctioned those attributes that marked the supremacy of the "National Union." The Civil War, then, brought to the Congress the authority to preside over the nation's currency as an expression of sovereign powers.

A. Barton Hepburn summarized historian George Bancroft's views on sovereign powers:

> [T]he dictum that the federal government had sovereign powers [was] to be revolutionary. Its powers were clearly limited. It had no

inherent sovereignty, but only that delegated to it by the Constitution. European sovereignties had *not* the power of making notes legal tender.[3]

This view is consistent with Marshall's view of sovereignty, as seen earlier. In addition, Bancroft asserted that it was understood that the authority to issue legal tender notes was denied to the federal government:

> This is the interpretation of the clause, made at the time of its adoption alike by its authors and by its opponents, accepted by all the statesmen of that age, not open to dispute because [it was] too clear for argument, and never disputed so long as any one man who took part in framing the constitution remained alive.[4]

Agreeing with Bancroft that the framers had intended to prohibit the Congress from issuing an irredeemable, legal tender currency, monetary historian A. Barton Hepburn also commented on the matter of sovereignty:

> The question, which was paramount, state or nation, was an active issue until settled by the sword and sealed in favor of the nation, by the surrender at Appomattox. . . .

> [Thus,] the courts were left free to discriminate between what the framers of the Constitution had done and what they thought they had done. . . .

> The law of self-preservation construed the Constitution broadly as to the power of Congress over currency, in the interest of preserving the government.[5]

The denial of the restrictive language contained in the Constitution overlooks the opinions of Madison, Chase, and others, as well as the intent of the framers—Taney even referred to the monetary claims of sovereignty by the states.[6] If the language was indeed restrictive, no claims of sovereign power over the monetary system seem valid. That would constitute a novel construction, which is precisely what Bancroft maintained, contrary to the position that the claims of sovereignty were always present in the Constitution, even if held in a dormant state.

References to sovereignty should be troubling to those who take the language of the Constitution seriously. Such references involve a classification approach to constitutional interpretation, tantamount to the claims of laissez faire, "outside the four corners" of the document. As a tautology, this begs the question, as one wonders what are the claims of sovereignty. Invoking sovereignty, therefore, serves as an escape route from the Constitution's language and the intent of the framers, while leaving no legitimate role for market determination in the construction of a monetary system that comports with the political system ordained by the Constitution itself. Otherwise, we are left to sort out the competing claims of sovereignty and to inquire what other unenumerated powers of George III reside with the Congress.

Among the other, competing explanations of the transition in constitutional interpretation of the monetary powers, one could surmise that the bimetallic standard so adopted was not enshrined in the document but was recognized, respectable international practice. The appropriate domestic standard would then change to accommodate changes in international practices among other "civilized countries." Here again, the arguments are not rooted in the instrument itself, and in general, international practices were shunned in the writing and adoption of the Constitution.

The assertion that the Constitution should be interpreted to accommodate changes in the concepts of money, or the evolution of technology or payments practices, fails to acknowledge that the founding fathers were closely acquainted with legal tender paper money, commercial banks, and national banks. The words themselves did not change, nor did they mean something different—legal tender paper money was not first created in 1862, as it predates the Constitution, as is true of a wide range of monetary practices.

Likewise, the assertion that the Constitution is a "living" document invites free-ranging interpretation, sanctioning political interpretations that suggest the review of decisions by Attorney General Edwin Meese to assure their compliance with the views of a democratically elected President. While also ignoring the express language of the instrument, this approach is empty of content, and devalues the historical experience. Constitutional interpretation has obviously flowed with the current in forming the prevailing consensus and perhaps it was "inevitable" that the Court's opinions would uphold the expression of this consensus by the Congress. To claim that 4 to 3 and 5 to 4 decisions were inevitable may press the issue a little too much, but one should scarcely argue that what happened was anything but inevitable.

This discussion, then, recognizes a change in the interpretation of the monetary provisions, that that interpretation is not grounded on the language or intent of the framers, that the reference to sovereign powers does not rest on solid ground, and that certain other interpretive modes seem inappropriate. Nonetheless, the monetary powers of the Congress are firmly grounded in a series of judicial decisions over a long history that gives a legitimacy to those claims of plenary power, although bounded by disciplining factors.

Alternative Explanations of this Transition

It might be informative to review how scholars in this field have bridged the gap between the express language of the Constitution and the prevailing exercise of the government's monetary powers.

Bray Hammond acknowledges that the expressed prohibitions of the state issues of bills of credit, declaring anything but gold and silver a legal tender, and the impairment of contracts were intended to apply to the federal government, as the latter was conferred only those powers specifically granted to it.[7] As transitional sentences, Hammond contrasts his earlier view, above, with the following discussion:

> I considered them in light of conditions and purposes coeval with their composition. But since the Constitution is the continuing basic law of the land, its meaning is a matter of jurisprudence; it means what the courts say it does, and the courts can not be merely historical when they pass judgment.[8]

The underlying rationale for the court's decisions, according to Hammond, ranges from an "act of sovereignty" to a reference to "the aggregate of powers" supported by the "necessary and proper" clause (not simply the monetary clauses) and buttressed in recent decades by invoking the commerce clause.[9] In offering such a rationale, the courts recognized certain changes in conditions, which Hammond cites in his comments on the decision in *Norman* v. *Baltimore and Ohio* (1935) and other cases:

> Those decisions removed whatever constitutional inhibition ever existed upon the power of Congress to authorize anything it wishes as money. Thus in the course of 150 years, changes in monetary and business habits, in governmental responsibilities, in statutes, and in jurisprudence have strengthened the Constitution's ban on issues of money by individual states but nullified completely the original intent that the federal government should have no power to make anything but the precious metals legal tender.[10]

This could be supposed a "calamity," according to Hammond, or, although wise at the time, a restraint that could not possibly endure.[11] While Hammond alludes to a number of bases for the changing interpretation of the monetary powers, suggested above, this argument would seem to be a balanced treatment of the constitutional transition, with which the author would largely concur.

Later in his book, however, Hammond offers some stronger, personal views: "In terms of the Constitution and of common sense, control of the monetary system irrefragably belonged to sovereignty,"[12] and "Jacksonian enterprisers deprived the federal government of its constitutional control over the monetary system,"[13] and Chase was initially moved "by the anomaly of a sovereign authority waging war in defense of its sovereignty without possessing that most ancient and elementary attribute of sovereignty—control of the monetary system."[14] The mainstream position, through Chase, clearly did not recognize those claims of sovereignty that, in their opinion, superseded constitutional principles, despite the supposed Hamiltonian tradition.

In contrast to the view of a historian, perspectives of the legal profession are offered by Gerald T. Dunne, who served as counsel to the Federal Reserve Bank of St. Louis, and James Willard Hurst, Vilas Professor of Law at the University of Wisconsin. As a matter of orientation, it should be noted that their readings of history differ sharply from Hammond's earlier perspective.

Dunne develops the theme that the money power is ultimately an attribute of sovereignty and that history moved ineluctably toward fulfillment of that claim, as stated in the *Case of the Mixed Moneys* (1604),[15] as the money power devolved to the Congress. In contrast to Hammond, Dunne emphasizes the absence of an outright prohibition of Congress's issuance of bills of credit, referring specifically to Randolph and Mason, in their preference not to tie the hands of Congress in unforeseen emergencies.[16] Randolph and Mason, of course, refused to sign the document, and they opposed the motion to strike that power, understanding that its approval would prohibit bills of credit.

In a position consistent with that taken on legal tender, Dunne also refers to the Convention's rejection of a proposal to forbid congressional impairment of contracts.[17] Thus, authority was not specifically granted but a proposal to deny the power was rejected. The power of Congress to grant charters of incorporation was also not approved, but in Dunne's estimation, the arguments were contradictory in terms whether, indeed, that power was already a matter of implication. In a similar vein, other money issues were not addressed at the convention, being perhaps too delicate for the framers to resolve.[18] Thus, Dunne supposes that powers not expressly prohibited were, in fact, granted.

Dunne then turns to Hamilton's proposal for a national bank as first a solution to the bills of credit "dilemma," which created a paper money under the authority of the United States but free of political control, and second a manner of achieving "its legitimacy." In Hamilton, Dunne finds the "legal basis of the transformation of monetary authority from a secondary to a plenary power."[19] This is derived, as Hamilton stated, "from the whole mass of the powers of the government and the nature of political society," and serves as a basis a century later for the Supreme

Court to validate the money power in its full magnitude.[20]

In the history of constitutional interpretation, according to Dunne, the "dilemma" often dodged rather than met, despite the arbitrary or capricious use of the monetary authority, was the "undeniable fact that monetary power was the power of a sovereign government; in the last analysis it must exist and can reside only there."[21] Dunne supposes that its existence means that it cannot be restrained by constitutional provision. So that "its abuse is simply irrelevant to the question of its existence."[22] The only check, in effect, is the ballot box, as the Court simply cannot provide protection given the fact that it can only act on cases brought before it, and as an appellate court, so that the passage of time effectively erases jurisdiction.[23] In short, the money power belongs to the Congress and the courts can offer no protection against any arbitrary exercise of that power.

Hurst also reviews the proceedings of the Constitutional Convention and reaches conclusions similar to Dunne's. He observes that the strict limitations on the states might well imply intent to give that power to the federal government—just the opposite of Hammond's interpretation—as "the framers put into the Constitution not a single explicit limit on what the Congress might do about money,"[24] such that "a fair inference might be that Congress should have a plenary authority over money as it had, for example, over the commerce among the states."[25] Following Hurst, no clear resolution was offered on paper money, legal tender, and chartering a bank. On paper money, Hurst concludes that the discussion was "clearly restrictive of federal authority to issue paper money," especially as a "regular constituent of the money supply," but ambiguities remain.[26] On legal tender, Hurst offers two arguments. First, "to coin money" implies legal tender to gold and silver, which is certainly the case. Second, the issuance of promissory notes "might well include authority to attach legal tender character to such government notes."[27] In this connection, however, Hurst misinterprets Madison, who suggested not attaching legal tender to notes, but that they might be issued devoid of legal tender standing. On chartering a bank, Hurst claims that "the convention left the matter ... fairly open to development in light of later experience,"[28] despite rejection of that power in the convention.

Hurst later summarizes his position:

> Within the standards set by the Constitution's language and the records left by those who formed and adopted that language, and within the scope which seventy-five years of political practice allowed for developing constitutional doctrine by legislative, executive, and judicial precedent, no formal change was required to accommodate the direct issue of government currency in national emergency, the chartering of national banks as agents of national governmental and economic goals, the preemption of the role of state-chartered banks in issuing currency, the resolution of the place of gold and silver in national patterns of money notation and value, or the subjection of past or future market transactions to the sovereign's power to fix the terms of a money system which was a necessary constituent of any market. The possible exception, where fair argument can be made that changes should have been by constitutional amendment, consists in the 1878 statute authorizing continuation and reissue of the United States notes in peacetime, to serve the regular needs of the economy, and the Court's validation of that statute in 1884.[29]

In Hurst's judgment, this statute did not lie in the realm incorporating the "necessary and proper" clause, "a realm in which our practice firmly legitimates growth by legislative and judicial precedent," in pressing our "informal practice of constitutional amendment to its limit," but perhaps not beyond that limit, in light of the "indicated constitutional intent that the national government fully control the system of money and that it enjoy broad authority to promote a truly national economy."[30]

The opinion of legal scholars may indeed accurately reflect the thinking of jurists today, but the claims of roots in the express language of the Constitution seem dubious. Court decisions, moreover, contain frequent allusions to sovereignty in the exercise of monetary powers by the Congress, but that too stands outside the document itself. An independent monetary authority does not conflict with any claims of sovereignty, however, as a sovereign power may choose to assign that authority to an independent body; otherwise it is not sovereign.

An Independent Monetary Authority

The Federal Reserve System is a much more powerful element in the U.S. financial system than could have been imagined when it was created, given the demise of the gold standard, and the central bank is indeed more centralized than the Balkanized structure adopted in 1913. The Federal Reserve is more responsive to the Congress, and perhaps less representative of the collective wisdom of the banking community. Its standing as an independent agency seems now to be well fortified, and consistent with a lengthy tradition of independence treated above.

The "independent" monetary authority, first of all, is not completely independent; it was created by and is accountable to the Congress. Its independence could be seen in three ways: (1) independence from the executive branch; (2) independence from the banking community and other private interests; and (3) independence within the boundaries drawn by laws, practices, and resolutions adopted by the Congress. We should expect, on the one hand, that independence carries responsibilities to remain judiciously free of influence from those constituencies, except within the legal framework that sets forth the Federal Reserve's policy objectives, as articulated, for example, in the Employment Act of 1946 and the Full Employment and Balanced Growth Act of 1978.[31] While disinterested in narrow partisan politics and private interests, the Federal Reserve, we should suppose, may very well share a coincidence of interests with those constituencies in serving its objectives, so that the communication of expectations and wishes should not be viewed as inappropriate. That, indeed, reflects the original structure of the organization: to entertain a plurality of opinions in formulating its policies in the public interest.

It has been argued that an independent monetary authority is tantamount to an independent Pentagon.[32] This clearly raises two constitutional issues related to separating the sword and the purse, a point of contention in the constitutional ratification debates. The President, not the Congress, is the commander-in-chief of the armed forces, a power limited, of course, by the authority of the Congress to appropriate funds and to declare war. The government's role in managing money, in contrast, is assigned to the Congress, not the President. Some commentators presume, of course, that the authority to control a politicized central bank should be vested in the President not the Congress, as Milton Friedman has contended. The Pentagon and the Federal Reserve System, moreover, are obviously very different entities, such that a politically "independent" central bank may be more responsive to the Congress than one closely governed by the President. Nonetheless, the arguments for an independent central bank under the authority of Congress are based on (1) the necessity of close acquaintance with developments in the economy and financial markets that the Congress simply does not possess; (2) the cacophony of views in the Congress; and (3) the lags between policy implementation and economic consequences, which would shift the costs of policy choices to the next generation (session) of policy makers (the Congress). Lest we forget, the purpose of an independent central bank is simply to reduce the chances of blatantly inflationary policies or the misuse of the bank for political motives, personal gains, or "constituent services."

International performance comparisons clearly indicate that independent central banks present a superior record in the management of a nation's currency. Statistical tests suggest that independent central banks conduct policies compatible with lower rates of inflation and tend to be less accommodative of budgetary deficits, thus exerting a disciplining force on fiscal policy.[33] As Chairman Martin once observed, "President Johnson might, indeed, have his Great Society, but he won't have a painless society," from which the listener could conclude that the Federal Reserve might not feel compelled to underwrite such venturesome fiscal policies.

Congress has frequently chided the chairman for advancing policies too closely aligned with the wishes of the presiding administration. The appointment process, of course, encourages that compatibility, at least to some extent. Whether Congress itself holds the power to appoint the governors would be a hard test of the separation of powers, despite any claims of Dunne and Hurst that the monetary powers reside with the Congress. The composition of the FOMC has been challenged, but remains intact.[34] (Prior to the Constitution, the Treasury came directly under the authority of the Congress, and some thought was given to that arrangement after the adoption of the Constitution[35]).

The Congress does not constitute a reasonable forum for the formulation of monetary policy and the committees scarcely seem equipped to manage monetary affairs, beyond setting guidelines and exercising oversight responsibilities. Congress has long recognized its incapacity to implement monetary policy, given the technical requirements of the task and the potential for abuse. While the Congress has seemed somewhat less inclined in recent decades to distrust itself, the role of critic seems more suitable than that of practitioner. Perhaps the risk of too intimate an association with monetary policy is best identified by Paul McCracken:

> If the Congress were to arrogate to itself more direct responsibility for monetary policy, the major immediate victims would be members of Congress. Central banks are usually most useful when least popular, and this would not seem to be a formula for longevity in that branch of government.[36]

Perhaps this explains why some Democrats in the Congress have favored the control of monetary policy by Republican secretaries of the Treasury, preferring Donald Regan over Paul Volcker, for example. There is no doubt that independence makes the accountability *of* the Congress somewhat nebulous, despite any assertions that there exists accountability *to* the Congress. This arrangement obviously blurs democratic sensitivities of policy, while protecting it from populist and other heresies. The Congress is just as politically sensitive as the administration, if not more so, but the Congress is an ongoing institution in a way that the administration is not. Long-run vision is scarcely an attribute of either, but the legislative process has clearly on monetary matters incorporated some sense of the long run. This attribute cannot be so easily identified among presidential administrations where the misuse of monetary policy would be more likely to occur, especially given the lags between an expansive policy and the adverse consequences.

Protection against Inflation

The best protection against inflation within a less unstable financial system would still seem to be found in the establishment of guidelines by the Congress for the implementation of policy by an independent monetary authority within a competitive market setting. The automatic long-run stabilizing qualities of a gold standard still seem to imply the transmission of financial market instability into the economy, a historically unsatisfactory trade-off for long-run price stability. Rules of a constitutional nature may also be destabilizing as the institutional setting evolves. Complete reliance on market determination of the money supply through a network of competing currencies—i.e., "free banking"—promises competitive alternatives to the government's money.[37] Thus, Continental Illinois may have issued its own "continentals" to compete with the Federal Reserve's currency. Actually, such competitive alternatives seem favorable, but whether such plans are workable outside the protective umbrella of government insurance of deposits is still questionable.

Certain policy changes would seem appropriate to reduce the appeal of inflationary policies and to offer the public further protection against inflation. A freer competitive situation would prevail if interest payments were allowed on all deposits, including bank reserves held by the Federal Reserve banks. The Federal Reserve might also be relieved of the duties to administer regulations designed to redistribute income—this is a fiscal policy matter that is not well managed through implicit transfers of income or wealth. This function obviously belongs to the executive branch. In any case, income redistribution statements and socially integrative statements should be required to accompany policies that convey implicit transfers. Indeed, stabilization policies imply stability in the distribution of income; redistributive flows emanating from monetary policy seem largely aggravated by such regulations.

Just as the New Deal banking regulations are being superseded by less confining regulations in a more competitive financial structure, so have laws governing private contracts and inflation-hedging devices become less restrictive. This is likely to prove more protective against inflation than political controls of the central bank, even though future exigencies may once again provoke the Congress to take action to close off these vehicles. That eventuality would seem remote at this time, however, as the Congress may feel constrained by history and by the fact that these devices would not be so clearly obstructive of the power of the Congress to regulate money. Thus, today private citizens have the right to buy gold and enter contracts providing gold clauses, contracts may have price indexation provisions, real interest rates are high and nominal interest rates are sensitive to inflation, and foreign currency holdings may be used to hedge against a depreciating dollar. With these protective devices, "free banking" is unlikely to offer additional protection and the gains to the government of inflationary policies are likely to be less attractive, even though in emergencies the private sector has been very receptive to private currency issues.

Summary

The transition in constitutional interpretation from the restrictive express language of the monetary provisions in the Constitution to a plenary status rests firmly on precedent, built on established practices, upheld by the courts, as well as recognition of the implied powers within the broad scope of that instrument and an aggregate of its express powers. Claims of any presumed attributes of sovereignty over money seem incompatible with the principles of government set forth in that document. Restraint in the exercise of monetary powers by the Congress is governed by market forces (including private substitutes for the government's money) and the political process. The Congress, of course, may choose to allow the existence of an "independent" monetary authority, one that conforms with the historical tradition, fits into the structure of the U.S. government, and presents a superior performance record among the fraternity of central banks. Protection of private interest rests on the political process and the use of a set of devices adaptive to any excessive inflationary bias in the policies managed by an "independent" central bank, that in a certain respect may eventually lay claims to being a Supreme Court of Finance.

The Federal Reserve does not coin money, nor do the powers exercised by the U.S. central bank rest on some supposed claim that it, in effect, coins money. Congress exercises that authority through the Department of the Treasury and its Bureau of the Mint. While serving a useful function, of course, that power has been substantially diminished by the Congress itself by the adoption of token coinage, from which profits are extracted and symbols of unity preserved. Yet, the Congress retains the power "to coin" money within the context given above, and it is this power that the Congress has wisely held beyond the reach of the one who wields the sword, but also, we trust, beyond the reach of those who might use it for sinister motives.

Notes

1. J. Laurence Laughlin, *The Federal Reserve Act: Its Origin and Problems* (New York: Macmillan, 1933), p. 216. Though he later questioned the validity of that comparison, the first such reference has been attributed to Laughlin:

[W]e must establish some institution wholly free from politics, or outside influence—as much respected for character and integrity as the supreme court—which shall be able, in a great emergency to use government bonds or selected securities, as a basis for the issue of forms of lawful money which could be added to the reserves of banks. (J. Laurence Laughlin, "Currency Reform," *Journal of Political Economy* 15 [January–December 1907], p. 609)

2. Irving Fisher, *100% Money* (New York: Adelphi, 1935), pp. 18–19.

3. A. Burton Hepburn, *A History of Currency in the United States* (New York: Macmillan, 1924), p. 266. Forrest McDonald concurs. Sovereignty in the eighteenth-century sense, he argues, was "absolute," and no one contended that the powers of the state and federal government were absolute. As apparent in the ratification procedure and the Tenth Amendment, sovereignty resided with the people of the states (Forrest McDonald, *Novus Ordo Seclorum: The Intellectual Origins of the Constitution* [Lawrence, KS: University Press of Kansas, 1985], pp. 278–80; "Novus Ordo Seclorum"—"a new order of the ages" appears on the Great Seal of the United States and is printed on the back of the $1 Federal Reserve note).

In commenting in 1934 on the legal provision that the Federal Reserve's gold stock be transferred to the Treasury, Princeton professor Edwin Kemmerer observed:

This policy is supported by a dubious legalistic argument which has been long dear to the proponents of cheap money in the United States, but little recognized abroad as regards paper money issues, the argument that the issuance of money is a function of sovereignty, and, therefore, should be done directly and exclusively by the Government, a corollary being that the gold reserve should be owned by the Government. ("Professor Edwin Kemmerer Analyzes the New American Dollar after the Devaluation of 1934," in *Documentary History of Banking and Currency in the United States*, vol. 4, ed. Herman E. Krooss [New York: Chelsea House, 1969], p. 2816)

4. George Bancroft, *History of the United States of America*, vol. 6 (New York: D. Appleton, 1890), p. 303. S. P. Breckinridge offers a very different view. The Constitution was not clear, she argued, a silence reflecting a dread of paper money, but a stronger dread of too narrowly limiting the power of Congress. A more accurate assessment would be that there was a certain reluctance to limit too narrowly the power of Congress, but a genuine revulsion to granting the power to issue a legal tender paper money (S. P. Breckinridge, *Legal Tender: A Study in English and American Monetary History* [Chicago: University of Chicago Press, 1903], p. 85). Arthur Nussbaum expressed a widely shared view: the majority at the convention, in his estimation, opposed federal bills of credit, but no express prohibition was approved so the matter remained open, leaving one to suppose that powers not expressly prohibited are granted to the government (Arthur Nussbaum, *A History of the Dollar* [New York: Columbia University Press, 1957], p. 118).

5. Hepburn, *A History of Currency in the United States*, p. 267.

6. Gerald T. Dunne, *Monetary Decisions of the Supreme Court* (New Brunswick, NJ: Rutgers University Press, 1960), p. 42.

7. Bray Hammond, *Banks and Politics in America: From the Revolution to the Civil War* (Princeton, NJ: Princeton University Press, 1957), pp. 92–94.

8. Ibid., p. 106.

9. Ibid., pp. 109–12.

10. Ibid., pp. 109–10.

11. Ibid., p. 110.

12. Ibid., p. 723.

13. Ibid., p. 742.

14. Ibid., p. 724.

15. Dunne, *Monetary Decisions of the Supreme Court*, pp. 3–5. Dunne quotes from the ruling: "as the king by his prerogative may make money of what matter and form he pleases and establish the standard of it, so he may change his money in substance and impression, and enhance or debase the value of it."

16. Ibid., p. 13.

17. Ibid., p. 14.

18. Ibid., pp. 14–15.

19. Ibid., p. 21.

20. Ibid., pp. 21–22.

21. Ibid., p. 100.

22. Ibid.

23. Ibid., p. 102.

24. James Willard Hurst, *A Legal History of Money in the United States, 1774–1970* (Lincoln, NE: University of Nebraska Press, 1973), p. 12.

25. Ibid.

26. Ibid., pp. 15–16.

27. Ibid., p. 16.

28. Ibid., p. 18.

29. Ibid., p. 195.

30. Ibid., p. 196.

31. Board of Governors of the Federal Reserve System, *The Federal Reserve Act: And Other Statutory Provisions Affecting the Federal Reserve System* (Washington, DC: Board of Governors of the Federal Reserve System, 1983), p. 13-001. A large volume of laws affects the operations and duties of the Federal Reserve, as set forth in this document.

32. Reference by Gerald T. Dunne to this statement in congressional testimony by James Meigs in 1973 appears in Henry G. Manne and Roger LeRoy Miller, eds., *Gold, Money and the Law* (Chicago: Aldine, 1975), p. 115.

33. King Banaian, Leroy O. Laney, and Thomas D. Willett, "Central Bank Independence," *Economic Review*, Federal Reserve Bank of Dallas (March 1983), pp. 1–13; Richard C. K. Burdekin and Leroy O. Laney, "Fiscal Policymaking and the Central Bank Institutional Constraint," *Kyklos* 41 (1988): 647–62; and King Banaian, Leroy O. Laney, John McArthur, and Thomas D. Willett, "Subordinating the Fed to Political Authorities Will Not

Control Inflationary Tendencies," in *Political Business Cycles: The Political Economy of Money, Inflation, and Unemployment*, ed. Thomas D. Willett (Durham, NC: Duke University Press, 1988), pp. 490–505.

34. Numerous studies have been conducted to sort out the factors contributing to the formulation of monetary policy and to explain the voting patterns of the FOMC. In a recent summary of this research, Munger and Roberts conclude:

> The literature we have reviewed is far from conclusive in characterizing the political pressures bearing upon the conduct of monetary policy. Although the motives of the principals are rarely in doubt, the avenues of manipulation of the Fed as an agent have never been clearly mapped. (Michael C. Munger and Brian E. Roberts, "The Federal Reserve and its Institutional Environment: A Review," in *The Political Economy of American Monetary Policy*, ed. Thomas Mayer [New York: Cambridge University Press, 1990], p. 93)

The absence of convincing evidence of political manipulation and of other consistent explanatory factors suggests that a multiplicity of forces operate in the policy-setting process, leaving room for supposing that the judgments of Federal Reserve officers on the state of the economy and financial markets, indeed, converge into a policy position, with dissenting opinions, of course, as the Federal Reserve contends. Monetary policy, nonetheless, should comply with the guidelines established by the Congress and be governed by the Congress's longer-run vision.

35. A. Jerome Clifford, *The Independence of the Federal Reserve System* (Philadelphia: University of Pennsylvania Press, 1965), p. 324.

36. Paul W. McCracken, "Reflections of an Economic Policy Maker: A Review Article," *Journal of Economic Literature* 23 (June 1980): 585.

37. Lawrence H. White, "Free Banking as an Alternative Monetary System," in *Money in Crisis: The Federal Reserve, the Economy and Monetary Reform*, ed. Barry N. Siegel (San Francisco: Pacific Institute for Public Policy, 1984), pp. 269–300.

INDEX

A.B.H. *See* After Bank Holiday

Act of October 6, 1917, 209

Act to Authorize Payments in
Stamps, 165

Act to Provide for a Copper
Coinage, 126

Act to Regulate the Circulation of
Copper Coins, 73

Adams, John, 114*n.35*

After Bank Holiday (A.B.H.), 219

Agricultural Adjustment Act of
1933

Thomas Amendment, 210

Aldrich Commission. *See* National
Monetary Commission

Aldrich, Nelson, 10, 180–81, 183

Aldrich Plan (bill), 10, 183–86,
203*n.15*

Aldrich-Vreeland Act of 1908,
157

American plantations token, 59

Andrew, A. Piatt, 168

Aristotle, 15

Articles of Confederation, 7, 13,
57–58, 64, 70, 82, 88, 97, 102,
129, 149

monetary provisions, 68, 80

Assistant Treasurer, 161–62

Attorney General, 187, 190

Baltimore, 101

Bancroft, George, 76–77*n.46*,
235–36

Bank of Augusta v. *Earle* (1839), 131

Bank of England, 35*n.18*, 64, 103,
232*n.47*

Bank of Ireland, 35*n.18*

Bank of New York, 70

Bank of North America, 64, 69,
103, 160

charter, 69

Bank of North Dakota, 138*n.56*

Bank of the United States. *See also*
Federal Reserve System, and
McCulloch v. *Maryland*

and Bank of North America, 69

bank notes of, 104

constitutional issues, 97–103

constitutionality of, 5, 8

granting of charter for, 5, 8, 12,
93, 97–103, 156

Jackson's veto of charter for,
108–9

opposition to, 30, 114*n.47*, 121

organization and operation of,
103–5, 112–13*n.2*, 114*n.35*

policies of, 29, 127, 132, 135–36

second bank, 105–8

shareholders of, 103, 107–9,
114*n.35*

third bank proposal, 111–12

token, 110–11

253

Bankhead-Pettengill bill, 220,
231n.40
Bank holiday, 209, 219,
228–29n.40
Banking
crises. See Financial crises
fractional reserve, 22, 26, 208
and seigniorage, 23
Banking Act of 1933, 188, 191
Banking Act of 1935, 187–88,
192
Bank note reporters, 128
Bank notes, 21, 24, 70, 105, 112,
126–33, 135
state, 9, 109, 111, 126–32, 135,
155–56, 158–61
Banks
colonial period, 64–65, 75n.29
commercial, 69–70, 74
Barnum, P.T., 19
Barter, 15, 19, 62, 218–19
Bavaria, 230–31n.36
Beard, Charles, 29, 36–37n.35
Bechtler gold, 123–24
Belgrade, 206n.48
Benton, Thomas Hart, 111–12
Biddle, Nicholas, 108
Bills of credit. See also
Continentals and Articles of
Confederation
colonial emissions of, 61–65,
75n.14
emissions unauthorized by
Congress, 3–4, 7, 80–85,
141, 238, 249n.4
and Federal Reserve, 179, 207
prohibited, 86, 160, 238
sanctioned, 106, 145, 149, 174,
159–60, 174, 240
and state bank notes, 9, 111,
129–32
state emissions of, 27, 33, 57, 66

Bimetallic standard, 8, 12, 93, 118,
120, 122, 237
bimetallism, 155, 170–74
Bits, 123, 163
half-bit, 133
Black, Hugo, 46–47
Bland-Allison Act, 170–71
Bland, Richard D., 170, 172
Board of Treasury, 72
Bondholders, 31
Bond portfolios, 3
Bond yields, 157
Bork, Robert, 50
Boulding, Kenneth, 30
Bradley, Joseph P., 148–49
Brandeis, Louis D. 203n.14
Brasher, Ephraim, 137n.18
Brassage, 18
Breckinridge, S.P., 90–91n.3,
249n.4
Brennan, Geoffrey, 36n.28
Brennan, William J., 50–51,
55–56n.24
Bretton Woods, 199, 212
Brimmer, Andrew F., 205–6n.47
Brisco v. Bank of Kentucky (1837),
130
Britain, 112
British
authorities (Crown), 59, 64, 66
coins, 57, 60
colonies, 59
constitution, 41
crown (coin), 71
gold coins, 72
policy, 172
pounds, 118
price record, 232n.47
Bronson v. Rodes (1869), 144,
213
Brown, Vernon L., 166, 219,
230n.32

ABOUT THE AUTHOR

Dr. Thomas F. Wilson is vice president and senior economist at Bank One, Indianapolis, IN. He is also president of the Association for the Study of the Grants Economy. Prior to joining the bank, Dr. Wilson was an associate professor of economics at Butler University (1970–80) and an economist at the Federal Reserve Bank of New York (1968–70).

Dr. Wilson was co-editor with Kenneth Boulding of *Redistribution through the Financial System* (1978), and has contributed articles to several journals.

Dr. Wilson earned his Ph.D. in economics at Columbia University in 1970 and was awarded a B.A. in international relations by the American University in 1962.